RELIGIOUS READING

RELIGIOUS READING

The Place of Reading in the Practice of Religion

PAUL J. GRIFFITHS

New York Oxford

Oxford University Press

1999

Oxford University Press

Oxford New York
Athens Auckland Bangkok Bogota Bombay Buenos Aires
Calcutta Cape Town Dar es Salaam Delhi Florence Hong Kong
Istanbul Karachi Kuala Lumpur Madras Madrid Melbourne
Mexico City Nairobi Paris Singapore Taipei Tokyo Toronto Warsaw

and associated companies in
Berlin Ibadan

Published by Oxford University Press, Inc.
198 Madison Avenue, New York, New York 10016

Library of Congress Cataloging-in-Publication Data
Griffiths, Paul J.
Religious reading : the place of reading
in the practice of religion / Paul J. Griffiths.
p. cm.
Includes bibliographical references and index.
ISBN 0-19-512577-0
1. Books and reading—Religious aspects—Comparative studies.
2. Books and reading—Religious aspects—Buddhism. 3. Books and reading—Religious aspects—Christianity. 4. Books and reading—India. 5. Books and reading—Africa, North. I. Title.
BL65.B66G75 1999
200—dc21 98-17108

1 3 5 7 9 8 6 4 2

Printed in the United States of America
on acid-free paper

This book is for Judith,
again and always

NOCH EIN WORT ÜBER BUCH UND LESEN. Die «Volksschott-Bewegung» wollte die unsichtbare Ikonostase zwischen Volk und Altar der Kanzel niederbrechen und dem Volk unmittelbaren Anteil am Altar und am Worte verschaffen. Sie rechnete zu wenig damit, daß ein Volk in die Kirche strömt, das nicht wie Augustinus oder wie Origenes zu lesen weiß. Für uns Moderne ist das Buch Unterhaltung, Zerstreuung, Belehrung, in der einern oder andern Form Ersatz für das wirkliche Leben. Wir verschwinden im Buch, vergessen beim Lesen uns selbst. Die Alten lesen, auch allein, mit lauter Stimme, sie realiserten das Wort im Zeichen. Etwas wie Scham oder Angst hält uns davon ab, uns selbst laut vorzulesen: es hätte existentielle Konsequenzen. Wir würden gezwungen, hörend «wahr» zu nehmen, sinnlich, geistig, geistlich. Unser Verhältnis zum Buch ist ein ganz anderes als noch bei Goethe oder Hölderlin, von Früheren ganz zu schweigen. Faktisch ist der «Schott» für uns eine Art neuer Ikonostase geworden. Wir verfolgen darin den realen Vorgang der Liturgie oder der Schriftlesung, wie der Feldherr der Manöver auf der Karte oder wie der reisende Snob die Landschaft im Baedeker. Wir beherrschen die Situation und stehen damit außerhalb. Wir haben das Wort schwarz auf weiß, aber das Wort hat nicht uns. Wir fassen, wir werden nicht erfaßt. Wir halten das Libretto in der Hand und könnten «Priester» und «Volk» soufflieren, aber wir sind nicht selber «Volk» oder «Priester». (Hans Urs von Balthasar, *Sponsa Verbi: Skizzen zur Theologie II* [Einsiedeln, 1961], 500)

And we're not performers, like Liszt, competing
against the world for speed and brilliance
. . . .
The longer I live the more I mistrust
theatricality, the false glamour cast
by performance . . .
. . . . . .
. . . there come times—perhaps this is one of them—
when we have to take ourselves more seriously or die;
when we have to pull back from the incantations,
rhythms we've moved to thoughtlessly,
and disenthrall ourselves, bestow
ourselves to silence, or a severer listening . . .
(Adrienne Rich, "Transcendental Étude")

Preface

SO FAR AS I CAN RECALL, I have always been able to read, to make sense of and be excited by written things. I know, of course, that there was a time when I could not read; it's just that I cannot remember it. But I was never taught, and have still not properly learned, how to read with careful, slow attentiveness; it is difficult for me to read with the goal of incorporating what I read, of writing it upon the pages of my memory; I find it hard to read as a lover, to caress, lick, smell, and savor the words on the page, and to return to them ever and again. I read, instead, mostly as a consumer, someone who wants to extract what is useful or exciting or entertaining from what is read, preferably with dispatch, and then to move on to something else. My habits of reading are mostly like my habits of purchasing: dazzled by the range of things I can buy, I spend all that I can as fast as I can, ecstatic at the excitement of contributing to the market economy and satisfied if I can assure myself of a place in that economy by continuing to produce and consume.

I'm not alone in this condition. Most academic readers are consumerist in their reading habits, and this is because they, like me, have been taught to be so and rewarded for being so. But I've also spent a good portion of my life trying to understand what it means to be a Christian, as well as much time studying literary works composed by Indian Buddhists. Both of these practices have gradually led me to see that consumerist reading isn't the only kind there is. It's also possible to read religiously, as a lover reads, with a tensile attentiveness that wishes to linger, to prolong, to savor, and has no interest at all in the quick orgasm of consumption. Reading religiously, I've come to think, is central to being religious. Losing, or never having, the ability so to read is tantamount to losing, or never having, the ability to offer a religious account of things.

This book is centrally concerned with the differences between religious reading and consumerist reading, and with what these differences imply institutionally, pedagogically, and epistemologically. It is not a disengaged book: it argues a thesis and does so with a tone that is at times (especially in the conclusion) like that used by Jeremiah in his more despairing moments. I argue that religious reading is a good and that consumerist reading is not only indifferent to religion, but actively hostile to it. I would like (though I do not expect) our educational institutions to pay attention to the argument and to reconsider the pedagogical dominance of consumerist reading. I would like also (though I expect this even less) those who have made the study of religion their intellectual avocation to show a proper humility before a mode of engagement with the world and with texts that their training has not equipped them to understand. These matters seem to me of desperate importance. The survival of properly religious institutional forms has much to do with their proper solution.

In the first chapter I sketch a theory of religion. A religious account of things, I claim, is one that seems to its offerers to be comprehensive (it takes account of everything), unsurpassable (it will not be superseded in its essential features), and central (it provides answers to, or ways of thinking about, whatever questions seem to its offerers to be central to the ordering of their lives). In chapter 2 I ask: If religion can reasonably be understood in this way, how will religious people typically use the literary works that they think of as having religious significance? Will their use of these works be wedded to particular technologies? Will they typically use their eyes to read or their ears to hear? What is the place of memory, of repetition, and of attention? In chapter 3 I turn to the question of authority. If religious reading requires, in some sense, submission to authoritative direction as to what is worth reading and how, what is this likely to mean in terms of (1) institutions in which religious readers might flourish; (2) epistemologies to which they might be committed? The institutional question is discussed by contrast with the present situation of American and European universities. In chapter 4 I treat two of the literary genres in which religious readers are most likely to compose and that they will most happily use: the commentary and the anthology. A formal analysis and definition of each is given, with many instances. Chapters 5 and 6 then provide detailed case studies of instances of these genres taken from (respectively) Buddhist India and Christian Africa under the Romans, together with a discussion of the pedagogical practices of the communities by which these works were composed and used. And in the conclusion I provide a final argument with heightened and (I hope) deepened rhetoric in which the contrasts between religious and consumerist reading are dramatized once again, and a plea is made for the recovery and institutional support of the former.

Acknowledgments

MY FIRST DEBT IS TO MY colleagues and students at the University of Chicago's Divinity School. They provided me with intellectual challenges and practical support during the years (1993–1997) when this book was one of my projects. My research assistants during those years (Nick Collier, Deepak Sarma, Trina Jones, Jonathan Gold) will see the fruits of their work here, and I thank them for what they did. I am grateful as well to the Jesuits of Aikiya Alayam in Madras (now Chennai), who made me welcome in the summer of 1996 and gave me what I most needed as this book approached its end: time to think and write, marked by the rhythm of the liturgy. Fr. Jeyaraj, the guestmaster there, will (I hope) find his spirit of hospitality and faith in these pages.

Parts of this work have been given as lectures or seminars at various places, most notably at the American Academy of Religion in November 1994 and November 1996; at the midwestern regional meeting of the Society of Christian Philosophers in April 1995; and at various places in South India in the summer of 1996. I profited from discussion and criticism at all those events. Some of the material in chapter 1 (in considerably different form) has appeared in the *Anglican Theological Review* 79 (1997). I am grateful for permission to reprint it here.

A number of people have read and commented upon all or part of this work in various stages of its writing; doing this is a work of supererogation, and I thank them wholeheartedly, even though I have done only some of the things they have urged on me. They are Jonathan Gold, Pat Griffiths, Judith Heyhoe, Greg Jones, Delmas Kiernan-Lewis, Charles Mathewes, Laurie Patton, Deepak Sarma, Allan Singleton, Charles Taliaferro, and Carol Zaleski. My children, Amy and John, have not read this work, but they have endured its writing with love, and for that I am grateful.

Above all else, I am grateful to God for the strength and (at times wavering) will to complete this book. I intend it *ad maiorem Dei gloriam*, and as an act of service to the Church.

Contents

RELIGIOUS READING

I

Religion

Religion as an Account

Defining religion is a little like writing diet books or forecasting the performance of the stock market: there's a great deal of it about and none of it seems to do much good.[1] This doesn't keep people from predicting share prices or prescribing eating habits, though it probably should. It won't keep me from offering a discursive definition of religion, either, though I may have a slightly better reason for it than does the usual diet-book author or stock-market prognosticator. Since I'm writing a book about religious reading, and since my understanding of what it is to be religious is different from that of many who call themselves religious, as well as from that of many academic professionals who think of themselves as studying religion, I can't avoid offering and defending my own understanding of religion.

I do this part of the work stipulatively. A religion is, for those who have it (or, better, are had by it), principally an account. To be religious is to give an account, where giving an account of something means to make it the object of some intentional activity—to tell a story about it, have some beliefs about it, direct some actions toward it, or the like. Mathematics, as an example of a human activity, gives an account whose chief objects are abstract entities and their relations, and whose main intentional activity is the construction, expression, justification, and ordering of beliefs about such objects and their relations. Being married, to take another example, is an account given by spouses (principally to one another, but also to others) of the history and current state of their relations, an account that involves the weaving of narratives, the regular performance of actions, the possession and nurturing of beliefs and affective responses, and much more.

Accounts that people offer may be distinguished one from another by their scope, their object, and the kinds of intentional activity they use. But there are no natural and inevitable distinctions among accounts. Decisions about the boundaries between mathematics and physics, or those between literary criticism and philosophy, are always indexed to the intellectual goals and interests of those making the distinctions. This is not to say that boundary decisions are completely arbitrary, that they have nothing to do with the accounts among which they draw boundaries. It is only to make the more modest claim that such decisions always and inevitably involve and are largely driven by the interests of those making them, and to suggest that other decisions are always both possible and defensible. Adjudicating rival boundary decisions must always involve reference to the interests implied by the decisions.

Nonetheless, paying attention to the scope, object, and kinds of intentional activity found in an account will typically give useful pointers as to how it might be demarcated from other accounts. Two accounts that differ significantly in even one of these matters are unlikely usefully to be classifiable as the same account, even though it will often be possible to imagine an account of which both are components. Consider, for instance, an account whose scope is whole numbers from one to 100, whose object is prime numbers within that range, and whose preferred intentional activity is squaring its objects. A giver of this account will, seriatim, find the square of each prime number within the chosen range. Imagine also an account identical in every respect, except that its object is even numbers within the same range. In spite of their deep similarities, these are likely, for most purposes, to be best thought of as different accounts, demarcated one from another principally by difference of object; though they might also for some purposes usefully be thought of as two components of a single account—perhaps the arithmetical account, or some such.

All human activities of cultural and conceptual interest are usefully capable of being understood as accounts in just this sense; and this means that religion must be capable of being so understood, since it is certainly of cultural and conceptual interest. If, then, to be religious is to give an account, what sort of account is it? I shall define it at a level of abstraction that makes the definition applicable to all particular religious accounts; and I shall define it by reference principally to how it appears to those who offer it. This is to say that I take the defining properties of a religious account to be both formal and phenomenal. They are formal because they are abstracted from the particularities of any particular religious account, and as a result address little if any of the substance of such an account. And they are phenomenal because they are not properties intrinsic to the account itself, but rather properties that explain how the account seems or might seem to those who offer it. These properties may also be nonphenomenal, just as the fastball that Frank Thomas of the Chicago White Sox hit out of the park last Friday may both have seemed to him to be traveling at 85 miles per hour (a phenomenal property) and have actually been doing so (a nonphenomenal property). But I shall not concern myself much with the interesting question of whether the phenomenal features of any particular account are also nonphenomenal features—for example, with the question of whether the Christian account, which indisputably possesses the property of seeming unsurpassably true to me, also possesses the nonphenomenal property of being unsurpassably true (of course, that I think it possesses the latter property follows ineluctably from the fact that it possesses the former).

There are a number of advantages to describing religious accounts in terms of their formal and phenomenal properties. First (and most important for me), concentrating at the formal level on how accounts of this sort seem to those who offer them permits me to avoid controverted questions about the substantive and nonphenomenal properties of religious accounts. I do not need to decide, for instance, whether, in order to be called religious, a particular account must involve reference to a transcendent reality (God, nirvana, or the like). Neither do I need to decide whether religious accounts, in order properly to be called such, must engage certain kinds of questions—as to how we humans should most authentically live, for instance. Second, my interest in this book is principally in the modes of learning and teaching that most effectively foster the ability to come to give, to maintain, and to nurture a religious account. This is a formal question that can be answered largely without reference to the substance of what is read when one reads religiously, a question that is in most respects better answered without such reference; and so it too benefits from the approach taken here.

Consider an analogy. It is possible to say useful things about the modes of learning best designed to produce fluency in speaking some language without saying anything about the characteristics peculiar to any. Japanese and English are, in many important respects, different from one another. Fluency in speaking one obviously does not provide fluency in speaking the other. And yet there are clear and deep similarities between the formal and phenomenal properties of being a fluent speaker of Japanese, on the one hand, and those of being a fluent speaker of English, on the other. It's beyond my scope here to describe what it seems like to a fluent speaker of some language to be such a speaker, but it is surely obvious that it does seem like something. And this is the same as to say that being a fluent speaker of some language has phenomenal properties that can usefully be considered at the formal level, in abstraction from the particularities of any natural language. Considering them in this way is just what makes it possible for those who want to think and write about language learning in general to do so in ways that are of use (even if of limited use) to the teachers and learners of any particular language.

There is something of a difficulty at this point, a difficulty suggested by the language analogy. It is that the phenomenal properties of being a speaker of (say) English are rarely a matter for articulation on the part of those to whom they belong. I don't usually think about what it's like to be a speaker of English, and couldn't say all that much about it if pressed. This is to say that I can articulate only some of what it's like to be such a speaker; and what I can and cannot articulate may vary from time to time. But I want to extend the category 'phenomenal property' to include properties of an account about which its offerers could say nothing, even if pressed. After all, as Thomas Nagel points out, it seems reasonable to think that it seems like something to a bat to be one, to think that a bat's experience has phenomenal properties.[2] And yet it is also true that the bat can say nothing about these, even to itself, while we nonbats might be able to say something.

In light of this, I use the phrase 'phenomenal properties of accounts' to include (1) properties that givers of the account do or can articulate; and (2) properties they can't (or don't) articulate, but which it seems reasonable to observers and interpreters of their accounts to attribute to those accounts, even if their givers would not themselves articulate them (and even if they would deny them if they heard others articulating them). This means that an account's phenomenal properties may be articulable or nonarticulable, and this distinction is closely matched by one between their being occurrent (the account actually does seem at the moment to its offerers to be of such and such a kind, and they both can and would say so), and their being implicit (the account implies that it should seem to its offerers to be of such and such a kind, but in fact it does not explicitly seem to them like that or like anything just at the moment, and they might deny that it seems like that or like anything, if asked). So I shall understand 'phenomenal properties' to embrace articulable, nonarticulable, occurrent, and implicit seemings, and this should be kept in mind as you read what follows, for I shall usually not signal all these distinctions. Bear in mind also that this way of talking about the accounts people offer is intended to explain only how they seem or might seem to those who offer them. The subjunctive mood in this second phrase ('might seem') covers the nonarticulable and implicit phenomenal properties of accounts.

Given all these qualifications, the phenomenal properties that religious accounts possess are three: comprehensiveness, unsurpassability, and centrality. The presence of these three will suffice to make an account religious; the absence of any one will suffice to prevent it from being so. This means that to say of people that they are religious, or have a religion, is just to say that they give an account that seems to them to have these three properties—to be comprehensive, unsurpassable, and central. It is to say that one of the things religious people do, perhaps in the end the only thing they do, is to give a religious account, to be religious.

It might be objected that the construal of religion offered here is neither the only possible nor the obviously best one. It is certainly true that it rules out much that has often been called religious. Activities that are often taken to be paradigmatically such (belief in a god or gods, making offerings to the ancestors, using sacrifice to cure disease, and the like) can, according to this construal, only properly be called religious when a good deal is known about the account of which they form a part. It is true also that much not typically included under the rubric of religion may be so included under this construal. For instance, it might be that a thoroughgoing (if somewhat old-fashioned) Marxist would turn out to be religious; or that an unusually obsessive follower of the Chicago White Sox might. But disadvantages of this kind are shared by all construals of religion. And as to whether the construal offered here is the best possible of those in the field: since the desirability of any stipulative construal of this kind must be indexed to its effectiveness in helping or allowing certain intellectual or practical goals to be met, this question reduces to the more fundamental and also more modest question of whether a particular construal does effectively serve the ends it was constructed to serve. This book is principally concerned to describe and advocate a particular form of reading; and for this end (though certainly not for all) I judge the construal offered here to be both flexible and effective.

Comprehensiveness

What then is it for an account to seem to its offerers to be comprehensive?—for this is the first of the three properties that an account must possess in order to be religious. For an account to be comprehensive it must seem to those who offer it that it takes account of everything, that nothing is left unaccounted for by it. Most accounts are not comprehensive in this sense. For example, one account that I give of myself is as a parent, the father of two living children. But this is not a comprehensive account because, first, it does not comprehend (indeed, has little to say about) the accounts I give of myself as teacher, writer, spouse, citizen of the United States, and many other things. It stands alongside some of these other accounts, neither accounting for them nor being accounted for by them. But it is strictly subsumed by, accounted for by, some of the other accounts I offer, most especially the Christian account, according to which both the fact of my being a parent and the details of my acting as such are accounted for in terms of (as I see it) the fact that I am a Christian. So the parenting account is not, for me (and I suspect this to be true for all who offer such an account) a comprehensive account, and as a result also not a religious account.

It is possible, indeed usual, for people to offer more than one comprehensive account at a time. I, for example, offer a Christian account that is comprehensive, and also the following (trivial) mathematical account: *everything is either a prime number or it is not*. This, like my Christian account, takes account of everything: of my being a parent (which is not a prime number), of my being a Christian (which is likewise not), of the number three (which is), and so forth to infinity.

These points may be put visually. Let a circle represent each account you offer. If you offer a comprehensive account, let that be represented by a circle within whose circumference all the other circles representing your noncomprehensive accounts are drawn. Some of these subsidiary circles (of which there will typically be a great many) may stand alone inside the great circle that represents the comprehensive account, neither subsuming nor overlapping nor being subsumed by any of the other subsidiary circles. But it will more frequently be the case that subsidiary circles will be related one to another by subsumption or overlapping. The full picture will typically be very complicated indeed. So the accounts that I offer of myself as parent, of the human activities of mathematics and music, of the physical states of affairs that partly constitute the cosmos, and of cultural facts like being an Englishman by birth who has become an American by choice are all (it seems to me) comprehended by the great circle of my Christian account. If you offer more than one comprehensive account, as I do, the line of your great circle's circumference will be increased in thickness for each comprehensive account you offer. Someone who offers a great many comprehensive accounts will have this fact represented by a great circle with a very thick line representing its circumference.

A couple of qualifications are necessary at this point. First, it is certainly not the case that everyone offers an explicit and articulable comprehensive account. That is, it may seem to you that no one of the accounts you offer comprehends all the others; if you're in this situation you're likely to deny offering such an account if a suggestion is made to you that you do. And this will mean that you are not, by my definition, religious, or are so only implicitly. Being explicitly religious is not, then, a necessary feature of human existence as such—and this conclusion is perfectly compatible with the truth of such claims as *all people were created by God*, and *all people have salvation made available to them through Jesus Christ*, and *God exists necessarily*. But it is rather less likely that anyone fails to offer an implicitly comprehensive account, and it is generally rather easy to persuade those who deny offering such an account that in fact they implicitly do. The easiest way to do this is to point at something (a book, say, or a table or a chair) and to ask whether it is what it is and not something else. The philosophically unschooled will rapidly agree that this is so, that everything must either be this thing or some other thing, and as soon as this is said a comprehensive account has been offered. The philosophically sophisticated may have more to say before they give their assent, or they may even withhold it altogether; but they, being sophisticated, will typically already have developed explicitly comprehensive accounts of their own. It seems a fair bet, then, that everyone offers a comprehensive account, though not that all do so explicitly.

The second qualification is that a comprehensive account, while it must provide rubrics under which the fact of all other accounts can be comprehended, need not determine just what the details of those other accounts are, and may often have nothing at all to say about those details. That is, it should not be supposed that offering a comprehensive account commits those who offer it to particular answers to all possible questions. Offering the Christian account does not, for example, commit me to any particular view as to whether Goldbach's Conjecture (that every even number greater than two is expressible as the sum of two primes) is true or not. But it does commit me to saying that the truth (or falsity) of this conjecture is one of the states of affairs eternally intended and known by God. Likewise, offering the comprehensive account *everything is either a prime number or it is not* commits me to no view about the relations between Father, Son, and Holy Spirit—except the view that such relations are not a prime number.

An account will be comprehensive, then, if and only if it seems to the person who offers it to take as its object strictly everything, and thereby to have universal scope. But some comprehensive accounts, like the prime-number account mentioned, are trivial even though their scope is universal. A trivial account is one that cannot organize a life. To find that an account is comprehensive is therefore not sufficient to make it religious; it must also appear to its offerer to be both unsurpassable and central, and as a result not to be trivial. I shall treat these two properties in order.

Unsurpassability

If I offer an account that seems to me unsurpassable, then I take it not to be capable of being replaced by or subsumed in a better account of what it accounts for.[3] So, for instance, one of the accounts I offer has my children as its objects. The chief elements of that account, its essential features, include beliefs such as that they are my children, bone of my bone and flesh of my flesh; that I love them; that I have nonnegotiable duties toward them and they toward me, duties produced directly by the fact of my parental relation to them—and so forth. It seems to me that this account is unsurpassable in its essential features, at least this side of death. This is not to say that the account will not change in its details; what I say and think about my children now, and how I act toward them, are obviously not the same in detail as what I will say, think, or do a dozen years from now. But the essential features of the account I offer will not, in my judgment, be changed, surpassed, or superseded. This is just what makes my account of my children unsurpassable for me. Unsurpassability, then, denotes an attitude toward what are taken to be the essential features of an account by the person who gives it.

When unsurpassability is coupled with comprehensiveness something close to a religious account is found. My account of my children, though unsurpassable, is of course not comprehensive, and as a result is not a religious account. My Christian account, by contrast, has both features. The importance of unsurpassability as a feature of religious accounts is that it highlights the fact that being religious, offering a religious account, is a commitment of a nonnegotiable kind. When coupled with comprehensiveness, such an account enters sufficiently deeply into the souls of those who offer it that the abandonment of its essential features is scarcely conceivable, and if conceivable, not desirable.

I take unsurpassability and nonnegotiability to be different ways of saying the same thing: if an account seems to you to be unsurpassable, this is just to say that you take what seem to you to be the account's essential features to be incapable of abandonment. This is to say neither that the formulation and expression of these essential features will not change, nor that they cannot be added to; the example of my account of my children shows this. But it is to say that any such changes or additions will not (or so it will seem to those who offer an unsurpassable account) involve or lead to the abandonment or alteration of these essential features. Christians, when considering the obvious fact that Christian doctrine appears to change over time, have often put this by saying that such apparent changes are to be understood as unfoldings, or unpackings, or flowerings (choose your metaphor) of what is already implied by Christian doctrine, and not as alterations or abandonments of it. Or, they have said that the content of the Christian account does not change, though its form may.[4] On such views (and they are typical of those found in religious accounts when their offerers become sufficiently reflective to pronounce on such matters), apparent change in the essential features of a religious account is always either developmental or cosmetic, and as a result is compatible with unsurpassability and nonnegotiability.

None of this is to say that religious accounts, once given, are never abandoned. You can cease to offer a religious account just as you can come to offer one. But it is to say that while a religious account is being offered, intrinsic to it is the feature that its offerer regards its essential elements as incapable of loss, supersession, or abandonment. This is a part of what Christians have meant by faith. But not even accounts that seem to their offerers both comprehensive and unsurpassable are necessarily religious. Some accounts of this sort may still be trivial, incapable of structuring the life of their offerer; or peripheral, not central to that life. This would be true, for example, of the prime-number account mentioned earlier. This account is, for me, both comprehensive and unsurpassable; but it is scarcely central to my life. Something more is needed, and it is centrality.

Centrality

For an account to seem central to you it must seem to be directly relevant to what you take to be the central questions of your life, the questions around which your life is oriented. Perhaps the account provides answers to these questions; or perhaps it prescribes guiding principles or intentional activities that contribute to answering, or provide ways of thinking about, these questions. Such questions may move in many areas. One is the general issue of how you should think about and relate to your fellow humans. Should you love them? Exploit them? Ignore them? Judge them to be perduring nonphysical individuals possessed of intrinsic worth? Treat them all the same, or some in one way and some in another? Another is the general issue of how you should think about and order your relations with the nonhuman order, both sentient and nonsentient. Should you treat sentient nonhumans significantly differently than you treat humans? Should you judge the nonsentient cosmos to be meaningful, or to be a collection of brutally irreducible states of affairs? Should you judge that what exists is limited to what you can perceive with your physical senses, and behave accordingly? And yet a third is the general issue of how you should think about yourself, and about what sorts of beliefs and actions you should foster in yourself, and what discourage. Should you make what seems to you to contribute to your own pleasure and happiness the central motivating factor in your decisions about what to do with your life? Should you judge that you are a perduring object of worth? Decisions about matters of these three kinds are life-orienting; they are also, when a decision already made about them is changed, life-changing. Not all may seem to everyone to be central questions, and the examples mentioned are only examples, not an exhaustive list. But they are ideal-typical representatives of questions central to the ordering of a life.

Most people do not explicitly ask themselves questions at this level of abstraction and generality. Doing so is characteristic of an uncommon level of reflection. But most people do explicitly ask and answer more concrete questions, and in so doing imply the asking and answering of abstract questions like these. For instance, a Hindu in Bihar might ask and answer a question such as this: Is my Muslim neighbor worthy of death just because he is a Muslim? A Muslim in Lyons might ask and answer the question: Should I wear the veil to school even though it is against French law to do so? A Jew in Hoboken might ask and answer the question: Should I marry a Gentile? A Christian in Leeds might ask and answer the question: Should I devote time and energy to becoming a concert pianist even though there are homeless and hungry people on the streets not a mile from my front door? Such concrete questions are likely to seem central to those who ask and answer them. And it is characteristic of religious accounts that they address such questions and that they do so in the context of offering a comprehensive and unsurpassable account.

That religious accounts must be central as well as unsurpassable and comprehensive is among the things that make it possible to be a person and yet not offer one. It's clear that not everyone explicitly offers an account that seems to them comprehensive, unsurpassable, and central; it's clear also that there are many who would deny offering such an account if asked. So some people, perhaps many, have no explicit and articulable religious account to offer. But perhaps they offer such an account implicitly, much as native speakers of English offer an implicit account of the grammar of the English language even when they can articulate little or nothing about that grammar. Perhaps, that is to say, offering religious accounts (being religious) is a necessary feature of human existence, a part of what it means to be human. Many have thought so, but it is not so. It is entirely possible to be human and to offer no religious account, even implicitly. I've already suggested that it is difficult, perhaps impossible, for anyone to avoid offering (at least implicitly) a comprehensive account. I suspect that similar things ought to be said about unsurpassable accounts: it turns out to be difficult not to offer at least one of these, even if it's of the pedestrian kind that denies (implicitly or explicitly) the possibility of offering an unsurpassable account—and in so doing, offers one. However, it is possible to fail to offer a central account with relative ease. Human beings can be (or can become) profoundly fragmented, their intentions and desires dispersed to such an extent that they do not, perhaps cannot, offer an account that seems to them directly relevant to what they take to be the questions around which their lives are oriented. For a deeply fragmented or dispersed soul, there may be no such questions: there may be only a series of disjointed, unconnected desires, chaotic in their proliferation and fragmentation. And in such a case, clearly, no central account can be offered, from which it follows that no religious account can be offered.

Being religious is therefore not an essential or intrinsic part of being human. It's important to note, though, that this is entirely compatible with the truth of claims such as *God created everyone* or *everyone's life comes from and is ordered to God*. These are metaphysical claims. Their truth (if they are true) does not require the truth of any claims about the phenomenal properties of the accounts that people offer—not even in the extended sense of phenomenal properties in play here. Returning to the analogy of language may help to show this. Suppose it's true that there is a deep structure common to all natural languages; it would then also be true that being a native speaker of English would imply (though distantly) the presence of that deep structure in every utterance. Analogously, if it's true that everyone's life issues from and is ordered to God, this fact will be implied by any account whatever (even one lacking in central questions). But in both cases the implication is a distant one and says nothing about the particulars of the account in question: it is applicable indifferently to all accounts. I am concerned here not with such distant implications, but only with those that have to do with the particulars of some account, the properties that differentiate it from other accounts, that make it the account it is and not some other. It follows that even if being a native speaker of English implies the presence and efficacy of a deep structure, and even if failing to offer a central account implies the existence of God, in neither case are these things among the phenomenal properties (implicit or explicit) specific to the accounts in question.

To reiterate: not everyone offers a religious account. But is it possible for anyone to have more than one religion (offer more than one religious account) at a time? The answer is no, and for strictly logical reasons. Bilingualism is possible, but bireligionism is not. It is, as I've said, possible simultaneously to offer more than one comprehensive and unsurpassable account. But the addition of centrality makes this no longer possible. For each person there is a finite (usually a small) number of questions that seem central, capable of organizing a life. Suppose you entertain two accounts, each of which seems to you comprehensive, unsurpassable, and central. Then either the two accounts will seem to you to be different in some of their essential features, or they will not. If the former, then it is both logically and psychologically impossible for you not merely to entertain but actually to offer both accounts. This is because you cannot offer, simultaneously and with conviction, different answers to what seem to you life-orienting questions. Suppose you entertain different answers to the (possibly) life-orienting question: Should I kill and eat apparently sentient creatures? One answer might be: Never. Another might be: Only if they have two or more senses. A third might be: Whenever no other food is available. The first answer is incompatible with the second and third. You may entertain, but you cannot offer, an account that embraces all three. The second and third answers are different but not necessarily or obviously incompatible. You may entertain and come to offer an account that combines both. But then you are offering a single account that includes a complex answer to this particular question. In no case are you offering two different accounts at the same time.

The anthropologist Dan Sperber makes a formally identical point in his discussion of symbol systems:

> [T]here is no multi-symbolism analogous to multi-lingualism. An individual who learns a second language internalises a second grammar, and if some interference takes place, it is on a remarkably small scale. Conversely, symbolic data, no matter what their origin, integrate themselves into a single system within a given individual. If one could internalise several different symbolic devices, as one can learn several different languages, the task of the anthropologist would thereby become considerably simpler. But the anthropologist, who little by little penetrates the symbolism of his hosts, is never able to pass from one symbolism to another as easily as he passes from one language to another.[5]

Sperber's point is that for a user of symbolic systems there is only one active system at a time. You can act, or engage in other complex forms of pretense, when you deploy symbol systems; but this is never the same as genuine and authentic use. Transition from pretense to genuine use is possible, but it isn't possible to pretend and genuinely to use at the same time. Similarly for religious accounts. Many can be entertained at a time, but only one can be offered. This is not to say, of course, that a religious account need contain elements drawn from only one of those complexes of human thought and action called 'Christianity' or 'Islam' or the like. If you say that you are a Jewish Buddhist, for example, you typically mean that you offer a religious account some elements of which are historically Buddhist and some historically Jewish. You do not mean, because you cannot, that you simultaneously offer two religious accounts.

Skill and Information

Giving religious accounts is a practice, a human activity. It follows that every instance of giving a religious account, every token of the type, is learned, and learned in a particular social, linguistic, and institutional context. We are not born giving religious accounts any more than we are born using language, even though we may have deep and partly genetic tendencies to come to do both things, and even though there may be facts about the cosmos in which we live that strongly suggest to us the desirability of doing the former. Unless we are placed in a social and institutional context in which certain pedagogical practices are in place, we shall not, because we cannot, become religious: we shall not learn to offer a religious account. Analogously, unless we are placed in a community of language users, we shall not, because we cannot, become fluent users of any language. Rather few of us fail to become fluent users of some language or another, and we understand a good deal about the conditions necessary for becoming such. But very many of us fail to become religious, most often because the necessary social, institutional, and pedagogical practices are lacking. This has perhaps been especially true for inhabitants of Europe and the United States since the seventeenth century, but it is now becoming increasingly true for people in other parts of the world.

None of this is to say that there is a deterministic relation between the presence of the relevant practices and the offering of religious accounts. The practices, whatever they turn out to be, may in some cases be present and yet no religious account be offered. Necessary conditionality is not sufficient conditionality; human free will, divine grace, and various other imponderables have their proper part to play. Paying attention to the practices constitutive of religious learning is therefore not intended to suggest a reductionist view of any particular religious account, or of religious accounts in general. It is not intended to suggest that when the learning practices have been analyzed there is no more to be said about religion. There is always the question of truth: is one, none, or several of the religious accounts offered true? But this is not my interest here.

Any kind of learning, including religious learning, results for us in one of two things: the acquisition and retention of information, on the one hand, or the possession of a skill, on the other. Each of these entails, in some measure, the presence of the other. Acquisition and retention of information is impossible without the possession and use of some skill that is not itself exhaustively accountable in terms of information. No human, for instance, can acquire and transmit information linguistically without being in possession of skills that go far beyond the information contained in dictionaries and manuals of syntax. The skills of reading or listening with understanding are complex and clearly not capable of analysis solely in terms of the possession of information. They involve dispositions and capacities that we do not fully understand, as is shown by the fact that we cannot program computers even to meet the test of producing a reasonable facsimile of reading or talking (one that could fool an averagely perceptive human observer), notwithstanding that the computer may have rapid access to a body of lexical and syntactical information many times larger than that possessed by any human. The same is true of other complex human skills. And even in the case of less complex skills, such as those of walking on two legs, riding a bicycle, making love, or playing the piano, skills in which the linguistic component is almost entirely (perhaps entirely) absent—even in the case of these it is at least arguable that the implicit possession of some information is among the necessary conditions for the exercise of the skill. You might need to know (even if you never need to formulate the knowledge) that pressing the pedal down will move the bicycle; that using the loud-pedal on the piano will make the noise continue; and that kissing the beloved will express your love and may be reciprocated.

There is, it should already be clear, a distinction between information presupposed by the possession of a skill and implied by its exercise, and information present to the minds of (or capable of being articulated by) possessors of that skill. Suppose you can speak a natural language; this is a skill that presupposes and implies all sorts of grammatical information, and yet you may be able to articulate little or none of it. Similarly for playing the piano or making love. This point can be clarified by speaking of three kinds of information. The first is occurrent: under this head comes all the information currently present to your mind. The second is dispositional: under this head comes information not at the moment present to your mind, but capable of becoming so when circumstance requires. And the third is implicit: under this head comes information implied in or presupposed by your skills, but not capable of articulation by you under any conditions.

Most of the information we possess is of the third kind, a good deal is of the second kind, and very little is of the first kind. This is as true of the information that belongs to religious accounts as of any other kind, and it is important to emphasize it, because only a tiny proportion of those who offer religious accounts have any but a vanishingly small proportion of the information implied by offering such an account either present to their minds or capable of articulation. Limiting the scope of this inquiry to information of the first kind would mean excluding the vast majority of people from learning to read religiously. I don't mean to do that, so when I speak of information in what follows I include all three kinds, though once again with the proviso that in the case of implicit information I am interested only in the kind specific to the account being studied.

Information and skill are never finally separable in practice. Nonetheless, it will be useful to have a fairly sharp distinction between them in mind when reading what follows, since I shall make some theoretical use of ideas about the difference between the two—between, as philosophers have tended to put it, following Gilbert Ryle and J. L. Austin, 'knowing how' (possessing a skill) and 'knowing that' (possessing some information).[6]

It should be pretty clear that offering a religious account will typically require much information and plenty of skill. Again, a good (though partial) analogy is with verbal fluency in some natural language. You need to know that a lot of things are the case (that, in Latin, nouns and adjectives agree, the subjunctive mood expresses possibility rather than actuality, and the like); and you need to know how to do a lot of things (how to construct a sentence with subordinate clauses, how to understand infinitives, and the like). So also with religious accounts. You need to know the grammatical and syntactical rules by which the account is structured, you need to know the semantic content of the claims made about human persons and the setting of their life, and you need to know what is prohibited, what permitted, and what recommended in the sphere of human action. These are all examples of knowing that. But you also need to know how to offer the account: you need, to a greater or lesser extent, to possess the skills required to elucidate the account, to instantiate it in your life, to develop the capacities and proclivities that will make it possible for you to act in accord with what is prescribed or recommended by the account. Offering a religious account involves learning to play the piano as well as becoming a musicologist; and the virtuosos, the Barenboims and the Goulds, are the saints.

These points can be and should be put more strongly. Offering a religious account is, principally and paradigmatically, a skill. It consists essentially in knowing how to do certain sorts of things. Only secondarily, and quite inessentially, does it involve the possession of occurrent or dispositional information. Just as there are many more players of chess than theorists of the game, so there are many more faithful Christians than theologians, many more good Buddhists than analysts of dharma, and many more committed and ecstatic Śaivites than expositors of Śaivasiddhānta. Knowing how to offer a religious account is, as Ryle put it, "a disposition, but not a single-track disposition like a reflex or a habit" (Ryle was of course not speaking of religion, in which he had little interest).[7] This means that the complex disposition that is possessing the skill of offering a religious account does not issue in a single set of predictable actions. This is what makes it different from a habit. If I have the habit of drinking coffee or that of splitting infinitives, these facts will be evident principally in my repeated performance of such acts. But if I have a sarcastic disposition, this will be evident in many ways, including the bitter put-down, the abrasive parody, and the self-aggrandizing critique; there is no single set of actions in which this disposition issues, which is why it isn't a habit but instead a context-sensitive set of behaviors, each of which evidences my possession of the dispositional skill of being sarcastic (not a desirable disposition to be enslaved to, of course).

Being religious is more like being sarcastic than like being a coffee drinker or a splitter of infinitives. It may certainly contain and be partly constituted by habits (for example, repeating the Nicene Creed on Sundays, or praying the Paternoster daily), but it isn't limited to them or exhaustively describable in terms of sets of them. Like being sarcastic, it issues in context-specific behaviors such as acting charitably in response to a particular need, responding with forgiveness to an act of hostility, or meeting an act of injustice with denunciation. Since being religious is a skill in this sense, it's possible to get better at it (or worse). You're not, then, simply religious or not; you're more or less religious. To say that people are good (faithful, perceptive, discerning, vigorous, active) Christians is principally to say of them that they do certain things and do them in such a way that understanding of what they do is evident, and that deep commitment to it can be seen. Such people practice Christianity well, and the analogy with being a good chess player, lover, or philosopher is close and deep. In all these cases, the terms of approbation have to do with what is done rather than with what is known—even though doing always involves and implies knowing.

Ryle again:

> Learning how or improving in ability is not like learning that or acquiring information. Truths can be imparted, procedures can only be inculcated, and while inculcation is a gradual process, imparting is relatively sudden. It makes sense to ask at what moment someone became apprised of a truth, but not to ask at what moment someone acquired a skill. 'Part-trained' is a significant phrase, 'part-informed' is not. Training is the art of setting tasks which the pupils have not yet accomplished, but are not any longer quite incapable of accomplishing.[8]

If indeed being religious (offering a religious account) is a dispositional skill, then, as Ryle points out, it will have to be inculcated, which is to say that those who have (or come to have) the skill will have to be trained. Reading of a certain kind will be an important part of this training; and it is the central concern of this book to make clear just what kind.

The Christian Account

An example may be of use at this point, since almost everything said so far has been abstract. What are the lineaments of some religious account, and how are the possession of information and skill required of those who try to offer it? I shall take the Christian account as my example because it is the one I try to offer, and as a result the only one upon which I am qualified to pronounce as a native.[9] It is for Muslims, Buddhists, Jews, and so forth, to say what the elements of their accounts might be. I shall have a good deal to say in later chapters about particular Buddhist artifacts that I take to illustrate some of the claims I shall be making about religious reading; but I shall be interested in those not for their substance but for their form, and I shall take pains to avoid normative pronouncements as to what should and what should not belong to a Buddhist account. Such restrictions do not constrain me when I write of Christianity, though of course any construal of that account I might offer is only one of many possible ones.

The sketch of the Christian account that follows is not meant to suggest that there is a single, unchanging account with just and only these features that has been offered by all Christians everywhere and always. *Semper, ubique, ab omnibus* (always, everywhere, by all) is a slogan with some uses and an important Christian lineage, but it should not be taken (and I do not take it) to indicate that the Christian account does not vary with time and place. That it does is obvious. But it is also obvious that there are features that have been and remain widespread among the accounts offered by those who call themselves Christians (though just what these are is matter for debate). It seems reasonable to think that when an account is offered from which some or all of these features are absent that account is no longer usefully thought of as a Christian account, much as the absence of any Latin-derived words in some idiolect probably indicates that the idiolect is no longer usefully thought of as English. It is features of this sort that the following sketch selects and calls essential.

The first and most fundamental essential feature of the Christian account as it appears to Christians is that the account itself is seen as a response to the actions of a divine agent who is other than those offering it. God, it seems to us Christians, has acted as creator, as guide of human history, and as redeemer of fallen and sinful humanity by becoming incarnate, dying, and rising from the dead. In order to learn how to offer our account, Christians must acquire both this basic item of information about it and the skills of responsive action that such a view of it implies. We Christians have been and continue to be acted upon, or so it seems to us; the account we offer is our response.

God's action requires a response from us. It is a response that we can give or refuse to give, wherein lies our freedom. And it is a response required of us not by compulsion, but by love: "For God so loved the world that he gave his only begotten Son, that whosoever believeth in him should not perish, but have everlasting life" (John 3:16). The response requires knowing that certain things are the case (what God has done, what God is like, what we are like, what we should do); it also requires knowing how to do certain things, the inculcation of skills that are difficult, learned slowly, learned hard, and never fully learned.

Principal among those skills is the ordering of the will and the appetites away from the self, away from self-centered gratification, and toward God first and other humans second. We come from God: the possibility of our existence and all its boundaries are from God and of God. This means that we are fundamentally restless and disordered until we come to see and acknowledge these facts, and to harmonize our wills with them. This restlessness and disorder is evident principally when we turn our wills and direct our appetites toward anything other than God. Things other than God are all of them necessarily and essentially good, since God made them. This means that they are proper objects of honor, affection, and use. But they are not, in themselves, proper objects of enjoyment, devotion, and reverence. Only God warrants those attitudes and responses, even though it's second nature to us to give them to things that are not God, which is to say that it's second nature to us to be idolaters. (Our first nature is given by God, and so is not idolatrous.) We must then, as Christians, inculcate the complex skill of directing our wills and appetites away from ourselves and our gratification, and toward God. Inculcating this skill and exhibiting it in our lives are proper and essential parts of the Christian account.

Closely associated with this necessity is the imperative to transform our attitudes toward humans other than ourselves. We have to learn to see each as an image of God, as created by God, and so as worthy of honor and affection. This involves learning the complex skill of discerning when to sacrifice our own interests (which are naturally dear to us, and which we naturally kill to defend and extend) for those of others, and when and how to witness to others in the hope that they might also become offerers of the Christian account, livers of the Christian life. Here, as so often, our paradigm is Jesus of Nazareth, who both gave his own life for others, and constantly taught and witnessed to them. But simple imitation is not possible, any more than simple imitation of Bobby Fischer's best games will make a good chess player, or simple imitation of Vladimir Nabokov's best novels will make a good novelist. The acquisition of a skill and the discernment to apply it well are what's needed.

The reordering of will and appetite away from self and toward God (first) and other humans (second) also has its application to the nonhuman parts of the created order, both sentient and otherwise. These also are God's creation, and are to be honored as such. They are not to be used solely for our gratification, not to be treated with casual violence or disrespect, and most emphatically not to become objects of idolatry, to be loved as if they were God. Seeing what all this means and applying it in the particular situations in which we find ourselves is, once again, a complex skill. It, too, is an essential part of the Christian account.

We Christians have often described and analyzed the inculcation of the skills mentioned in the immediately preceding paragraphs under the rubric of the training of conscience. All humans have a conscience, an internal witness and judge that instructs us in what we ought to do. But for most of us it is undeveloped, "weak" as St. Paul puts it (I Corinthians 8), clouded or obscured by sin and self-will. Inculcation of the skills I've mentioned (indeed, the whole process of religious learning for Christians) can usefully be understood as enlivening the lazy conscience.

Three kinds of practice are typically used by Christians as tools for the inculcation of these skills. The first is worship; the second, prayer; and the third, reading or hearing the Bible for nourishment. These are not finally separable one from another. All worship involves prayer, all prayer is a form of worship, and proper use of the Bible is both prayerful and worshipful. But it may nonetheless be useful to say a few words on each separately.

Worship, the first of these three, is a communal and individual returning of praise and love to the God who has acted in such a way as to make possible and to require the offering of the Christian account. Worship is, as we Christians have developed it, a complex and highly ordered collective activity. When, for instance, Catholic Christians offer the sacrifice of the mass, we perform actions that require a high level of understanding and skill. There are skills of bodily movement: knowing how and when to genuflect, to kneel, to stand, to make the sign of the cross, and so forth. There are skills of voice: knowing when and how to sing, to chant, and so forth. And there are skills of thought and attitude: knowing when and how to compose the mind, to direct the thoughts, to order the emotions and the will. All these skills presuppose and express a broad range of knowledge that: knowledge that God has acted in such and such a way; knowledge that such and such a response is appropriate; knowledge that the bread and wine on the altar have a peculiar significance—and so forth. The knowing how and knowing that evident in Christian worship are learned and inculcated by repetition; their inculcation produces a particular skill that is in turn part of the process by which the will and the appetites are ordered to God.

Prayer, the second practice used by Christians, has both communal and private aspects. Whether done with others or alone in your room behind closed doors (Matthew 6:6), it, too, is a returning of love, praise, and service to God. Its paradigm is the Paternoster, the prayer given by Jesus (Matthew 6:9–13; Luke 11:2–4), and its shortest and most pithy form is direct address to God in the form "Your will, not mine, be done." Like worship, it acknowledges and represents the facts about what God has done for us, and in so doing inculcates the skill of responding properly to those facts. It is part of the process by which our wills and appetites become aligned with God.

The third practice integral to the Christian account is the use of the Bible. We Christians possess what we take to be a peculiarly authoritative witness to God's actions and intentions. This authority is construed in various ways, but common to them all (or at least to all that warrant being described as Christian) are the ideas that the Bible has greater authority than any other work, that the reading of it should provide Christians with a set of tools and skills we can use to interpret the world, and that the world is to be interpreted in terms of the Bible, written into its margins, so to speak, rather than the other way around. Technically, this is to say that the Bible is a *norma normans non normata*, a norm that norms but is itself not normed. Here, too, many skills and much information are required: we Christians need to learn the skill of reading the Bible in a particular way, as well as a good deal of information about the Bible and about reading. George Herbert, in these lines from "The H. Scriptures I," puts the Christian's attitude to the Bible well:

> Oh Book! infinite sweetnesse! let my heart
> Suck ev'ry letter, and a hony gain
> . . . .
> . . . heav'n lies flat in thee,
> Subject to ev'ry mounters bended knee.[10]

Sucking is another learned skill (as also was sucking at your mother's breast); learning it and practicing it contributes to the more fundamental and difficult skills of reorienting the will and the appetite.

The immediately preceding paragraphs have provided a very schematic outline of the Christian account. It has been meant only to illustrate the points made earlier about skills and information as integral parts of religious accounts. Similar schematic outlines could be given of Buddhist, Hindu, or Confucian religious accounts (though not by me). It should be clear even from this schematic version of the Christian account that it appears comprehensive, unsurpassable, and central to Christians. It also exhibits some other features likely to be found in religious accounts. It presents views about the setting of human life, and it presents them in such a way as to account in broad terms for every aspect of that life. All religious accounts are likely to do this. It presents views, also, about the nature of human persons, and about how we should conduct ourselves, and it does this in such a way as to embrace all dimensions of that life. This, too, is likely to be something that any comprehensive, unsurpassable, and central account will attempt. It also presents methods (worship, prayer, reading the Bible) intended to remind those who offer it of what they are doing, and to inculcate in them the skills needed for doing it well. It's unlikely that any religious account can get away without doing this, too. Enlivening the conscience, sharpening discernment, honing skill—whatever the preferred vocabulary, religious accounts must contain methods for doing this. That is, any religious account must contain a pedagogy. A final point about the Christian religious account that may also be applicable to others: central to its pedagogy is the teaching of a method of reading. What is read, for Christians, is primarily and paradigmatically the Bible, and this, of course, is specific to the Christian account. But it may be that the way in which its reading is taught is not specific in this way: perhaps all religious accounts recommend the kind of sucking at the nipple of the works important to them that George Herbert commends to Christians.

Religious reading (the methods of reading preferred by religious teachers and learners) is the central topic of this book. But it should be abundantly clear from what's been said about the nature of religious accounts, as well as from the sketch given of the Christian account, that the pedagogical methods appropriate to the inculcation of the skills and the acquisition of the information required for giving any particular religious account include much more than reading. In the case of Christian worship, for example, these methods may range from the didactic/discursive (the catechetical class for new or prospective Christians) to the kinesthetic (hands-on participation in worship without formal discursive instruction in the meaning of what is being done or the proper way to do it). A complete study of religious learning would be an enormous task, since it would have to deal with a huge range of pedagogical methods at both the formal level and at the level at which these methods are actually used in the transmission of particular religious accounts. This is not what I intend in this book; it could not be done in a single work.

Instead, I shall focus the inquiry by asking how those engaged in religious teaching and learning read: what kind or kinds of reading most appropriately belong to the formation, preservation, and development of the skills required for the offering of a religious account, and how are these taught? (I have in mind a somewhat extended sense of the term 'reading', as will become apparent.) Answering this question—and it is a sufficiently large question by itself—won't come close to dealing with the whole topic of religious learning, of how religious accounts are transmitted and appropriated. But it will illuminate some important aspects of that larger question. It will shed some light upon how the lexicon and syntax of a religious account are typically acquired, and upon how skill in deploying them with understanding is typically developed. It will also raise some critical questions about the contemporary dominance of certain views about the significance of reading and the best way to read.

2

Religion and Literary Work

Composition, Display, Storage

Literary works must be composed somehow. It is part of their nature to be woven, constructed, fabricated, collected together out of disparate elements. Most of these meanings are implied by the Latin *textere*, from which the English word 'text' is derived. I prefer 'work', or 'literary work', though, to emphasize the importance of human agency and human labor, and to de-emphasize the idea of textual autonomy, which is a fundamentally irreligious idea.

Works will usually be displayed after (or simultaneously with) their composition; more rarely they may be stored after they have been displayed; and those that have been stored may sometimes be taken from storage for redisplay. How may these things be done? Which tools and techniques can be used, and which are likely to be used? These questions are important because engaging them will allow resolution of (or at least some useful ways of thinking about) controverted and significant issues connected with the cultural and practical significance of speech, memorization, and writing; engaging these questions will also provide some useful conceptual tools for matters to be taken up later in this book. Asking questions about composition, storage, and display separately is important in another way as well: it helps to restrain the common tendency to think that the tools used for one of these functions must also be those used for the others.

First display is the pivotal moment in the life of a literary work. It occurs when such a work is made available in a fixed and bounded form, a form in which it can enter storage. In the case of a work displayed aurally, the moment of first display occurs when the last syllable is uttered; in the case of one displayed in writing, it occurs when the last graph (letter, character, word) is written. There are other somewhat more recherché possibilities: a work may be displayed in purely visual ways, as an ordered sequence of images that are not representations of words (consider silent movies or patterns of gestures used in ritual activity); it may be displayed, I suppose, though it is harder to think of examples, solely as an ordered sequence of olfactory, gustatory, or tactile signs. A meal might be thought of as a displayed work in this sense, as might the communicative patterns of touch shared by lovers. But whatever the sensory modalities, a work will have been displayed for the first time just and only when it is available in principle for public consumption in bounded form.

I'll be concerned in what follows only with displayed verbal works (literary works on a fairly broad construal), works that use words in one form or another. A displayed verbal work, then, is one that could be (though need not actually be) consumed (read, heard, tasted, memorized) by a public just as it stands. Display has inaccessibility as its contrastive term. An undisplayed work is one that cannot be consumed by a public just as it stands. It is hidden, unavailable, inaccessible; further work must be done before it can be read, heard, or memorized.

To say that a work is displayed when it is available in fixed and bounded form may seem to suggest that it is obvious where the boundaries of a work are to be located, where the *incipit* and the *explicit* are to be written. But these things are not at all obvious. Deciding where a particular work begins and ends is, like all such matters, a question of convention, of the point of making such decisions for those who need or want to make them. Two extreme positions are possible. One is to say that all the words ever uttered or written form a single gigantic work—that there is no reasonable way to divide them into separate works. The other is to say that no work is ever larger than whatever the minimum semantic unit is taken to be (the word, the character, the phrase, the sentence)—that there is no reasonable way to aggregate them into separate works. Between these extremes are many possibilities. As I write these words, and in writing them add to words I have just written, I might say that each word written marks the completion of a new work; or I might say that the work of which these words are parts will not be finished until I write "the end"; or I might say that what I write is itself a part of everything else I have written and will be complete only when I cease to write, perhaps as a result of death. The point is that any decision I (or anyone) might make about this is not one we are compelled to by the character of the works we read or write. (Similar questions arise for many religious readers in thinking about the boundaries between commentary and work commented upon.) My definition of first display, then, is meant in a purely formal sense: a particular work is available in a bounded form when someone decides, for some purpose or other, that it has taken such a form.

Verbal works can be displayed in only two ways. The first is by speech, understood as the creation by the human voice of semantically loaded patterns of vibration in the air; and the second is by the partial encoding of such patterns in some other form, most commonly (but not necessarily) visual rather than aural. This second option will usually mean writing, which I here understand to mean the making of marks upon some enduring physical surface (carving upon stone, metal, or the like; scratch marks upon paper, palm leaves, parchment, or the like; patterns of electrons upon a cathode-ray tube), when such marks are understood by some community to encode or represent (though always partially and imperfectly) the spoken words of some natural language. But it need not involve writing in this sense. It may mean the encoding of speech in some other aural form (such as Morse code), or in some other visual form (such as semaphore), or in some form intended for tactile reading (such as Braille). But these cases are likely to be atypical, communicative conventions evolved for very specific purposes, and always parasitic upon speech or writing or both.

The definition just given suggests that display by writing is secondary to and parasitic upon display by speech, because it requires that writing be understood as a secondary means of encoding or representing the primary data, which are given by speech. And this is the case even though, in some settings, writing may be almost the only working mode of display and storage. The principal reason for saying that writing is secondary to speech in this sense is that, for both individuals and social groups, writing has speech among the necessary conditions for its development, while the reverse is not true. There are no instances of individuals or groups being in possession of writing but not of speech. This is not, of course, to say that writing, once it finds a place in the life of some individual or group, may not develop properties, semantic and other, that are neither determined by nor in any significant way related to properties of the speech habits already possessed by that individual or group. Neither is it to say that writing is a device capable of representing all the properties of speech. Nuance, irony, humor—all these can easily be conveyed by tone of voice, facial expression, bodily posture, or gesture. Written language can represent these aspects of spoken language only with difficulty and without subtlety, usually by the use of visual devices such as layout, underlining, italicization, alteration of the size and shape of some graphemes relative to others, and the like.[1] Finally, asserting the primacy of speech over writing in the limited sense intended here does not mean that any particular instance of writing always encodes or represents some instance of speech. Writing can of course be a tool of composition and storage that represents not speech but thought.

Given this understanding of display, the essential point of which is the in-principle public availability of a bounded work, what of composition? This process will always occur either before display or simultaneously with it. For most works, composition and display will be virtually simultaneous: the last moment of display (the moment at which the bounded work is made public) will be the same as the last moment of composition, and the processes by which such a work is composed will not easily be separable from those by which it is displayed.

Consider ordinary conversation. The (short) spoken sentence "How do you do?" is, for most native speakers of English on most occasions of its use, composed and displayed at one and the same time. The same may be the case, though much less frequently, for longer and more complex works. Consider the performance art of an action painter, the inspired recitation of a bardic singer, or the speaking in tongues of a Pentecostal Christian. But composition (especially of long and complex works) may also occur before, sometimes long before, the acts of speech or writing whose completion signals the moment of their display. That is to say, composition sometimes includes acts that occur prior to or alongside acts of display, and that are intentionally directed toward the completion of that display. Composition in this sense will usually include mental acts: deliberation, volition, intention, choice, and so forth. It may also include physical acts: writing a draft, scribbling phrases on paper, speaking words aloud.

Questions about display are therefore not the same as questions about composition. The former are about the means by which a particular work is first made available to a public, while the latter are about the (often private) processes of thought, artifice, memorization, or draft, that may have gone on before this happens. For instance, to say that some work is displayed aurally is perfectly compatible with saying that it is the product of a lengthy process of conscious artifice using nonaudible methods (memorization, writing, gesture); it is compatible also with saying that it is the result of an onrush of afflatus. The improvisations of a skilled jazz pianist are usually spontaneous in something like this fashion: they are prepared for in a very nonspontaneous way (the pianist listens to other pianists, practices a lot, and so on), but the display of a musical work (a performance) may use none of these methods, even when they are among the necessary conditions for its occurrence. Similarly, the works displayed by rhetors in ancient Greece, by preachers in contemporary gospel churches, and by some politicians and lecturers may often be entirely aural in display, but have behind them much intentional work, and therefore a long process of composition that need not be exclusively or at all audible.

The third and fourth concepts that need explanation are intimately linked: storage and redisplay. Once a work has been displayed it may be stored in some way for later redisplay. Most, of course, are not stored intentionally. The vast majority of verbal works that we produce are ordinary aural conversational ones without sufficient interest or potential for future use to suggest that it is worth anyone's while to put effort into storing them. But some are stored nonetheless, either by accident or with intent. A work has been stored when, after its first display, it exists in some form that permits, in principle, its redisplay or reuse.

The possibilities here are many and complex. A beginning can be made by going back to the question of display. Recall that there are two possible modes under which a work may be given its first display: aural and visual, which in the case of works using words effectively comes down to speech and writing. I shall consider these in order.

First, how may a work given its first display aurally, in speech, be stored? This must be done by an act separate from that which gave it its first display. This is because, as Augustine puts it, uttered words last no longer than the vibrations in the air in which they consist;[2] it is therefore necessary, if you want to store the uttered words, to do something else with them, typically to institute the use of letters, graphemes, which are representations of or signs for the sounds that make them up. But storage need not occur only by writing: *litterae*, in

Augustine's terms, are not its only instruments. It may occur in a wide variety of ways including the use of the memory, of electronic technologies, and of writing.

These different ways of storing and redisplaying spoken works can be classified variously. One way of doing this involves appeal to the extent to which storing a work requires intentional action on the part of human agents. Memorization and writing both score high on this scale. It is true that memorization of a displayed work in such a way that its recall is easy sometimes occurs without anyone intending that it should (the lyric of a song heard just once may lodge in the mind in such a way that it is difficult to get rid of); and it is also true that on some views of memory, all or almost all works, whether first experienced aurally or visually, are lodged in the memory involuntarily, even though their recall may often be difficult or impossible in practice. But for the most part, the kind of memorization that carries with it the possibility of recall at will requires considerable intentional effort, as is evident from the demanding techniques for developing it commended wherever it is an important form of storage.

The same is true for storing aurally displayed works in writing. Court stenographers do their job with considerable intentional effort, as do reporters taking shorthand notes; this method of storage almost always requires a professional class to do it efficiently, one that may do nothing other than store works composed by others. By contrast, the intentional effort required for storing an aural work on tape using electronic methods is minimal. Since religious readers typically give a moral value to intentional effort directed to a good end, they will tend to value the storage methods that rank high on this scale (memorization and writing), and will have a correspondingly negative evaluation of those that score low.

Another way of ordering or classifying methods of storage and redisplay has to do with the extent to which redisplay requires devices other than those used for storage. Works stored in manuscript form, or as printed books, are redisplayed just as they stand: they are, without further intervention, permanent possibilities of communication for people with the proper skills. But this is not true of works stored as microfiche, or as digitized computer-readable code. To read a microfiche you need not just the fiche but also a reading device. To read the matter stored on your floppy disk you need not just the disk but also a central processing unit and a monitor. And to hear the words recorded on your telephone answering machine you need not just the tape but also a player. There are interesting marginal cases: the compact edition of the *Oxford English Dictionary*, though in most senses a printed book, is not a permanent possibility of communication for normally equipped people: you need a magnifying glass to read it. Whatever is decided about such interesting cases, there is clearly a spectrum along which stored works can be ordered according to the quantity and complexity of devices needed to make their redisplay a practical possibility. And since there will be a strong correlation between stored works at the high end of this spectrum, and variables such as the expense of the devices and the nature of the institutions needed to make it possible to produce and maintain them, this, too, will be an important ordering principle to consider in thinking about the institutions in which religious reading is likely to flourish.

In the case of works given their first display visually, in writing, there is a similar range of possibilities for storage and redisplay. The work may be read aloud and then memorized, written down again, or recorded electronically. The same ordering principles can be applied here as to the possibilities for storing and redisplaying works that were given their first display aurally. But this suggests an important point about writing upon a medium that can be read from without the use of further mechanical devices. Writing in this sense is unique in that it, and it alone, is a technique for composition, display, and storage all at once. A work may be composed (in part at least) by writing on paper, or palm leaves, or parchment; a work so composed is simultaneously and already displayed and stored, the latter for as long as the physical medium upon which it is written lasts. None of the other techniques mentioned has this property. Thought is a mode of composition and storage, but not of display; speech is a mode of composition and display, but not of storage (or only of very short-term storage); and the various electronic methods of recording are modes only of storage and (sometimes) of (re)display, but not of composition. Writing upon a directly readable medium therefore holds a unique and pivotal place, a place that goes some way toward explaining the dominance it has come to have in contemporary western culture as a tool for literary composition, display, and storage.

This brief discussion suggests that works may be composed, displayed, stored, and redisplayed without the use of writing, and without literacy in the narrow sense. It also suggests, by making clear the conceptual distinctions among composition, storage, and display, that the use of a particular set of tools and techniques for one of these implies nothing about the use of those same tools and techniques for any of the others. It's important to emphasize this point because of a tendency among contemporary scholars, most of whom do their thinking in a context in which writing is dominant for the composition, display, and storage of all works, to assume that wherever writing is present at all it will assume the same dominance it has come to have for us. That it need not is obvious. It's not difficult to imagine a context in which writing is one mode of storage among others, but not the most important; or a context in which it is effectively the only mode of storage, but in which the preferred mode of display is aural; or one in which it is used for composition, but never for storage; and so on.

Rolf Köhn, in his study of the practices surrounding the composition, display, and storage of letters in medieval Europe, offers a fine illustration of how complex the relations among these variables can be.[3] In a typical case, he suggests, those who wanted to send a letter and were not versed in Latin (and likely not literate in any language) would visit a scribe and dictate to him (in the vernacular) what the letter should say. Composition in such a case is likely to be either in thought (composers decide what they want to say as they walk to the scribe's house) or in speech (they discover what their letters will say as they dictate to the scribe); first display, of course, will be entirely aural. Storage (of at least a translated version) is in writing; once written by the scribe the letter exists as a document, a *scriptum*. This document would then typically be sent to its recipient by messenger, usually with an accompanying oral message, memorized by the messenger and delivered aurally along with the document. The document would then be taken by the recipient to another scribe and read aloud (again in the vernacular, although not necessarily the one spoken by its composer) by the scribe to the recipient. Here, then, a work stored in writing is taken from storage and redisplayed aurally (with added complications provided by the necessity for translation). Neither composer nor recipient makes any use of writing, which in this example is a tool of storage only.

We do not need to go back to medieval Europe to find examples of this sort. As I was thinking about the material in this chapter, I heard on FM radio in Chicago an actress deliver what she described as one of Sojourner Truth's speeches on the rights and dignity of black women. Sojourner Truth was an illiterate itinerant preacher in the United States in the early nineteenth century. Since she was illiterate, her compositional practices could have included neither writing nor reading. She must have composed in thought or by speech, and displayed her works aurally. Then, presumably, some written record was made of her words—they were stored in writing. And then, for the purposes of the radio broadcast I heard, this written record was taken from storage and redisplayed aurally. Even in a writing-dominated culture like ours, writing is not always dominant as a means of composition and storage. What little I know of Sojourner Truth has come to me aurally, and her words were themselves ordered and delivered without the help of writing.

These examples (and it would not be difficult to multiply them) call into question the assumption of writing's inevitable dominance. Another questionable (and at least equally common) assumption is the view that the existence and use of writing makes possible the composition of kinds of works (works with certain specifiable formal characteristics) that in principle cannot be composed orally or by thought. The correlate of this assumption is the idea that 'oral texts' (a phrase that, as usually used, does not make the necessary distinctions among composition, display, and storage) have clear and specifiable properties that mark them off from written works. There is a cluster of issues here, the discussion of which has generated an enormous literature in the last thirty years. Since it is important for my argument about religious reading to consider whether religious people, in learning to read, are necessarily tied to some particular tool or technique (to interpreting marks on paper, say, or to recitation, or to memorization), I must now devote some space to a discussion of the relations between orality and literacy.

Orality and Literacy

Debates about the significance of literacy and its relations to orality typically have three axes.[4] The first has to do with the nature of literary works, with their formal features and what these features may reveal about the tools and techniques used for their composition, storage, and display. The second has to do with cognitive psychology and epistemology, with the effects the presence and use of a particular tool or technique may have upon the thought patterns, epistemological habits, and compositional practices of its users. And the third has to do with social organization, with the effects the presence and use of a particular tool or technique (writing, printing, electronic storage) may have upon social institutions of various kinds. There is an enormous literature on all three, but there are nonetheless common threads that make it relatively easy to disentangle the issues, and to isolate desirable and undesirable strategies for dealing with them.

One such thread is the tendency to tie the three issues together by making very strong claims about all of them. So, for instance, it is sometimes argued that there are formal features of works (their length, say, or the degree of complexity of their internal organization, or the presence in them of repeated formulaic elements) that signal with a very high degree of probability which tools were used for their composition and storage. It is also sometimes argued, as a correlate of this claim, that the presence and use of a particular compositional tool is determinative of the cognitive psychology of its users: that, for instance, users of technologies of thought rather than technologies of writing will, in some important respects, live in a different cognitive world than do those who live in a world like ours, "a world on paper," to borrow the title of David Olson's recent work on this topic. And as a final connecting link it is occasionally argued that the presence of writing, for example, acts not merely as a necessary condition for the existence of certain forms of social organization (such as the bureaucracy of the nation-state), but also as their sufficient condition.

Defenders of strong views such as these will typically place great emphasis upon the determinative force of technology. In the case of writing, if these views are defensible, almost everything of interest about a culture (the cognitive psychology of its members, the nature of the works they compose and store, and their modes of social organization) will be more or less directly traceable to the presence or absence of this tool. The presence or absence of a particular tool of composition, storage, or display becomes, on these views, a panacea for all explanatory difficulties. Such tools are presented as floating free of specific cultural settings and as always producing the same effects no matter what the local variables. Like space aliens who always turn the locals into identically gray and willing slaves no matter what they were like before the aliens got there, tools and techniques of composition, storage, and display are seen as turning every culture they touch into one more token of whatever type is under discussion—a writing culture, an oral culture, an electronic culture, and so on.

Most of these elements can be seen in comments on this topic to be found in the works of European intellectuals writing in the eighteenth century. A classic example is the following passage from Gibbon's *Decline and Fall of the Roman Empire* (Gibbon is contrasting the Germans of the third century with the Romans of the same period):

> The Germans, in the age of Tacitus, were unacquainted with the use of letters; and the use of letters is the principal circumstance that distinguishes a civilised people from a herd of savages incapable of knowledge or reflection. Without that artificial help, the human memory soon dissipates or corrupts the ideas intrusted to her charge; and the nobler faculties of the mind, no longer supplied with models or with materials, gradually forget their powers; the judgment becomes feeble and lethargic, the imagination languid or irregular. Fully to apprehend this important truth, let us attempt, in an improved society, to calculate the immense distance between the man of learning and the *illiterate* [emphasis Gibbon's] peasant. The former, by reading and reflection, multiplies his own experience, and lives in distant ages and remote countries; whilst the latter, rooted to a single spot, and confined to a few years of existence, surpasses, but very little, his fellow-labourer the ox in the exercise of his mental faculties. The same, and even a greater, difference will be found between nations than between individuals; and we may safely pronounce that, without some species of writing, no people has ever preserved the faithful annals of their history, ever made any considerable progress in the abstract sciences, or ever possessed, in any tolerable degree of perfection, the useful and agreeable arts of life.[5]

Almost all the elements of a deterministic view of the relations between writing and cognitive psychology are present here. Without writing, says Gibbon, memory and judgment fail, imagination is impoverished, historical memory becomes corrupt, work in the abstract sciences is impossible, and civilization is absent. Gibbon continues, interestingly, in the same chapter of *Decline and Fall*, to liken letters to money: both, he says, are conventional media of exchange, the former for ideas and thoughts, the latter for material goods. And "both these institutions, by giving a more active energy to the powers and passions of human nature, have contributed to multiply the objects they were designed to represent."[6] Literacy, for Gibbon, is the conceptual equivalent of a cash economy: the latter expands what you can buy, and the former expands what you can think. Both expand what you can want. Nonliterates are impoverished (literally) because they can neither think nor buy very much. Gibbon's thought on these matters was likely influenced by that of his friend Adam Smith: the postulation of a similarity between a culture's material economy and its conceptual economy was becoming a commonplace throughout the eighteenth century in Europe, and is still of some theoretical importance in coming to think about the significance of reading and writing, not least among pedagogical theorists.

Similarly strong arguments on the determinative importance of writing have been revived in a number of works published during the last three decades. Jack Goody and Ian Watt (who may here serve as representatives of this work) argue, in an essay published in 1963,[7] that cultures without writing tend to be homeostatic, by which they mean that there are stringent restrictions upon the kinds of information that can be transmitted in such cultures (no change here from Gibbon's views), and that this affects perceptions of the past, and of temporal process generally. They distinguish logographic systems of writing, defined by their use of pictograms as well as phonetic representations (for example, Chinese and Akkadian), from those that use fully phonetic alphabetic syllabaries (of which the paradigm is Greek after the eighth century BC or so). The latter, they say, make possible forms of social organization ruled out by the former, for these reify both the social and the natural order and as a result sit well with a stable and hierarchical social order. Alphabetic cultures, by contrast, permit a distanced and critical attitude to social structures, and are as a result conducive to individualism and the development of democracy.

Goody and Watt's overall purpose in this essay is to trace putative connections between the adoption of the alphabet in Greece in the eighth century BC and the widespread social transformations there in the following two centuries. For them, writing establishes a new relation between the word and its referent, a relation that fosters the development of a conceptual distinction between myth and history, as well as the possibility of empirical science. Epistemology and taxonomy in their systematic forms are as a result both taken to have alphabetic literacy among their necessary conditions (no Plato or Aristotle without the alphabet), as also is democracy (no *polis*, either). We are still very close to Gibbon and Smith here, although there is no clear evidence in Goody and Watt's work that they are aware of this lineage.

Similar arguments are made by Walter Ong in a number of works.[8] Like Goody and Watt, Ong argues that writing restructures consciousness, and although in the end he pays much more attention to the technology of printing than to that of writing, his work issues in the claims that these technologies have had dramatic effects upon what he likes to call the noetic economy of the West, and that such effects have been a direct outflow of the technology by itself and would have occurred no matter what other variables had been in place. Some still hold such strong views. Olson, for instance, has recently claimed that systematic thought about the structure of a language has the existence and use of writing among its preconditions,[9] a claim falsified at once by the example of Pāṇini, the Indian grammarian, who thought deeply and systematically about the structure of the Sanskrit language, but who did so without using writing and possibly even without knowing of its existence. Olson also thinks that storage of long or complex works in memory rather than in writing requires the presence in the work of specifiable formal features, for example, metrical or poetized speech.[10] Although Olson's main goal is to explain the cognitive and institutional effects of the presence of writing (and printing) in the West (and his comments on many aspects of that story are of great use), he still exhibits a strong tendency to hypostatize and give independent power to particular tools and techniques of composition and storage.

These strong views as to the cognitive and social significance of writing, and as to the possibility of determining compositional technology on the basis of a work's formal features, are almost certainly mistaken, or at the very least too crude, as many studies of specific cases of the effects of writing have begun to make clear. The most that can be said with any degree of plausibility is that a particular set of tools and techniques for composition, display, and storage may, in certain settings, have significant effects upon such things as cognition, compositional practice, the formal features of literary works, and social organization.

Certainly, particular instances of such causal relations can be shown with a very high degree of plausibility. The case can be made, for example, as it has been by Elizabeth Eisenstein in her study of the uses of printing in Europe, and by Robert Darnton in his work on the publication of the *Encyclopédie* between 1775 and 1800, that there were strong connections between the introduction of print technology and certain kinds of social change in early modern Europe. And a study by C. A. Read and others shows that the acquisition of alphabetic literacy (in addition to pictographic literacy) has strong effects upon the ways in which native readers of Chinese handle and relate to their language.[11]

But to point to examples of such causal connection is very different from claiming that the presence of a particular tool or technique will always have specific and identical effects no matter what other variables are in place. Making the more limited claim should lead to studies of the effects of particular technologies in particular settings, and of the relations between these effects and other local variables. And, as might have been expected, such studies, insofar as they have been carried out, suggest strongly that the effects of particular tools and techniques, whether of composition, storage, or display, are very different in different settings. The monolithic views are simply not adequate.[12] Two brief case studies—of what Milman Parry and Albert Lord have argued about the Homeric corpus, and of what is currently argued about the uses of writing in ancient and classical India—will serve to illustrate the inadequacy of monolithic views.

The Parry/Lord Theory

A locus classicus for the view that there is a strong and direct correlation between the formal features of literary works and the techniques use to compose, display, and store them is the so-called Parry/Lord theory as to the oral composition and display of the Homeric epics.[13] Milman Parry originated this theory in a series of articles written in the late 1920s and early 1930s. He argued that the *Iliad* and the *Odyssey* could be shown to have been composed and displayed without the use of writing solely on the basis of their formal features—most especially their repeated use of stock epithets or formulaic expressions to identify dramatis personae ("great-hearted" or "swift-running" for Achilles; "lord of the silver bow" for Apollo; and so on). Parry took these formal features to suggest composition-in-performance by the poet (or singer). Each performance of the *Iliad,* on this view, was a set of improvisations around a known plotline, given literary form by the use of stereotyped formulae. This view was developed and given further precision and subtlety by Parry's student, Albert Lord, in a number of works published over more than thirty years. It has been and remains one of the chief topics of discussion among those working on the Homeric corpus, as well as among those interested in the complex of issues surrounding orality and literacy.

Lord's version of the theory argues that features of oral composition and display observable in the practices of bardic reciters of epic narratives in Eastern Europe (specifically, the improvisatory nature of each performance and the repetitive use of stock formulaic elements as an ordering device) are features whose presence is guaranteed by and in turn guarantees the predominance of oral composition and aural display. If you have oral composition and aural display, runs the claim, then you will have these features; and wherever you find these features you will also find oral composition and aural display. This is true for the bardic singers of Eastern Europe, argues Lord, and it is also true for the Homeric corpus: in the case of the latter it is possible to infer the techniques used for its composition and display from the formal features of the work as we have it. For Parry and Lord it is definitionally true of oral works (or at least of oral epics) that they have no fixed verbal form, but are instead created anew (and differently) on each occasion of their performance. The singer of tales, to use Lord's phrase, does not reproduce a memorized work, but instead performs a set of variations on a theme, putting different verbal flesh on the same narrative skeleton on each occasion of performance.

This proposed strong connection between the presence of formulaic elements (stock epithets, repetitions with structural significance, and so on) and improvisatory oral composition and aural display can be shown not to obtain in a number of ways. The first is by indicating works that have these features and yet whose composition and display have much to do with writing. Donald Fry's studies of Caedmon and Larry Benson's work on the literary character of Anglo-Saxon poetry do this for medieval England, and Dennis Green and Werner Hoffmann do it for medieval German literature.[14] The second is by indicating examples of lengthy epic narratives displayed aurally that possess the formulaic elements pointed out by Parry and Lord, and yet whose display has few or no improvisatory elements, but rather is a matter of reproducing a memorized and largely invariant set of words. John Smith's ethnographic work on the performance of the Pābūji and Devnārāyan epics in Rajasthan provides just such an instance, as do ethnographic reports by Arthur Grimble of the composition and display of epic poetry in the Pacific Islands.[15] In this latter case, composition is done by an individual alone; a preliminary version of the poem is then displayed aurally to a small group for comment and criticism; revisions are made by the poet, again in solitude; the final version is then memorized and displayed aurally on subsequent occasions, essentially without further verbal variation.

These examples, if they hold up, suffice to destroy the determinism of the strong form of the Parry/Lord theory. They show that long narrative works displayed aurally should not be assumed to have been improvised rather than memorized. Neither should the presence of formulaic elements in a work be thought to rule out the use of writing for its composition and display.

The Parry/Lord theory is an example of an unnuanced deterministic view about the relations between tools and techniques of composition, display, and storage, on the one hand, and other variables such as the formal features of literary works, the cognitive psychology of their users, and so on, on the other. The facts mentioned in the immediately preceding paragraphs strongly suggest that it does not carry conviction. This is not to say that the Parry/Lord theory is entirely mistaken or uninteresting: Parry and Lord did succeed in identifying and describing with precision a particular mode of composition and display that is independent of writing; they erred definitionally, though, in claiming that all composition and display done without writing share these features, and that all works with the formal features found in Homer and in the songs of the Eastern European bards are the product of just this kind of composition and display. In fact, as the examples mentioned have shown, not all writing-free composition and display need be of the inspired-improvisatory kind identified by Parry and Lord: some may make use of a fixed, memorized set of words and be the product of much effort prior to and independent of display. And, equally important, not all works with formulaic epithets need be composed or displayed without writing: Kipling's Just-So stories and Dr. Seuss's children's stories provide striking twentieth-century examples.

Writing in Ancient India

The Parry/Lord theory rests, as do most such, upon strong intuitions about what can and cannot be done with techniques of composition, storage, and display that do not include writing. These intuitions are usually not supported with evidence; they rest largely upon unexpressed inferences from what is possible for us, compulsive users of writing that we are, to conclusions about what must have been possible for them. These intuitions are very often called into question by evidence from particular cases, and an especially interesting example is ancient India.[16] What then do we know about the ancient Indian uses of writing?

Suppose we consider 'ancient' to mean the millennium preceding the birth of Christ. Writing was, it is true, used in the region before this: there are survivals of a non-Sanskritic written language used in the second millennium before Christ on some seals from Harappa (in what is now the Punjab) and Mohenjodaro (in Sind). The script used on these seals has not been deciphered, and while it is certainly evidence of the use of writing on the Indian subcontinent at a very early period, its survivals are so few and its significance so uncertain (it has not been deciphered) that its existence is of only marginal relevance to the question under discussion.

Leaving aside these Indus Valley materials, we know that during the first millennium before Christ in India a very large body of literature was composed, displayed, stored, and repeatedly redisplayed. Much of it was in some form of Sanskrit, and much also in various Sanskrit-related languages, generically called Prakrits. These works include examples of many genres. The Veda itself, however its limits are defined, includes the *Rigveda*, a collection of more than ten thousand verses of praise, homage, lament, and cosmogonic or cosmological speculation. Ancillary to it, and by some definitions part of it, are the *Brāhmaṇas*, enormous collections of theory about ritual and instruction in ritual performance. Various technical treatises for help in using and learning the Veda were also composed in this period, notably the *Anukramaṇī*, which are lists that provide information about each hymn in the Veda—its first word, the number of verses in it, its meter, and the names of the deities addressed in it.

Quite apart from the Vedic corpus and its ancillaries, technical treatises on numerous subjects began to be composed in this period. A notable example is

Pāṇini's treatise on grammar called *Aṣṭādhyāyī*, a work comprising almost four thousand algebraic statements (each called a sutra) in which is given a complete analytical description of the Sanskrit language as it was spoken around 500 BC (if the usual guesses about Pāṇini's dates are right). This treatise soon attracted commentators, and by the beginning of the Christian era two large works of exposition (by Kātyāyana and Patañjali) had been completed and were in circulation. Buddhists, too, composed and stored a vast array of literature during this period, including narratives, histories, discourses attributed to the Buddha, rules of discipline for monks, and manuals of philosophy.

This is only a small portion of the literary work composed and stored in India during this millennium. The evidence available as to the uses of writing during this period is sparse and capable of varying interpretations, so no definitive statement on the significance of its use is possible, and perhaps none ever will be. There is a tangle of different issues connected with this large topic, including questions about the origins of the two principal scripts used in India after the third century BC, about possible references to writing in Indic works from the ancient period, about the interpretation of accounts given by Greek visitors to India at and after the time of Alexander—and much more.[17]

It is useful to approach the question in two different ways. First, what hard evidence is there as to the question of when writing began to be used in India, and for what? Hard evidence would be material remains (inscriptions or manuscripts) that can be dated with something other than guesswork. Second, what soft evidence is there as to the use and significance of writing in ancient India? Soft evidence would be mentions or descriptions of writing in works of the relevant period, or clear indications from within such works that writing must have been used in their composition or storage.

The earliest hard evidence for the use of writing in Sanskrit or Sanskrit-related languages in the Indian subcontinent is the edicts that the Emperor Aśoka caused to be inscribed in the third century BC on rocks and pillars in various parts of the subcontinent, ranging from the extreme northwest to the far south, and including both eastern and western coasts. Some of these inscriptions are written in Brāhmī script, and some in Kharoṣṭhī, and they are all in various forms of Prakrit (no Sanskrit inscriptions with a date earlier than the second century BC have yet been found in India). Further, they all have to do with broadly political and administrative matters. The earliest surviving manuscripts written in Indic scripts and languages (the only other kind of hard evidence there could be) have been found in Central Asia and date from the second century after Christ. Manuscripts found on Indian soil are much later, usually more than a millennium later.

The only other material remains that may indicate the use of writing in Indic scripts at an early date are some pottery shards unearthed in Sri Lanka and tentatively dated to the sixth century BC by the use of radiocarbon methods. These shards have fragments of writing in Brāhmī script incised upon them. But their dating is not firm: there are very few shards, and it appears possible that they have been disturbed by intrusion from other layers at the site where they were found.[18]

There is, then, no hard evidence for the use of writing in Brāhmī or Kharoṣṭhī script in India before the third century BC, and none for the use of writing for the composition, display, or storage of literary (i.e., nonadministrative, nonpolitical) works before the early centuries of the Christian era. None of this means much by itself, of course. The climate of most of India is not conducive to the survival of manuscripts written on palm leaves or birch bark, which were the two favored materials for writing until the introduction of paper well into the second millennium of the Christian era. So the absence of early witnesses certainly doesn't mean there were none. Is there, then, any softer evidence on the matter? Do any works from the relevant period mention writing or imply its use?

There is no explicit mention of writing, and no clear implication of its use, in any part of the broadly Vedic corpus, most parts of which had been composed by the time of Aśoka. There are a number of places in this corpus that have been taken by both western and Indian scholars to suggest the use of writing; but I follow Harry Falk's recent study in concluding that there is no clear textual evidence for the use of writing in the Vedic corpus.

Moving now beyond the Vedic corpus, there are some possible mentions of writing in Pāṇini's grammatical work (which probably predates Aśoka). In sutra 3.2.21 Pāṇini uses the term *lipikara/libikara*, which some take to mean 'scribe', 'one who makes writing'. But in fact the meaning of this term is far from clear; it may mean not 'scribe' but 'artist', or 'painter'. Even if it does refer to writing (which is possible), the most likely interpretation is that Pāṇini, in using it, signals his knowledge of the writing habits of the Achaemenids, within whose sphere of influence northern India then was (there is some evidence to suggest that the term *lipi/libi* is itself an Iranian loanword, which further supports this view). Pāṇini's use of the term does not suggest that he used writing himself: if it refers to writing at all, it suggests rather that he identified the use of writing with foreigners.

The other place is sutra 4.1.49, where Pāṇini gives the word *yavana* ('Greek') as an example of a term to which the affix *-āni* can be added to make a feminine noun (in this case *yavanāni*). The earliest surviving commentary on this sutra, by Kātyāyana (perhaps from the time of Aśoka) takes *yavanāni* to mean 'Greek writing' (*yavanāl lipyām*), which (probably) means writing in Kharoṣṭhī script. It is not quite clear that this is in fact what Pāṇini meant by the term, but this evidence does at least indicate that the fact of writing was known to a Sanskrit grammarian in India in the third century BC, at a period roughly the same as that of the Aśokan inscriptions.

The evidence from Pāṇini and his commentators therefore gives almost no grounds for thinking that they used writing themselves. It does give grounds for supposing that, insofar as they thought about the matter, writing was for them something that foreigners did.

The only other explicit mentions of writing in works from this period are in the Buddhist rules of monastic discipline, the *Vinaya*. While these mentions raise difficult interpretive questions of their own, the most thorough and careful studies strongly suggest that the places from this corpus in which writing is clearly mentioned are relatively late, certainly post-Aśoka.[19]

There is some interesting evidence from Greek historians on the use of writing in India before Aśoka. Following the conquests of Alexander in the second half of the fourth century BC, references to India begin to appear in Greek literature. For example, Megasthenes, who was the Indian envoy of the Syrian Seleucid monarch from 302 to 291 BC, spent several years at the court of Candragupta I, the first Mauryan emperor, in what is now Bihar. Based on his years there, he wrote a work describing Indian customs, geography, political habits, and much else. This work, usually called *Indika*, has not survived independently; but it can be consulted in the lengthy extracts from it quoted by other Greek authors, principally Strabo. Some of these fragments have suggestive things to say about Indian uses of writing.[20]

In one (#27), Megasthenes, in describing the legal practices of the Indians, says that they make no use of letters (of *grammata*, of writing) and must therefore rely upon their memories when arguing cases in the law courts. In another (#33), he discusses the functions of philosophers at the royal court, and mentions their composition and aural display of opinion without using any terms that imply the use of writing for these purposes. And in yet a third fragment (#34), Megasthenes mentions the presence on Indian roads of mileposts to mark distance and the directions in which other roads might be found. This may imply the use of writing: perhaps the information was engraved upon the posts. But it need not. Perhaps these pillars, like the punch-marked coins of the same period, communicated what they had to communicate without writing, by using visual devices of some kind.[21]

The evidence offered by Megasthenes largely supports the idea that in the India of the early Mauryas writing was not a significant tool of composition, display, or storage. It was used, if it was used at all, solely for administrative and political purposes—and this in spite of the fact that by 300 BC a large body of complex, ornate, lengthy, and technical works had already been composed in Sanskrit. A century ago, Max Müller, the German Indologist, put this point trenchantly:

> Where the art of alphabetic writing is known and practised for literary purposes, no person on earth could conceal the fact, and I still challenge any scholar to produce any mention of writing in Indian literature before the supposed age of Panini. To say that a literature is impossible without alphabetic writing shows a want of acquaintance with Greek, Hebrew, Finnish, Estonian, Mordvinian, nay with Mexican literature. Why should all names for writing, paper, ink, stylus, letters, or books have been so carefully avoided if they had been in daily use? Besides, it is well known that the interval between the use of alphabetic writing for official or monumental purposes and its use for literature is very wide. Demand only creates supply, and a written literature would presuppose a reading public such as no one has yet claimed for the time of Homer, of Moses, of the authors of the Kalevala, the Kalevipoeg, or of the popular and religious songs of Ugro-Finnish or even Mexican races. To say that the art of writing was kept secret, that the Brâhmans probably kept one copy only of each work for themselves, learnt it by heart and taught it to their pupils, shows what imagination can do in order to escape from facts.[22]

It's likely, then, that writing was not used for composition and storage in India before Aśoka, and probably not for several centuries thereafter; that the

Brāhmī script, if not actually invented for administrative purposes by Aśoka's regime, is not likely to have been in use much before his time; that neither it nor Kharoṣṭhī were used at all widely, even for administrative purposes, until well after Aśoka; and that, during the first millennium BC, literary works were composed and stored very largely, if not exclusively, in the heads of Brahmins and Buddhist monks, and displayed with their mouths.

This does not, naturally, say anything about the use of writing in India after the beginning of the Christian era. In this period, references to the tools and techniques of writing multiply, and there is considerable hard evidence of various kinds. But even after the birth of Christ, literary references to the tools and practices of writing are relatively rare. It is possible to read hundreds of pages of material composed between the third century AD and the thirteenth without discovering any references of this sort; and if Müller's words are to be taken seriously, this should at least suggest that the authors and compilers of Indian works found writing to be insignificant to their own thinking about literary composition and display for long after writing had become well known and widely used in India. Although writing did come increasingly to be used as a tool for storage, the physical objects produced in that way were meant at least as much to be given ritual and magical significance as to be read. The memory and the mouth remained (and in some circles still remain) the essential tools for the storage and display of literary works.

Some still express disbelief in, or at least surprise at, the likelihood that India was effectively preliterate until the third century BC, and not much addicted to the use of writing for long thereafter. Richard Salomon, for instance, in acknowledging that this probably was the state of things, says (as recently as 1995):

> But can we imagine such a state of affairs, given what we know (admittedly not too much) of the state of society and culture in India, especially in the northeast, before this time [sc. the third century BC]? If we can put any trust at all in the traditional lore of the *Purāṇas* and the testimony of the Pāli canon, Magadha was the site of great and prosperous empires, notably that of the Nandas, decades if not centuries before the foundation of the Mauryan dynasty around 320 B.C. Can we believe that these dynasties with their legendary riches, and the remarkable intellectual and cultural life of India in the time of the Buddha and Mahāvīra, existed in a totally illiterate sphere?[23]

Salomon knows that we must imagine and believe these things. But the tone of wonder in his rhetorical questions shows how deeply the iron of writing's dominance has entered into our souls.

The conclusion that the use of writing for the storage of literary works does not predate the third century BC, and was not widely evident until long after that, has the advantage of being approximately in accord with what the Buddhist tradition says of its own use of writing, for it is in this tradition that we have the earliest clear reference to the use of writing as a medium of storage (though still not, notice, for composition). It is in two verses found in historical chronicles composed in Pali, a Sanskrit-related language used in Sri Lanka for the composition of Buddhist literature:

> Previously, wise monks handed down the threefold collection of sacred works orally (*mukhapāṭhena*), together with its exposition. But then, seeing that sentient beings were degenerating, they assembled and caused [all these works] to be written in books (*potthakesu likhāpayum*) so that the doctrine would last for a long time.[24]

The chronicles attribute this event to the reign of King Vattagāmaṇī in Sri Lanka, probably between 89 and 77 BC. This falls (just) within the period of interest to me here, and although it happened in Sri Lanka rather than India, it seems not unreasonable to include that island, by courtesy and for these purposes only, in India. Suppose we judge the event described in these verses to have occurred in the first century BC. The clear implication is that until then the large corpus of Buddhist literature had been displayed only aurally and stored only in memory. Nothing is explicitly said about composition; but if writing was not used for storage and display, it is unlikely to have been used for composition, either. Suppose, on the other hand, that the event described did not occur when the chronicles say it did, but was instead fabricated a couple of centuries later by the authors of the Pali chronicles. In this case we can conclude only that Buddhists composing in Sri Lanka during the early centuries of the Christian era thought it reasonable to have and to present such a view of the uses of writing. But even this is evidence in support of the view that writing was not a significant tool of composition and storage in India during the first millennium before Christ.

A final point about these verses. The verb they use to denote writing (*likhāpayum*) is in the causative: it is not the monks who do the writing; they have it done for them by someone else, by professional scribes. This secondhand use of writing does not require those who compose and recite and direct others to record in writing to themselves be skilled in the making and deciphering of scratch marks on palm leaves, any more than my ability to compose material with the help of a computer requires me to understand and be able to reproduce the technology that produced my computer. The religiously learned, on this view, do not need to be literate in the narrow sense.

This small excursion into ancient India supports by illustration the conclusion that monolithic and deterministic views of the relations between literary genre and particular techniques of composition and storage, whether defended by Gibbon two hundred years ago or Goody last week, are deeply mistaken. And this is important because, while religious reading does require, or at least strongly suggests the desirability of, composing and storing works in some very specific genres (florilegium, chrestomathy, enchiridion, commentary, catechism), it does not follow from this fact that those engaged in religious reading are tied to the use of particular tools and techniques of composition and storage. Religious reading has a strong elective affinity for some tools and techniques (for example, for the arts of memory), not because of a deterministic relation between these tools and composition in certain literary genres, but for a combination of ethical and practical reasons, about which I shall soon say more.

The existence of particular literary genres in specific cultural settings does suggest the presence there of certain attitudes toward literary work; it may also indicate predispositions toward the use of some tools and techniques over others; but it neither determines nor is determined by the presence and use of these tools and techniques. It's important to note, as well, that if deterministic views of the relations between the formal features of literary works (genre, length, internal complexity, and so forth) and the tools and techniques used for their composition are not correct, then the use of certain genres by religious readers doesn't require the possession of literacy in the narrow sense. It doesn't require the capacity to make semantically laden marks on permanent media of storage; nor even the capacity to decode such marks made by others. Religious readers, paradoxically, need not know how to read.

How Religious People Read

Religious learning involves reading. More than that, it is largely constituted by reading. But reading religiously is in many ways deeply different from the kinds of reading taught in the schools of contemporary nation-states, like those of Western Europe and North America, in which universal adult literacy is either a reality or an aspiration.[25] Religious reading requires and fosters a particular set of attitudes to what is read, as well as reading practices that comport well with those attitudes; and it implies an epistemology, a set of views about what knowledge is and about the relations between reading and the acquisition and retention of knowledge.

You may read for a wide variety of reasons: for religious learning, for academic prestige, for the acquisition of information, to relieve boredom, to excite your emotions, or to demonstrate a skill. If you read for any of these reasons, you will, if you are lucky and well taught, use the most appropriate technique for your purposes. Religious reading, like any other kind of reading, is done with a purpose: the acquisition or development of the skills and information necessary for offering a religious account. As a result, religious readers are likely to find particular techniques and methods congenial and others problematic. In this they differ not at all from those who read for entertainment or titillation.

It's important to emphasize these facts because of a widespread tendency, especially evident among professional readers in western institutions of higher education, to assimilate all forms of reading to a single standard model, which is through and through consumerist. All other forms of reading are then judged in terms of the extent to which their practices and goals approximate to or deviate from those of this standard consumerist model, and forced to follow its norms. This is a mistake because it implies that the superiority of one mode of reading (the consumerist mode) is self-evident, and that as a result all other modes should be judged in terms of it and assimilated to it. But this is an odd conclusion to come to. The sumo wrestler's program of diet and exercise is different from the gymnast's, and for good reasons; why should not the religious reader's way with reading be different from the consumerist's, for equally good reasons?

That religious reading and consumerist reading are different is (or will soon become) obvious; it is also clear that the latter has assumed a position of unquestioned dominance among professional readers (who are also usually those who teach and theorize about reading), as well as in the pedagogical practices used by those charged to teach religion, to transmit religious learning in religious institutions. This is unfortunate, unnecessary, and for religious learning disastrous, because coming to offer a comprehensive, unsurpassable, and central account has the skills of religious reading among its necessary conditions, and these are in large part antithetical to those fostered by consumerist reading.

What then of religious reading? How is it to be characterized? Reading is usually understood to mean the visual consumption of ordered patterns of print on a page (or script on vellum; or scratch marks on palm leaves; or hieroglyphs on granite; or ideographs on plates of silver; or pixels of light on a liquid-crystal screen). In other words, it is usually understood to require written objects to be read, and so to entail the specific technical skill of extracting meaning from such objects. But religious reading is a practice both more and less specific than this. It has to do primarily with the establishment of certain relations between readers and the things they read, relations that are at once attitudinal, cognitive, and moral, and that therefore imply an ontology, an epistemology, and an ethic. This kind of reading requires neither written objects nor the technical skill of extracting meaning from them, though it will commonly be connected with both, and may, if certain other cultural and institutional variables are in place, require their production and use. Religious reading, then, though it does require literary works if these are understood generously as ordered systems of signs, does not require written works. It may take as its object, that which it reads, a work displayed only as an ordered pattern of sounds in the air (something spoken or musical); or one displayed only as an ordered pattern of three-dimensional shapes (a sculpture); or (just conceivably) one displayed only as an ordered pattern of tastes, smells, or tactile stimuli—as in the case of the teachings of the Tathāgata Sugandhakūṭa, which, according to the *Vimalakīrtinirdeśasūtra*, are given not in words but only by means of smells.[26] But it will, in every case, imply a distinctive set of relations between religious readers and their works.

The first and most basic element in these relations is that the work read is understood as a stable and vastly rich resource, one that yields meaning, suggestions (or imperatives) for action, matter for aesthetic wonder, and much else. It is a treasure-house, an ocean, a mine: the deeper religious readers dig, the more ardently they fish, the more single-mindedly they seek gold, the greater will be their reward. The basic metaphors here are those of discovery, uncovering, retrieval, opening up: religious readers read what is there to be read, and what is there to be read always precedes, exceeds, and in the end supersedes its readers. There can, according to these metaphors, be no final act of reading in which everything is uncovered, in which the mine of gold has yielded all its treasure or the fish pool has been emptied of fish. Reading, for religious readers, ends only with death, and perhaps not then: it is a continuous, ever-repeated act.

The second, and almost equally important, constituent of the relations between religious readers and what they read is that readers are seen as intrinsically capable of reading and as morally required to read. Their capacity for retrieving the riches of the work by an act of reading is something intrinsic to them: they are essentially and necessarily readers, to the point where *homo lector* can be substituted for *homo sapiens* without loss and with considerable gain. Nonreaders, on this view, are precisely those who have largely renounced their humanity, their defining characteristic; and it is typical of religious readers that for them the act of reading is, in George Steiner's nice phrase, an "unmistakable witness to the ambiguous mastery of texts over life."[27] The work's intrinsic stability and fecundity as a resource is therefore matched by the reader's intrinsic stability and ingenuity as a discoverer or uncoverer. Both works and readers are ordered; it is this that makes acts of religious reading possible, and this that guarantees their continuation and fruitfulness.

Religious readers therefore treat what they read with reverence. Since the literary work is what it is for them, they will necessarily adopt toward it an attitude incompatible with those implied by consumerist uses of literary works. Consumers treat what they read only as objects for consumption, to be discarded when the end for which they are read has been achieved. Consider, as an illustration of this attitude, the consumerist reading done by professional academics in Europe and America at the end of the twentieth century: the attitude toward works implied in their practice is based on metaphors of production, consumption, use, and control. Academic readers consume the works of others and produce their own; they are defined and given status by the body of literature they control and upon which they are accredited to give authoritative (expert) voice for proper reward; they cite and mention (rather than religiously read), and are in turn judged largely by the extent to which the works they produce (again, the industrial metaphor, the image of mass production) are cited and mentioned.

Or, as a rather different but complementary contrastive case, consider the reading practices of the (usually male) user of sadistic pornography, or the (usually female) user of romantic fiction. Such readers read only to produce certain effects: sexual arousal, perhaps, in the case of the pornography user; or emotional titillation in the case of the romance user. When the required effects have been produced, the objects read have no more useful work to do. They can be discarded: returned to the circulating library, sold back to the used bookstore, or given away. The use of textbooks in schools, universities, and colleges is similar, as is that of most of the occasional writing found in magazines and newspapers: readers read such works to gain ephemeral information, to titillate rather than to cultivate, to entertain rather than to transform. All these are forms of consumerist reading.

Reverential religious reading is quite different. For the religious reader, the work read is an object of overpowering delight and great beauty. It can never be discarded because it can never be exhausted. It can only be reread, with reverence and ecstasy. The Bible is, as Bernard of Clairvaux put it in his thirty-fifth sermon on the Song of Songs delivered in the 1130s, the wine cellar of the Holy Spirit (*spiritus sancti apotheca*); and since it is, no one should be surprised if people spend a lot of time in it and study it curiously to see what it can do for them. In the same sermon he says that it is tasty matter for rumination that fattens his stomach (*replentur viscera mea*) and makes all his bones sing with praise (*omnia ossa mea germinant laudam*).[28] Anselm of Canterbury expressed similar sentiments about the words of Christ in the opening paragraph of his meditation on human redemption composed at the beginning of the twelfth century:

> Taste the goodness of your Redeemer, burn with love for your Savior. Chew the honeycomb of his words, suck their flavor, which is more pleasing than honey, swallow their health-giving sweetness. Chew by thinking [*mande cogitando*], suck by understanding [*suge intellegendo*], swallow by loving and rejoicing [*gluti amando et gaudendo*]. Be happy in chewing, be grateful in sucking, delight in swallowing.[29]

Images of rumination, of eating, and of digestion are everywhere in medieval Christianity. The words of the work read (paradigmatically, but not only, the Bible) are the sweetest possible food, it is said; you cannot tire of chewing, of sucking, of savoring them once you have come to think of them in this way. Bernard and Anselm show, in using such figures, not only reverence for their works, but also active delight in them, and these attitudes are entirely typical of those that religious readers bring to what they read.

Neither are such attitudes limited to Christians. Buddhists, too, have shown (and show) reverence for and delight in their literary works. A commentary composed by Asaṅga in the fourth or fifth century after Christ in India, the *Mahāyānasūtrālaṅkārabhāṣya*, says that the words of the work on which it comments provide supreme pleasure, like something made from beaten gold (*ghatitasuvarṇādivat*).[30] And, in the *Vajracchedikāsūtra*, a work said to have been spoken by the Buddha, there is the following exalted claim about the benefits of studying the work:

> And again, Subhūti, suppose that a being turned toward awakening, a great being, having filled immeasurable and incalculable world-systems [*aprameyāsamkhyeyalokadhātu*] with the seven precious things, were to give them as a gift to the Tathāgatas, the Arhats, the Perfectly Awakened Buddhas; and then suppose that a man or woman of the right lineage, having taken up from this perfection of wisdom [i.e., from this very work] a verse of even four lines, were to memorize it, teach it, and master it [*catuṣpādikam api gāthām udgṛhya dhārayed deśayet paryavāpnuyād*], and were to explain it in detail to others [*parebhyaś ca vistareṇa saṃprakāśayet*]—the latter would certainly produce immeasurable and incalculable merit, vastly more than the former.[31]

If learning and teaching a four-line verse from a particular work produces more merit than giving away whole world-systems filled with jewels, it seems reasonable to assume that the work in question is an extremely valuable object. And such judgments about the value of works read are integral to the construction of a comprehensive, unsurpassable, and central account—a properly religious account.

It may be (although the matter continues to be disputed) that the term *religio* derives from *relegere*, 'to reread'. This was Cicero's view, though it was opposed by Lucretius and later by Lactantius, both of whom prefer to derive *religio* from *religare*, 'to rebind' or 'to reconnect'. No resolution of this debate has been reached by philologists, but the derivation from *relegere* is rhetorically pleasing since it allows the conceit that what makes rereading religious reading is (semantically) that this is what religion means. Or, as René Gothóni puts it:

> [Religious] action is the *intellectual activity* [emphasis original] containing unceasing re-reading, reflecting and reviewing the testimonies of the sacred traditions. . . . [*R*]*eligio* is, then, a faculty or talent to be cultivated.[32]

Anne Klein, in her study of Tibetan oral commentary, makes similar points:

> [T]he modern secular construct of 'reading' seems inadequate to describe Tibetan textual engagement. The face-to-face and often ritualized encounter with the person whose oral commentary is integral to the experience of text is one differentiating factor; another and even more significant difference is what occurs through repeated practice of the text, that is, through performing the procedures it teaches, including recitation, visualization, and conceptual training. One is not so much reworking the written text—although this is a crucial and fundamental practice in many quarters—as reworking the self. Nor does the usual meaning of 'reading' illuminate the nonconceptual processes of calming, breathing, concentration, and mental intensity so central to meditative textual practices.[33]

Consumerist readers and religious readers have, then, very different attitudes to reading. The dissimilarities can be put in a different light by emphasizing the importance of writerly creativity for consumerist readers, and its almost complete lack of importance for religious ones. Consumerist readers who have the courage of their convictions understand themselves to be writers as well as readers; religious readers who know what they are doing do not. But I mean writing here in a rather special sense. I do not mean to limit the word to a practice that involves making visible marks on some more-or-less permanent medium of storage; I mean, rather, a practice that is quintessentially creative, a process that brings order and structure where there was none, whose description involves appeal to images of making, of construction, of conceit (in both the literary and affective senses of that word), of ornamentation, and of artifice. Focus on the root metaphor of writing as essential to, even constitutive of, human beings, makes us, as writers, the center of our own epistemological and ethical interests. The practice of writing, understood in this way, is the only creative act, the only act by means of which order and structure can be given to things. There is no order or meaning other than that inscribed by the act of writing and created by writers, and this means that writers, when writing, inscribe always and endlessly themselves, their own potential for creating order. This is a familiar, now almost a tired, theoretical trope: everything, even (especially) philosophy, is a kind of writing, as Richard Rorty puts it in his discussion of Jacques Derrida,[34] and the proper object of all intellectual inquiry is, in the end, rhetoric. Even consumerist readers of pornography or romance are, in reading such stuff, writing their own sensuality or their own emotional life, creating it and giving it form, even if unsubtle and undifferentiated form.

There are fundamental and crucial differences here. For religious readers the world is a textualized field of endlessly uncoverable ordered riches. For consumerist readers/writers the world is also textualized; but it is an endlessly constructable field of play, and not just any play, but most especially the free play of signifiers that can be ordered at whim into lightly orgasmic objects of *jouissance*, of sexual or sensual pleasure. Writers, according to this interpretation, are radically autonomous, subject to nothing other than their own creative impulses, and constrained by nothing other than the limitless potential of the signifiers to be arrayed to serve and please them. To take a financial analogue: religious readers draw upon a very substantial savings account, but have to balance the books as they go and can do so only by handling currency; consumerist readers/writers have to hand a credit card without limit. They need never touch cash, and they get their pleasure solely from engaging in the process of production that, for them, is also the process of consumption. In this they are, as Fredric Jameson claims, most at home in the culture of late capitalism:

> [O]ne's sense, particularly when dealing with foreigners who have been enflamed by American consumerism, is that the products form a kind of hierarchy whose climax lies very precisely in the technology of reproduction itself, which now, of course, fans out well beyond the classical television set and has come in general to epitomize the new informational or computer technology of the third stage of capitalism.[35]

This is typical of the attitude of consumerist readers and writers to the activity of writing. It is important to have written, to be writing, and to project the process of writing into the future. The product of writing (the literary work) is relatively unimportant, just as the artifacts to be consumed in late capitalist cultures are unimportant relative to the process of anticipating, lusting after, and consuming them. Religious readers are, by contrast, strictly feudal: for them, the object is of central importance and the processes of production are of marginal interest. Recall, once again, Gibbon's connection between literacy and the kinds of trade made possible by symbolic representations of wealth like coins and banknotes.

There is some superficial similarity between religious reading and the kind of consumerist writing I've been describing. Both are deeply text centered, and that this is the case goes some way toward explaining the attraction of religious reading for some contemporary writers. Geoffrey Hartman, a literary theorist, has some perceptive comments to make about this in his discussion of Midrashic exegetical practice:

> Of course, literary commentaries and Midrashic ones have their differences. But these are not easy to define except by pseudo criteria. The very advance of contemporary theory toward Midrash makes Jewish scholars more zealous to avoid contamination. There is fear that the motive for Midrash will be reduced from *Everything is in the text, and what the text signifies is its relevance to the actions or thoughts of the interpretive community* to *Everything is text, and the text is a structure of imaginary relations, a tissue without issue.* I acknowledge the danger, but why be frightened by those who insist on being superficial?[36]

Hartman's distinction between "everything is text" and "everything is in the text" is crucial. Religious readers believe the latter (and read as if they did) but not the former. According to them, the textualized world is intrinsically other than the human, ordered independently of it, and capable of acting upon it. But according to consumerist readers/writers, the nonhuman effectively dissolves into the human. Ontology becomes epistemology, and the self becomes the all-absorbing (perhaps in the end the only) topic of philosophical interest. And this in turn means that writers read only (or at least typically) in consumerist mode, to serve their writerliness.

These contrasts may offer some suggestive possibilities for classifying movements in the history of thought, categories to be used in painting, with very broad brush strokes, the allegiance and methods of particular schools of thought and particular thinkers. Writing, as I've just described it, is the root metaphor of late modernity and postmodernity, while reading is that of the premodern, dominant in the West until the sixteenth or early seventeenth century. Then, with Montaigne, Descartes, Spinoza, and Locke, religious reading began to be transformed into writing; and writing has been the dominant metaphor for our intellectual practices for at least the last half-century, coupled as it so often is in philosophy with what Alvin Plantinga has, in a number of works, usefully called creative antirealism.[37]

More can be said about the intellectual practices that constitute the ideal type of religious reading. The first additional point to emphasize is the role of memory.[38] If religious reading involves the kind of inexhaustibly repetitive rereading that I've pointed to, then inevitably memorization of what is read will often occur. A work can be reread only so often before it becomes stored in the memory to be capable of recall (rereading) at will without further need for external stimuli. Religious readers, unlike consumerist writers, will therefore have a large body of works at memorial command. But although such memorial storage would occur anyway, as a by-product of the ordinary practices of religious reading, it will typically be actively sought and inculcated through the intentional use of mnemotechnical devices. Large bodies of material can be stored and recalled with relative ease and rapidity by religious readers trained in the use of such devices. The ideal-typical community of religious readers will therefore harbor virtuosos of the arts of memory, and will require even of its nonvirtuoso members feats of memory that are almost unbelievable to and certainly unattainable by, most contemporary writers.

Use of the memorial arts is important for religious readers for more than these practical reasons, however. For such readers the ideally read work is the memorized work, and the ideal mode of rereading is by memorial recall. This is because a work whose potential for being understood and used is both inexhaustible and nonconventional, intrinsic to it and endlessly extractable from it, is worth inscribing on the tables of the memory, worth storing where neither moth nor rust can damage or destroy it, and where the only threat to its continued existence is also a threat to the continued existence of its reader. The religious reader becomes textualized (an embodiment of the work) principally through memorization. Ezekiel's eating of the prophetic scroll ("Son of Man, eat that thou findest; eat this roll, and go speak unto the house of Israel. So I opened my mouth, and he caused me to eat that roll," 3:1–2) is a representation of the kind of incorporation and internalization involved in religious reading: the work is ingested, used for nourishment, incorporated; it becomes the basis for rumination and for action. And here again the contrast with the practices of the consumerist readers/writers who presently dominate the academy is very striking: the memorial arts are scarcely used or recommended by them because their ideal is not retention but production, and ideally production that gives the illusion of being ex nihilo. Consider, as illustrative of this difference, the following view of the importance of memory, found in Hugh of St. Victor's *Didascalicon*, composed around 1120:

> We should, therefore, collect together brief and reliable portions of all that we study [*in omni doctrina breve aliquid et certum colligere*] and consign them to the treasure-chest of the memory [*arcula memoriae recondatur*], so that later, when there is need, we might derive the remainder [of what we have studied from them]. We ought often to replicate these [portions], and bring them out from the stomach of the memory [*de ventre memoriae*] to be savored so that they might not be lost by long inattention. So I ask you, reader, not to rejoice immoderately if you have been able to read much; and if you have been able to understand much not to rejoice because of the extent of your understanding, but rather because of what you have been able to retain [*sed retinere potueris*]. For otherwise there is benefit neither in much reading nor in much understanding.[39]

The necessary condition for all other fruits of religious reading, according to Hugh, is placing what has been read in the treasure chest of the memory. Only when it is there can it be ruminated at leisure; and only as a result of such rumination can it issue in understanding. Any other kind of reading is merely passing the time, running the eyes over words in a daze of impatience.

Hugh's claim about memorization suggests that he takes it to have a moral sense, and he is entirely right to do so. A memorized work (like a lover, a friend, a spouse, a child) has entered into the fabric of its possessor's intellectual and emotional life in a way that makes deep claims upon that life, claims that can only be ignored with effort and deliberation. Just as spouses make claims upon each other that can only be ignored or removed with pain and intentional action in divorce, so also memorized works are present and efficacious until uprooted by forgetfulness or deliberate erasure. In this they differ in degree, and probably also in kind, from works that have been read only as a consumerist reader reads. Those works sit inert upon the shelf, usually forgotten, and remembered, if remembered at all, not for their flavor and fabric, but for their title and place of publication. The claims of such works are minimal and strictly instrumental; the claims of memorized works are much greater and are properly moral.

George Steiner makes a similar set of points:

> Memory is, of course, the pivot. 'Answerability to' the text, the understanding and critical response to *auctoritas*, as they inform the classic act of reading . . . depend strictly on the 'arts of memory'. *Le philosophe lisant*, like the cultured men around him in a tradition which runs from classical antiquity to, roughly, the First World War, will know text by heart (an idiom worth thinking about closely). They will know by heart considerable segments of Scripture, of the liturgy, of epic and lyric verse. . . . [T]he classic reader . . . locates the text he is reading inside a resonant manifold. Echo answers echo, analogy is precise and contiguous, correction and emendation carry the justification of accurately remembered precedent. The reader replies to the text out of the articulate density

> of his own store of reference and remembrance. It is an ancient and formidable suggestion that the Muses of memory and invention are one.[40]

Steiner's style is precious. But what he says is both correct and profound. On his view, readers who memorize possess (have in part become) the works they have read: they are a rich echo chamber, a "resonant manifold," in which new acts of reading reverberate. Here again we are very far from the world of the consumerist reader, and quite close to that of the religious reader. An unsurpassable, comprehensive, and central account (a properly religious account) is best given and developed from inside just the kind of resonant manifold that Steiner intends.

Inhabiting such a manifold is, as Steiner suggests, an integral part of what it meant to be an educated person in Europe from Plato until the quite recent past. But such a habitation is not limited to those he calls "cultured men." Literacy is not a requirement for it; neither is subjection to the formal methods of the schools, whether those of Athens, Rome, Bologna, Paris, Oxford, Vikramaśilā, or Nālandā, or those designed to produce happy consumers in late twentieth-century America. All that's required is a well-stocked memory, and that can be had by the many, the proletariat, the formally uneducated, those with neither time nor money to go to school. In Hippo, for instance, a small town at the edges of a rapidly vanishing empire at the beginning of the fifth century after Christ, Augustine was bishop and a very frequent preacher. Many of those who heard him preach, mostly unschooled and technically illiterate as they were, could resound to his scriptural allusions, complete (often loudly and enthusiastically) his half-quotations, and generally give evidence of possessing a Steinerian resonant manifold (at least so far as Scripture was concerned).[41]

Partly because of this positive view of memorization as an important element of religious reading, and partly because of the difficulty and expense of book production in the premodern period, mnemonic technique was highly developed and widely used everywhere before the sixteenth century. In both medieval India and medieval Europe its use was essential to all learning. While the details of the techniques vary somewhat from place to place and from time to time, memorization's essential features remain the same, controlled as they partly are by human physiology. These essential features are three: first, the imaginative creation of a storage system, a set of loci each of which is identified and tagged by an image; second, the division of the matter to be memorized into small units of an ideal size for quick storage in memory and rapid recall therefrom; and third, repetitive reading, usually vocalized or subvocalized, and accompanied by rhythmic bodily movement, of the units tagged for memorization.

First, the places for storage. These need to be very deeply incised upon the pages of the memory, for they provide the basic structure that makes possible the storage and recall of everything memorized. There are many ways in which such places can be created and maintained. Some have used the houses on a street or the rooms in a house as the images to mark the storage places; others have used such things as the letters of the alphabet (preferably one that belongs to an unknown language), or numbers, or the mythical beasts in bestiaries. Common to them all is the creation of an articulated system of storage places, a system in which each place is related in an ordered way to every other. This is important because the point of memorization for religious readers is not just to make possible verbatim reproduction of the memorized material, but also to permit its manipulation, sorting, and reordering. Only an articulated system of storage will permit this. Suppose you're using images of the rooms of a house as your storage sites; you'll need to know the order of and relations among these rooms in order easily to be able to recall what's in the third room on the left in the first-floor hall and place it next to what's in the fourth bedroom on the third floor. You need to be able to take a mental walk through your articulated system of storage places, looking into each in turn; but you also need to be able to move instantly from one to another, and only an articulated system will allow you to do so.

The second feature of mnemonic technique is division of the matter to be memorized into bite-sized pieces, short enough for rapid memorization and easy recall. 'Gobbet', with its connotation of sufficient smallness for chewability, is a good word for these; this is what undergraduates at Oxford used to (and perhaps still do) call the short chunks of Greek or Latin they were asked to translate at sight. The matter to be memorized needs to be divided into gobbets largely because of strictly physiological constraints upon memory. Empirical work upon memorial capacity strongly suggests that the amount of information capable of being focused upon and comprehended at one time is definitely limited, to a number of units somewhere between five and nine.[42] The nature and extent of these units is somewhat flexible; they may be words, syllables, short phrases, or the like, but it seems likely that the upper limit of a gobbet of English designed for memorial storage is probably around twenty words. Memorization of a long work must then proceed by dividing it into small units and placing these one at a time into storage places. The articulated system of storage places may often be multilayered in order to accommodate large quantities of matter. This might mean that the third room on the left in your memorially imagined house contains the first of T. S. Eliot's *Four Quartets*, but since that is a long poem (eight pages), its pieces are distributed around the room, each linked to an imagined item in the room. So the lines "Garlic and sapphires in the mud / Clot the bedded axle-tree" might be linked to (memorially stored in) an image of an olive-wood jewel case on the mahogany writing desk to the left of the fireplace.

The third feature of mnemonic technique, vocalized or subvocalized repetitive reading, needs little elaboration. Vocalization slows reading; it makes impossible the archetypally consumerist half-attentive skimming of a work, or the gutting of a book for its matter, and as a result helps the religious reader to read with the kind of attention that makes possible memorization and the nourishment that goes with it. Vocalization or subvocalization (the murmur, the *japa*) may aid memorization in other ways, too. Like the rhythmic bodily movements with which they are often associated (bobbing the head, walking up and down) by religious readers, they may help to fix the matter to be memorized in its storage places by providing an extra set of cues for recall. When the bodily movement is reproduced, this will help to recall the material you want to get at. Neither vocalization nor bodily movement are essential for memorization. But each is helpful, and both are widely used by mnemonic artists.

An example may be helpful. Hugh of St. Victor, in his *De tribus maximis circumstantiis gestorum* [On the Three Chief Mnemonic Categories for History] composed in about 1130 as a preface to his *Chronica* (a detailed conspectus of biblical chronology),[43] describes a method for memorizing the Psalms. To do this, Hugh says, the best storage places are the numbers 1–150 (for there are 150 Psalms). To each of these you'll attach the *incipit*, the first few words of each psalm; these are your images to mark the storage places and to fix them in your mind. So, for instance, the image for Psalm 62 (following the enumeration of the Hebrew Bible and of most Protestant Bibles) will be the number 62 coupled with the words '*nonne Deo*' (the Latin *incipit* of the psalm). Under the image for each psalm you must then visualize a subsidiary set of numbers, beginning at one. Attached to each of these subsidiary numbers will be a gobbet: the words of the verse to which the subsidiary number corresponds. These are the mnemonic units, and they should each contain no more information than can be retrieved and scanned at a glance (perhaps twenty words is an ideal upper limit). It is likely that the divisions of the text of the Psalms into sense lines (and later into verses) were originally created in part for just these mnemonic purposes: the number of words in a sense line is generally close to the ideal for a mnemonic unit. The verses in English Bibles use the divisions that were standardized only in the sixteenth century, after the production of printed editions, and these typically contain more words than the sense lines of Bible manuscripts in late antiquity. This is one indication that by the seventeenth century the Bible was beginning to be read without attention to the demands of memorization.

Recall of the memorized units can then proceed in any order and by any combination. Asked to recall Psalm 62:6, for example, you call up the image "62-nonne-Deo" in your background grid, open the list of subsidiary attached memorial images and reproduce the matter found there: "For God alone my soul in silence waits; truly, my hope is in him" (14 words). You will not need to run through the matter in 62:1–5 in order to access 62:6; this is because you have provided an address or a label for the information in 62:6 that makes it possible for you to go straight there. If you have the whole of the Psalter memorized in this way, you will be able to reproduce the matter in widely separated parts of it as quickly as you can that in contiguous verses. It will be no more trouble to string together Psalm 1:4, 10:8, and 149:1 than it will be to string together 1:1–3. You will also be able to do such things as recite particular psalms backwards (that is, with the verses in reverse order, though with the words in normal order within each verse), or produce a work containing the third verse of every psalm. And, of course, any body of literary matter, however large, can be treated in this way, though where it is not already divided into the necessary gobbets, this will have to be done first.

One sign that a work is probably designed for memorial storage is the presence of markers dividing its matter into gobbets. Indian works of many kinds typically have such markers, most commonly dividing the work into *ślokas*, verses whose meter (called *anuṣṭubh* in Sanskrit) requires eight syllables per quarter-verse (thirty-two for the whole verse). Nāgārjuna's philosophical treatise called *Mūlamadhyamakakārikā* [Basic Verses on the Middle], for instance, composed in India in the first or second century after Christ, contains 447 verses of this sort, divided into twenty-seven chapters.[44] Each verse is close to the ideal size for a mnemonic unit (though there is evidence from the way the work is treated by the commentators that the half-verse, usually containing sixteen syllables, was the basic mnemonic unit). Precisely the same mnemotechnical device described in the preceding paragraph for use in memorizing the Psalms could be applied here, and no doubt was.

This method of memorization, while it certainly requires effort to begin with, to set up the architecture of the mnemonic system and to fill it with matter, produces a system of recall far faster, more efficient, and more flexible than those in use for retrieving information from books or manuscripts. If you have stored all of Asaṅga's *Mahāyānasūtrālaṅkāra* [Ornament of the Sacred Works of the Great Vehicle] or of Peter Lombard's *Sentences* in the treasure chest of your memory in this way, it will be available to you with a rapidity, thoroughness, and ease that far exceed those belonging to the cumbersome and inefficient method of turning the pages of a book—or that of retrieving it from a CD-ROM or the databases of the Internet. These are practical advantages in addition to the moral advantages valued by religious readers. And it is important to add that since religious readers, unlike consumerist readers, will usually read what they read slowly and many times over, the initial labor of memorization will be partly completed by the act of religious reading itself.

Memorization using techniques of this kind need not issue in or be aimed at verbatim storage and recall. It may also be used to store and recall the substance or gist of a work: its structure, its main arguments, its vocabulary, and so forth, but not every one of its words. For instance, forms of aural display of verbal works in contemporary western culture (the sermon, the lecture, the political speech, to mention the most prominent examples) may involve the verbatim display of a previously composed work, as when a sermon is read from a script (or, more rarely, spoken from memory). But a sermon or lecture may also be a nonverbatim reproduction of a previously composed work: a display of its argument, its illustrations, and some of its phraseology. Memorization by number grid may serve this kind of display as well as it serves verbatim display; but what will go into the grid's loci, its storage places, in such a case will be ideas and themes rather than gobbets. Every preacher who has composed a complete script and then, to avoid reading from the pulpit, reduced that to note cards as a jog to the memory, has used a mnemonic aid to bring about the aural display of the gist of a previously composed work. Mnemonic artists may do the same, but will have the cues written on the tablets of the memory rather than on note cards.

The importance of memory in religious reading further weakens the connection between such reading and techniques for composition, display, and storage that rely upon the making of marks upon some physical medium—that is, of writing as usually understood. If the ideally read work is the memorized work, religious readers will typically not give much importance to writing as a medium of storage—at least, not for the purposes of reading and redisplay in general. And the extent to which writing is important as a means of composition and display will depend in part upon local material culture (how expensive and difficult is it to create manuscripts and books?), and in part upon the extent of literacy (how many locals possess the skill of decoding marks made on papyrus or birch bark?). Where it is difficult and expensive, in materials or labor or both, to create books and manuscripts, as it was throughout most of the world until the sixteenth century, the significance of such objects as tools for religious reading will be small. And where literacy is not widespread, as was almost always the case for religious communities (and largely still is), books will have a correspondingly reduced significance as tools of religious learning. Harry Gamble's recent work on the topic suggests that no more than 15 percent of Christians were literate, even minimally, during the first five centuries of the Christian era;[45] the percentage was almost certainly lower in both medieval India and medieval Europe. And there are now many Christian communities in the United States in which a majority of the people cannot read the Bible with easy comprehension. In such situations, if religious learning is to be affordably available to all who want it, then the tools and techniques required for it must be cheap and not restricted to those with the unusual skill of being able to decode marks made on permanent media of storage. The human mouth and the human memory fulfil these requirements. Written books, material objects, typically do not.

However, even where written objects are of marginal importance for religious learning, they may have other important functions. They may, for instance, have considerable ritual significance, given them in part by their rarity and expense but in part also by the weight of the matter in them. This is evident in the tendency of Buddhists in medieval South Asia to enshrine their manuscripts in memorial mounds very much more often than to read them;[46] or in that of Buddhists in China to engrave sacred works on walls in places where no one could read them even if they wanted to.[47] These practices ensured the inaccessibility of written objects for reading, but also showed their importance in other respects. Manuscripts of the Bible in medieval Europe were also given more ritual than pedagogical uses, as, arguably, is true of most printed Bibles in Christian homes in contemporary Europe or the United States. Their presence has more significance than their use. Books or manuscripts may also be given strictly magical or divinatory uses, as was frequently the case for early Christian use of manuscripts of the Bible.[48]

The way of reading outlined in the immediately preceding pages, with its emphasis on repeated rereading and memorization, and upon the establishment of a certain kind of moral relation between reader and work, does not require either the presence or the absence of any particular technology of composition, storage, or display. It is theoretically compatible with many such technologies. Nonetheless, it comports better with some than with others. Technologies that make it easy to compose, display, store, and redisplay very large quantities of material are likely to sit less well with properly religious reading than are those that do not. And so it is scarcely surprising that, to take just one example, the technological changes that have gradually increased the ease and speed of storage and display of literary matter in Europe since the twelfth century have also gone along with a gradual reduction in the cultural prominence and pedagogical significance of religious reading.[49] A typical sixth-century Latin manuscript, for example, was written without punctuation, differentiation between upper and lower case, word separation (or any other breaks), cursive script, and so forth. Such an object is slow to write and even slower to read. It is in fact almost impossible to read without vocalization,[50] and because of this it scarcely qualifies as an object that displays what it stores. Compare this with a late twentieth-century printed book, with its many aids to rapid and silent reading: word, paragraph, and chapter divisions, tables of contents, indices, and so forth. These objects can be produced quickly and read quickly; they do display what they store. Religious reading sits better with the former than with the latter, which is one part of the reason why it has declined. But religious reading is not made impossible by the late twentieth-century printed book (or by the CD-ROM), only more difficult.

A final point is that the works in a religious reader's well-stocked memorial library are unlikely to be individuated in the same way as the objects on our library shelves. The content of a book (a material object) is bounded both physically (by its covers) and legally (by copyright law). The content of a memorized work is not so bounded; indeed, the mnemotechnical devices used to make possible the memorization and easy retrieval of large quantities of matter work against such bounding and sit much more easily with fluidity. This is because large quantities of matter must be broken up into gobbets in order to be stored in memory in the appropriate way, and these, together with the ordering schemata used to make their retrieval possible, are likely to be the basic units of the religious memorial library. Divisions among works will therefore tend to be of less importance than they are for a print-dominated culture, though there may be reasons in particular religious communities for paying attention to the boundaries of particular works that counteract the opposing tendencies of religious reading.

The entire body of literary matter that constitutes a religious reader's library will, mostly as a result of religious reading practices, tend to be treated as a single fabric composed of interlocking parts that can be retrieved and recombined variously as the occasion demands, without respect to the fact that they may have come from different works. Such a state of affairs is sometimes called intratextuality, according to a strong version of which every element of a given body of works becomes part of the interpretive context within which every other element is read and understood, so that religious readers read, recall, and teach what is functionally a single work, even if one that is internally differentiated, composed of works that may have come from the minds of different authors at different times.

Religious reading and its concomitant memorization need not always be presented in positive light. One of the most horrifying portraits of obsessive monomaniacal madness in twentieth-century literature is that of the fictional Peter Kien in Elias Canetti's *Die Blendung*. Kien is the apotheosis of the religious reader and mnemonic artist, as the following sketch of his capacities makes clear:

> He did indeed carry in his head a library as well-provided and as reliable as his actual library. . . . [H]e could sit at his writing desk and sketch out a treatise down to the minutest detail without turning over a single page, except in the library in his head [*ausser eben in seiner Kopfbibliothek*]. Naturally he would check quotations and sources later out of the books themselves; but only because he was a man of conscience. He could not remember any single occasion on which his memory had been found at fault. His very dreams were more precisely defined [*Selbst eine Träume hätten eine schärfere Fassung*] than those of most people. Blurred images without form or color were unknown in any of the dreams which he had hitherto recollected. In his case night had no power to turn things topsy turvy; the noises he heard could be exactly referred to their cause of origin; conversations into which he entered were entirely reasonable; everything retained its normal meaning. It was outside his sphere to examine the probable connection between the accuracy of his memory and the lucidity of his dreams.[51]

In Canetti's novel, the reader's mind is shown becoming coextensive with what he has read, becoming textualized, which means that any intrusion of a non-bookish reality that cannot be read and memorized must end in disaster. Kien's lucid dreams and his eidetic memory for words on a page are no match for the destructive capacities of calculating stupidity, for the intrusion of an untextualized world. Kien ends in madness: he and his library are burned. Canetti's novel is much more (and much less) than a parable about the fate of religious readers; it was first published in 1935 and must be understood in part as a reflection of the European political situation at that time. But it can usefully be read as a dramatic (and unremittingly negative) presentation of religious reading, as a reductio ad absurdum of the ideal-typical sketch given to this point. The *Kopfbibliothek*, like all other human creations, can be demonic as well as life giving, but that this is so does not call into question my earlier claim that memorization creates a moral relation between work and reader that is unique, profound, and transformative. Stocking the *Kopfbibliothek* is among the proper ends of religious reading, and the best possible basis, as I shall argue more fully later, for composition in the archetypally religious genres.

How Religious People Compose

If you read as a religious reader, you will compose as one, for religious reading is connected very closely with composition. It's difficult for religious readers to separate the one from the other, since they seem to such readers to be symbiotically linked. The very practices that constitute religious reading are themselves also compositional practices. John Dagenais calls the reading that was typical in medieval Europe "lecturature" (reading that is also composition), and this is a beautifully appropriate term for what I'm calling religious reading.[52] Lecturature is typically not passive, not done with the principal goal of amassing information or sharpening writerly skills. It is done, instead, for the purpose of altering the course of the readers' cognitive, affective, and active lives by the ingestion, digestion, rumination, and restatement of what has been read.

The ways in which these goals are met have direct and obvious effects upon what and how religious readers compose.

The first such effect comes from the mnemotechnical devices employed by religious readers. These techniques require the work read to be stored in memory in such a way that it can easily and rapidly be retrieved, and this in turn, as I've shown, requires the work to be divided into gobbets and these gobbets to be ordered according to a scheme that makes their retrieval rapid and easy. This aspect of religious-reading-as-composition explains, or goes a good way toward explaining, some typical religious compositions, compositions in genres whose existence and function is otherwise difficult to understand, and which, for precisely that reason, are largely ignored by contemporary western scholarship.

One such is what in the West is called the florilegium or the anthology, the bouquet of flowers, small but fragrant textual blooms culled from many different works and arranged together into a new work for the delectation and improvement of other readers (I'll say more about this genre in chapter 4). The composition of works of this kind makes perfect sense if those who use them deploy mnemotechnical devices as part of their ordinary reading practice, and if these devices require that works read be stored in gobbets. In such a case, the stored gobbets will be capable of easy recall from storage independently of their location in a larger work (which is not to say that such location is necessarily or always forgotten by or irrelevant to religious readers), and therefore capable of recombination in an infinite variety of ways.

Another genre best understood as a typical product of religious reading is the commentary (again, more on this in chapter 4). Both the ethical and the practical demands of memorization suggest that composing commentaries will be important for religious readers. Ethically, writing a work upon the pages of the memory gives it an importance that can be given by no other kind of reading; such importance consists in large part in the demand it makes on religious readers by its presence in their memories, a demand that can be met in one way by composing a commentary. Practically, the presence of the whole work in the memory, coupled with its storage in the form of gobbets, any one of which can be recalled and juxtaposed to any other, will suggest and enable the composition of commentaries that have two important formal features, both of which are typical of religious commentaries. The first is that the religious commentary will take as its initial object precisely the gobbets into which the work has been divided for memorization, which means that it will treat in the first instance small units of the work, and only then, if at all, take up the treatment of larger units or of the work as a whole. The second is that a comment on any one of these gobbets will typically presuppose knowledge of them all, and may be incomprehensible without such knowledge.

Religious reading-as-composition, then, will most often produce commentaries and anthologies. But which tools and techniques are most likely to be used for compositional purposes by religious readers? Writing (in the narrow sense) may, but need not, be their principal tool; they are more likely to use some combination of mnemonic and oral/aural technique. Although making scratch marks on paper or using a keyboard seem to most late twentieth-century writers quite indispensable to composition, especially for long and complex works, there is much evidence to suggest that this was not so (and is not so) for religious composers. The connection between writing (in the ordinary sense) and composition is at best a contingent one. Long and complex works have often been composed in thought and displayed aurally, by dictation, as the following examples will illustrate.[53]

Suppose we consider first Thomas Aquinas. There is very considerable evidence that he usually displayed his works for the first time aurally, and that they were then reduced to writing ('reduction' is a good metaphor for religious readers to use about writing) by a scribe taking dictation. It's likely that Thomas used writing to some small extent in making drafts or memoranda, and that he sometimes had such *scripta* before him as he dictated to an amanuensis. Indeed, we know that he did use writing for some purposes because we possess some fragments written in his hand.[54] But it does not seem that writing was ever, for Thomas, a tool of central importance for composition. There are a number of pieces of evidence for this conclusion. First, the early biographies of him are unanimous in their witness that not only did he frequently compose a work from the beginning without writing, immediately dictating it to a scribe or scribes, but even that he was capable of dictating materials from different works in progress to different scribes on the same occasion rather like a chess master playing many games at once—so, at least, some of the early hagiographies suggest.[55] Second, all the surviving autographs are from an early part of Thomas's career, the most likely explanation for which is that as more and better scribal help became available to him as his career progressed and his fame grew, he made almost exclusive use of it for the purposes of composition.

There is, in addition, some relatively hard evidence that Thomas used dictation as a mode of composition. One early manuscript (of Thomas's *De Veritate*) is, if Antoine Dondaine's detailed study of it is right,[56] best understood as a scribal transcription of Thomas's first aural display of the work, complete with erasures, second thoughts, and other marks more usually associated with autographs. As Dondaine puts it, in this case at least it seems best to think of Thomas giving shape to his thought with the hand of his amanuensis rather than with his own.[57] An added fact of importance is that the autographs we possess show clearly that writing was never, for Thomas, intended as a mode of display. He wrote in a hand aptly called by those who have tried to read it *littera inintelligibilis*; it would have been almost entirely illegible to anyone except himself even in the thirteenth century, and this seems typical of those who used writing and yet were not professional scribes.

For Thomas, then, the preponderance of evidence very strongly suggests that writing was never a tool for display; that it was a tool for composition of only marginal significance; and that its main use was for short-term storage. Thomas, a prolific composer of works of great length and considerable internal complexity, composed mostly in thought or orally, in the scriptorium or dictation chamber; and his principal tool of storage was memory.

Thomas was not at all unusual in these things. The same was largely true of Origen and of Augustine, both of whom used dictation as their principal tool of composition and display,[58] as did virtually all Christian composers during the first 1,400 years of Christian history. There are exceptions. Jerome, for example, did not like dictating to a scribe, and the same was true of Guibert of Nogent in the twelfth century.[59] But it remains true that dictation was the standard mode of composition and display in Europe until at least the fourteenth century. Composition by dictation requires, naturally, scribes capable of taking notes at dictation speed, and this in turn means, almost inevitably, the development of systems of shorthand and of a professional class expert in their use. And from late antiquity on such systems and such people were widely available, as Herbert Boge and Harald Hagendahl have shown, a fact that strongly supports the view that writing was not an important tool of composition in the early centuries of the Christian era.[60]

Neither need we restrict our attention to premodern times. Charles Dickens, for instance, when he was working on *Hard Times* in the 1840s, used quite frequently to compose and deliver political speeches, usually in support of reform in the system of public education. Here is Peter Ackroyd's description of how these speeches were usually composed and delivered:

> Dickens never made or kept notes but seemed to speak spontaneously and effortlessly, all the more extraordinary since the speeches themselves are as graceful and fluent as anything he ever wrote. . . . He had an astonishing verbal memory. He did not make notes because he memorised everything he wished to say, and this for speeches that lasted some twenty or thirty minutes. Even after he had finished, he could still repeat what he had said verbatim to reporters anxious for clean copy. . . . How did he achieve this? The morning before he was due to speak, he would take a long walk and in the course of that journey he would decide what topics he was going to raise. He would put these in order, and in his imagination construct a cart wheel of which he was the hub and the various subjects the spokes emanating from him to the circumference; during the progress of the speech, he said, he would deal with each spoke separately, elaborating them as he went round the wheel; and when all the spokes dropped out one by one, and nothing but the tire and space remained, he would know that he had accomplished his task, and that his speech was at an end. . . . One of his closest friends noticed that at public dinners he did indeed dismiss the spoke from his mind by a quick action of the finger as if he were knocking it away.[61]

Dickens's political speeches, for the most part, had no existence as written works until verbatim written records of what he had said were made by newspaper reporters present at their delivery. These speeches were composed mentally, stored mnemonically, and delivered aurally. It is interesting to note that Dickens's mnemonic technique appears to have been designed to produce a fixed set of words that could be displayed easily only in linear fashion. The unit of matter represented by each spoke of the wheel is locatable and reproducible only in its proper place within the speech as a whole. His appears not to have been a random-access method like Hugh of St. Victor's scheme for memorizing the Psalms.

I mention Dickens not because he was a typical religious reader but rather to signal the possible endurance and use of such techniques even when an attitude to works of literature that best grounds them and gives them sense is absent. Dickens was a member of the last, or perhaps the penultimate, generation of western intellectuals to have made much use of these techniques; they have not survived in the intellectual life of the twentieth century.

Here is a final example, this time a contemporary one taken from Daniel Perdue's study of debating techniques among Tibetan Buddhists, of a very positive evaluation of the ability to hold in the memory a mass of information, and to deploy it constructively in an act of composition:

> The disputants come to the debating courtyard . . . with no aid but their own understanding. One does not peruse books at the time of debating, and books may not be brought to the debating courtyard. There is a joke among debaters that if one has studied a topic and knows where to find the information in a text or in one's notes but is not able to explain it, then such a person "has his learning in a box" (where the books are stored). Rather, the debaters must depend on their memorization of the points of doctrine—definitions, divisions, illustrations, and even whole texts—together with their own measure of understanding gained from instruction and study.[62]

Bearing these examples in mind, I suggest that religious compositional practice, while it does require tools and techniques for composition and storage, does not require writing (in the ordinary sense) for either. It is likely, given the assumptions about reading that inform it, to lean more heavily toward the use of thought and speech as the principal tools of composition, and toward memorization as the principal tool of storage.

There are important contrasts with the technologies of composition and storage favored by contemporary consumerist readers/writers. From the sixteenth to the late twentieth century, technologies of storage have been print centered, and technologies of composition have focused on the making of marks on paper. It has become part of the ordinary mental furniture of academics and intellectuals of all kinds to think of a literary work as just and only the kind of thing that is composed on paper and in solitude, then printed, and finally stored to be reread, cited, dissected, and analyzed at will. The trope of the solitary writer, like that of the innocent child, is a cliché, but one found everywhere from high to popular culture; it is mirrored in current copyright laws and publication practices. Academic assent to it is evident in views about the sanctity of authorship and its concomitant, the heinousness of plagiarism, as well as in the ways that academics assess, evaluate, and reward one another. The key measures of worth in the academy are the volume of publication and the extent to which that publication is cited by others. And both these measures assume compositional techniques that require paper and storage methods that require print, as they also assume a strong view about the proper boundaries of works and their proper relations to authors.

All this is changing at the end of the twentieth century as electronic technologies for composition and storage become increasingly dominant. I shall not venture prophecies about the future of these technologies and their effects upon academic practice and academic views about reading, writing, authorship, and the legalities of copyright and publication. But it is clear that their use comports very well with the intellectual life understood through the metaphor of writing (in the broad sense); and the quotation given earlier from Fredric Jameson's work on postmodernism makes the connection quite explicit. But whether print- and paper-centered technologies maintain their dominance, or whether they wither away in favor of electronic technologies, one central and irreducible difference between western academic compositional practice and ideal-typical religious compositional practice will remain. Consumerist readers/writers, whether using print or electronic media, see their works as without intrinsic value, to be discarded as soon as consumed, or perhaps consumed and then stored for a while. Works of literature are, in these respects, just like automobiles. The mnemonic arts are irrelevant, and the modes of reading that foster and require those arts are a positive drawback. Indeed, religious reading is best understood as intrinsically opposed to (perhaps even incompatible with) the dominance of technologies intended to maximize the flow of information, of consumable and discardable semantic units. There are causal connections of a complicated kind between the rise of print technology from the sixteenth century onward and the decline in religious reading; and while the axiological and epistemological implications of the rise of computer technology in the last fifteen years are in many important respects different from those of print technology, the two share a profound lack of hospitality to religious reading and composition. If anything, the more recent electronic technologies are less hospitable to religious reading than the older print technology—and much less than manuscript technology.

The presence of these technologies in our culture is not the sole reason for the decline in the importance we give to religious reading and composition. Just as writing (in the ordinary sense) does not by itself have the transformative power attributed to it by its apologists, so also print and electronic technology must be placed in a certain context and combined with other variables in that context before they can become dominant. It also follows from these considerations that those who wish to preserve or recover religious habits of reading or composition in contemporary western academia need not forswear the use of print or electronic technologies altogether. But such people must pay close attention to the ways in which such technologies are used. These technologies should be closely circumscribed servants rather than lively masters, and it may be that such circumscription will be hard to maintain because of the power of conformist and consumerist pressures in academia and elsewhere. These pressures are so powerful because they have assimilated intellectual work to the processes of production and consumption that now dominate almost every department of life in late capitalist cultures like ours. Resisting such pressures means resisting much that is woven deeply into the fabric of our lives.

3

The Context of Religious Reading

Institutions

To be religious is to offer a comprehensive, unsurpassable, and central account. Offering such an account requires the possession of both information and skills, and these are not innate: they have to be acquired, which means that they have to be learned and taught. Religious reading is one of the more important skills involved in offering a religious account, and it, too, needs to be learned and taught. What can be said about the institutional forms within which the teaching and learning of religious reading can take place?[1]

An institutional form is a pattern of social arrangements with some principal end or purpose. Using this definition, the family is an institutional form (a particular pattern of social arrangements) whose principal end is procreation and the raising of children. So is the limited liability corporation; its principal end is the generation of capital. And so is the Buddhist monastic order; its principal end is the production of merit for those who are not members of it. None of these claims about principal ends is likely to be acceptable to all those who belong to families, limited liability corporations, or the Buddhist monastic order. That this is so shows only that the difficulties of individuating patterns of social arrangements one from another and of saying what the principal end of any is (these are two parts of the same question) are exactly parallel to the difficulties involved in individuating religious accounts (discussed in chapter 1) or literary works (discussed in chapter 2). There, as here, are no natural kinds, and decisions about where to draw the boundaries between one pattern of social arrangements and another, one institutional form and another, one literary work and another will be made in dependence upon the interests of whoever is cutting the cake.

Nevertheless, institutions do need to be individuated and sorted into kinds if they are to be thought about at all, and using the Aristotelian/Thomist tool of looking at ends (goals, purposes) to do so is as good a way to begin as any (and considerably better than most). So I suggest the following: a pattern of social arrangements to which we affix the name 'educational institution' has as its end the transmission of skills and information from one group of people to another; and in order to do this, to achieve its end, any such institution will need the following: a curriculum, studied by students; a pedagogy, deployed by teachers; and some method of certification, by which the successful completion of the curriculum is marked. When all these are in place we have an educational institution.

Skills and information can of course be transmitted without educational institutions in this sense. Most are. The quotidian skills of social interaction, of farming, of cooking, of speech, and of dress—all these are transmitted in most societies most of the time quite effectively in the absence of educational institutions devoted to them. The highly differentiated societies of Europe and North America at the end of the twentieth century are unusual, perhaps, in the extent to which they have developed educational institutions even for some of these skills. This is especially evident in the United States, where the best evidence of possessing a skill is typically not thought to be exercising it, but holding certification of having been educated to possess it. But even in the United States, a great many skills and much knowledge are transmitted without benefit of institutional training. This typically happens within some pattern of social arrangements whose principal end is not the transmission of the skills or information in question. In the family you learn table manners; in the factory you learn how to curse. Institutions usually have effects ancillary to (and sometimes even opposed to) their principal ends.

What about religious reading? Will this skill and the information that goes with it and is required by it typically be transmitted with or without institutions devoted to that purpose? It's hard to generalize about this. Certainly it is possible to become a skilled religious reader without training by an institution devoted to producing such readers. This will most often happen if all or most of the social arrangements of which you're a part (family, work, and so forth) are made up of religious readers who communicate their skill by example and precept. In such a situation you may need an educational institution to teach you to read religiously about as much as you needed one to learn how to speak your mother tongue. It's normal, then, for most religious readers to have gained most of their skills as such without religious educational institutions, just as it is normal for most poets to have gained most of their skills as such without going to poetry school.

But there will be many cases in which communities of religious readers find it necessary to establish and maintain institutions for teaching religious reading. Most of these will involve a need for specialists, virtuoso religious readers: if a community values or thinks it needs such people, it is likely also to think it needs institutions specifically devoted to their training. A community might come to think it needs specialist readers (readers who do nothing other than read, whose principal social function is the exhibition and transmission of readerly skills) for many reasons. Suppose the practice of the community has attained a sufficient degree of complexity over time that the kinds of reading skills reachable in passing, as it were, in the context of social arrangements not specifically devoted to their inculcation, are likely to be insufficient to master it. Then the community will need specialists who have mastered it and can rule on disputed questions having to do with it. Brahmanical Hinduism is in this case, clearly: specialists in the use of proper Vedic mantras are indispensable, and they need a great deal of training. So is Anglican Christianity: the *Book of Common Prayer* is by now too complex (despite Cranmer's hopes for it) to be used with understanding by a nonspecialist religious reader.

Specialists are also likely to be needed when a community of religious readers has political power. Knowing how to read in such a way as to be able to rule on political matters is not likely to be a skill available to nonspecialist readers. The Confucian examination system in China from the sixteenth through the twentieth century or the specialist education given incarnate lamas in Tibet until the Chinese annexation of the 1950s provide examples. Most long-lived communities of religious readers will come to judge that they need specialist readers for one or another of these reasons. This certainly applies to many Jews, Christians, Buddhists, Muslims, Hindus, and Confucians.

When specialists are needed, then, institutions devoted to religious learning, and to religious reading as a part of religious learning, will also exist. They may exist, however, even when specialists are not needed, or when some community of religious readers has reasons specific to itself for judging that such specialists are a bad thing—perhaps because their presence might be taken to imply that the community thinks that not all its members need a degree and kind of education in religious reading that can only be gained from time spent in an institution of religious education. Perhaps the catechumenal process developed by Christians from the second through the fourth century is an instance of a pattern of social arrangements whose primary end is to transmit information and skills, and exposure to which is required of all members of the community, not just of specialists. Christians have always been uneasy about differentiating between learned élites and the rest in a way that suggests the former have a better chance at salvation, or are more loved by God. There is, or can be, a parallel uneasiness about the education of specialist religious readers.

It follows from all this that when communities of religious readers do possess institutions for religious education, one of the variables by which to classify them is that of what proportion of the community is required to use them. Another is that of whether the institutions are local or translocal. Most religious communities have institutions of the local sort: the synagogue's bar-mitzvah preparation class, or the transmission of Vedic learning from teacher to student in a particular Indian village are examples. These are institutions for people who happen to live where they are; they do not draw from further afield. Some religious communities have only these, either because all the members live in one small area, or because, even though they have widely scattered members, they have seen no need for educational institutions that could be used by members from any location, and that might have a normative teaching function for all. But some communities of readers do have educational institutions of this translocal kind. Perhaps the Buddhist monastic institutions of Nālandā and Vikramaśilā were of this sort; they certainly attracted students from as far afield as China and Indonesia in the seventh and eighth centuries.

Asking whether a particular community's educational institutions are local or translocal, then, provides another set of conceptual tools by which to order thought about them. Answers will usually involve saying something about the function of specialist readers in the community: if a community has and uses translocal educational institutions, it will also typically have and make use of specialist readers, just as it will if it does not require identical levels of reading skill for all its members.

There is nothing about religious reading as a skill that requires for its transmission any technology more complicated than the human tongue, ears, and brain. In this it differs, for example, from the skill of architecture or that of cookery. But, as I showed in the discussion of religious reading in chapter 2, there is also nothing about religious reading that is in principle incompatible with particular tools and techniques of a more complex kind. Communities of religious readers may very well be intimate with print technology, or computer technology, or with other technologies required for the administration of large, translocal institutions. Whether this is so will depend upon variables specific to the community and its situation, and will often have to do with the methods used by a particular culture for the composition, storage, and display of verbal works.

So much for what institutions for teaching and learning religious reading are, and for analytical questions to ask of particular instances of such institutions—variables by which they might be ordered and thought about. These are important preliminaries; but more important is to say what the skill of religious reading requires of the institutions devoted to its teaching. Whether these are local or translocal, required of all or some, high-tech or low-tech, what does the fact that they are institutions for teaching and learning religious reading require?

The key elements here are authority, hierarchy, community, and tradition. The presence of these in institutions of religious reading will inevitably have effects upon how curriculum is decided, how teaching is done, and how certification is granted. The use of authority in the determination of curriculum will usually be the most evident. Minimally, this means the presence of some acknowledged constraints upon what and how religious readers should read and compose, as well as (by entailment) upon the kinds of conclusions that can properly be drawn and taught from this reading and composition. Authority of this kind is present in all human discursive practices—even in those of consumerist readers who, following a broadly Cartesian epistemology, might in unguarded moments think of themselves as freely deciding what they will read and drawing their own unfettered conclusions from their reading. But even though such authority is always present, its presence is not always acknowledged; it is part of modernist error in almost all fields of intellectual enterprise to refuse to acknowledge it, and to think, instead, of modernist intellectual practices as self-constituting and self-founding, and as a result standing in no need of external authority to constrain their pursuit and outcome. This flight from authority is part of the story of modernity, intellectually speaking.[2] Here is John Locke's rhetorically powerful defense of this flight, in the *Essay Concerning Human Understanding*:

> The fourth and last wrong Measure of Probability I shall take notice of, and which keeps in Ignorance, or Errour, more People than all the other together, is that which I have mentioned in the fore-going Chapter [iv.19], I mean, the giving up our Assent to the common received Opinions, either of our Friends, or Party; Neighbourhood, or Country. How many Men have no other ground for their Tenets, than the supposed Honesty, or Learning, or Number of those of the same Profession? As if honest, or bookish Men could not err; or Truth were to be established by the Vote of the Multitude: yet this with most Men serves the Turn. The Tenet has had the attestation of reverend Antiquity, it comes to me with the Pass-port of former Ages, and therefore I am secure in the Reception I give it: other Men have been, and are of the same Opinion, (for that is all is said,) and therefore it is reasonable for me to embrace it. A Man may more justifiably throw up Cross and Pile [i.e., toss a coin] for his Opinions, than take them up by such Measures.[3]

Locke's rejection of the view that you can be justified in having a certain belief just and only because you've received it from an authoritative source is obviously and dramatically incorrect (I'll say why in the next section of this chapter). But it seemed obviously correct to him and to his successors, and that this was so shows, once again, the depth of the divide between religious and consumerist readers.

Religious readers, then, do not differ from consumerist ones in the extent to which their reading is constrained by authority; but they do typically differ in the extent to which such constraint is acknowledged, and, often, in the substance of the convictions underwriting the exercise of authority. Religious readers will, as a result, usually be clear about the fact that their reading practices presuppose a select list of works worth reading, things that must be read, and read religiously; as well as a concomitant (and much longer) list of works not worth reading, things that ought not be read, or at least not religiously. The ideal type of such approved lists is the canon; its complement is the index, in the sense of *index librorum prohibitorum*. Religious readers will typically openly embrace both, at least in situations (like ours) when there are many possible works to be read, not all of which have anything to do with the religious account being learned, and some of which may be, or appear to be, actively opposed to it or detrimental to its learning. In such situations, the presence of canon and index will be an open and important part of religious pedagogy.

But even where there are few nonreligious works available, and perhaps none that appear irrelevant or opposed to the religious account in question, there will still typically be a hierarchy of works worth reading, with those at the top forming a canon or some functional equivalent thereof. An open use of canon and index may, but need not, go with the presence of sanctions against those who refuse to read the canon and instead delve into works on the index. Such sanctions, extending even to the extreme of murder, have been used from time to time by some religious communities. But the use of such is not a necessary part of the open acknowledgment of the presence of constraining authority, and as a result not intrinsic to the ideal type of religious learning.

The constraining authority may also work itself out in various particular ways: a papal pronouncement ex cathedra is distinct, institutionally speaking, from the pronouncements of a university syllabus committee as to what must be read in order to gain a doctoral degree; and both are distinct from teachings given by the Dalai Lama as to whether a particular doctrine is or is not properly Buddhist, or decisions issued by a federal appeals court as to whether a particular publication is or is not obscene. So the ideal type is compatible with a wide range of particular institutional forms; but some form of acknowledged authority will be strongly present in every kind of properly religious pedagogy.

The importance of this emphasis upon authoritative determination of what is to be read (of curriculum) is fundamental for institutions that teach religious reading. This is because deciding what to read is the most basic decision religious readers can make; from it flows almost everything of importance about the religious accounts they offer, and without it no religious account can come to be offered. The fact that I am a religious reader of the Christian Bible and not, say, of the Qur'ān is among the most important factors in what makes my religious account different from that of a Shi'ite Muslim. Choice in what to read is not a positive value for religious readers generally, nor for the curricula of institutions that teach such skills. Of course, that there are options in what to read religiously is not usually something that enters the head of religious readers. As the Brahmin boy sits at the feet of his teacher to learn that day's portion of the Veda, he does not typically wonder whether he ought to be learning the Epistle to the Colossians or the Lotus Sutra. And, as the Baptist in Sunday school class in Birmingham, Alabama, stands to recite the Ten Commandments, she doesn't typically wonder whether next week she might not turn her attention to learning a portion of the Analects. For most religious readers, the choice of what to read religiously is made based upon the authoritative curricular decisions of an institution of religious learning—and made without the fact that they are being made coming to consciousness.

Sometimes, though, religious readers do become aware that there are other works that could be read than the ones they read, and that these other works (or at least some of them) are indeed read by others, whether religiously or not. In such a case, if they are part of a pattern of social arrangements designed to give instruction in religious reading, they will typically need authoritative guidance from that institution. Here's an example of how this might work. In late 1957, Flannery O'Connor, the American Roman Catholic novelist and short-story writer, began to host at her house a weekly meeting of people interested in talking about theology in modern literature. One of the works suggested for discussion was by André Gide, whose writings were at that time on the Catholic Church's Index. O'Connor, remarkably for a Catholic intellectual in that place and time, saw fit to consult the hierarchy as to whether she could be granted permission to read Gide. The hierarchy's response is not recorded in O'Connor's correspondence; but the decision made is less interesting than the fact that she felt sufficiently bound by the authoritative direction of her Church as to what she should read to ask its permission to read something forbidden. It is true that she seems to have asked in the hope and expectation that she would be granted permission: she says, perhaps with tongue in cheek (but perhaps not), that one of her reasons for asking is that "all these Protestants will be shocked if I say I can't get permission to read Gide."[4]

This is an example, and a rare one, of an almost-contemporary American writer with a high profile thinking of her intellectual life as properly subject to constraint by external authority. It may strike you as odd, atavistic, feudal, immature; if it does, this is more evidence that we have moved very far from understanding the intellectual life as a religious reader would. It is perhaps worth noting that O'Connor was one of the great religious reader-writers of this century, so she also serves as a counterexample to the idea that submission to authority leads inevitably to intellectual mediocrity.

Institutions of religious reading are likely to locate authority both in a body of works, as already suggested, and in a hierarchically ordered group of individuals, as the case of O'Connor illustrates. And here enters hierarchy, the second key characteristic of institutions designed to teach religious reading. The authoritative people in the hierarchy will be the teachers and interpreters of the works to be read; they will also, at least ideally, themselves be serious religious readers, and perhaps also composers of works in the classic religious genres. Institutions of religious reading require teachers whose authority as such is not questioned, and submission to whose authority is itself a part of progress in religious learning. This theme has a prominent place in the works and practices of almost all religious communities. The rules governing the life of the Buddhist monastic order, for example, require formal training under the direction of an authoritative preceptor before ordination as a full member of the community can occur; and the relations between preceptor and novice are as hierarchical and authoritative as it is possible to imagine. And Buddhist works describing the path from bondage in samsara to liberation in nirvana almost always pay a good deal of attention to the functions of the *kalyāṇamitra*, the good friend who acts as teacher, guide, and interpreter of the doctrine. Here is a representative passage on this topic from a Buddhist anthology, Śāntideva's *Śikṣāsamuccaya*, composed in India in the seventh century:

> [A]pprehension of the true doctrine [*saddharmaparigraha*] is said to be the service and respect due those reciters of the doctrine [*dharmabhāṇaka*] who are entirely involved in religious practice [*pratipattisāra*] and who explain the sacred works in the proper ways. It is sitting near them; getting up before them; bowing and doing homage to them; obeying them; protecting them; receiving them; giving them the necessities of robes, begging bowls, beds, seats, and medicines for sickness; giving them reverence; protecting them as your master; praising them; and protecting them from criticism.[5]

Teachers, this passage says, provide exegesis and interpretation of works to be read religiously. And they do so authoritatively. Both their teachings and their persons are to be treated with utmost respect, and such treatment is itself part of the practitioner's proper doctrinal understanding. While O'Connor probably did not treat her bishop in all the ways commended in this passage, there are some clear similarities between her attitudes to her hierarchy and those recommended in this passage.

But why exactly should religious learning require authoritative works, authoritative teachers, and the hierarchical structures that permit the institutions in which both can flourish? These are needs that all pedagogical practice must meet in some degree; contemporary western schools, colleges, and universities are all more or less authoritarian in these senses. They all require submission to an institutionally defined and enforced idea of what is worth reading and knowing, and they all appoint and license authoritative interpreters of this material. But since the public and professed ideology of these institutions is still mostly in accord with Enlightenment ideas about the unfettered individual's free search for truth, the presence of authority is typically not made much of, not elevated to the status of a good. Authoritarian decisions and teaching practices are, in contemporary secular educational institutions, treated a little like the janitorial staff: a necessity, but not what the institution understands itself to be about. For institutions of religious learning things are (or should be) very different. Recall that a religious account is, in the eyes of those who offer it, comprehensive, unsurpassable, and central. Learning to offer such an account is, therefore, learning to engage in a strictly imperialist enterprise. All phenomena not themselves part of the religious account are to be interpreted by religious readers in light of their religious account, in the terms provided for them by their account. And this is one (perhaps the most important) dimension of discursive imperialism: the desire to write everything that is not already part of your account into its margins.

Now, the kind of imperialism intrinsic to religious accounts requires a strong authoritative hand, evident to all who want to learn to offer a particular religious account. This is because religious accounts cannot, by their very nature, permit opposing or different accounts to remain unaccounted for, or to continue to be offered by the religious reader. Their secular counterparts, by contrast, very well can: learning to offer the account offered by cultural anthropologists in a contemporary university need not involve giving any explicit account of, say, the religious convictions and practices of nationalist Theravāda Buddhists in Sri Lanka (unless these should happen to be the object of anthropological study; and even then any normative account given of their claims will tend to remain implicit). So the pedagogy of cultural anthropology can let its authoritarianism remain implicit precisely because its self-understanding does not include the ambition to offer a comprehensive, unsurpassable, and central account (it may be that some cultural anthropologists do harbor such ambitions; but insofar as they do, they are religious). This is not an option open to religious pedagogues; they must rule on, marginalize, and incorporate all those rival accounts of which they come to know, and must be explicit in their exercise of authority as they do.

But there is more. Recall that religious reading requires the establishment of a particular set of relations between the reader and what is read. These are principally relations of reverence, delight, awe, and wonder, relations that, once established, lead to the close, repetitive kinds of reading already described. The questioning of authority and the concern with preliminary issues of method and justification (intellectual attitudes and concerns typical of modernity) make the establishment of such relations almost impossible because of the endless deferral of commitment that such attitudes bring with them. Commitment to some body of works as an endlessly nourishing garden of delights is essential to religious reading; and authoritative direction as to which works are of the right sort is a necessary condition for religious engagement with them. But concern with method (what does it mean to read religiously?) or with epistemology (how can I be warranted in reading this work religiously?) preempts and makes effectively impossible the act of religious reading, as well as the authoritative direction that undergirds it. Hence religious learners and teachers need to be self-conscious and explicit about the place of authority in their decisions about what to read religiously. This is not a need central to the practices of consumerist readers.

A final comment on why religious learning requires authority—or at least on why it needs a more explicit and self-conscious use of authority than do the pedagogical practices of modernity. These latter are predicated not only upon the assumption that the individual is the locus of value but also upon the assumption that a central goal of education is the maximizing of the individual's knowledge of alternatives and capacity to choose among them. Recall Gibbon's explicit connection of writing and money as tools for extending choice, and Fredric Jameson's linking of consumerist writing and consumerist attitudes to purchasing products. For religious pedagogy, by contrast, choice and alternatives are not significant values, and are certainly not to be maximized. Pedagogically, modernity is the cafeteria-style university catalogue of courses from which consumers (provided they have paid their tuition fees) can choose what most pleases them; it is the row of paperback editions of sacred works from a dozen religious traditions jostling one another on the bookstore's shelves. Religious pedagogy, by contrast, is the single curriculum, identical for all, like that in place in Nālandā in India in the eighth century, or at Clairvaux in France in the twelfth; and it is a single set of sacred works that cannot be placed on a par with (much less on the same shelf as) others. Religious learning therefore requires explicit appeal to authority in ways that consumerist pedagogy does not. The former wants to make choices for its learners, while the latter wants to equip them to choose for themselves from the cornucopia of material and intellectual blessings produced by the limited liability corporation and the other institutional appendages of late capitalism.

Authority and hierarchy are not simple univocal categories, of course. Each may be present in a particular institutional setting in a wide variety of ways. There is a tendency on the part of those who are suspicious of the idea that authority has any proper place in pedagogy to smooth this variety into uniformity by equating authority with self-validating authority. On such a view, the deliverances of a particular authority (whether work or person) are to be taken as true simply in virtue of their origin in the relevant source; if the authority really is self-validating, then there is no conceivable need for further checks. But this is not the only kind of authority there is, and so also not the only kind that must be present within institutions of religious learning. The sources of authority in an institution of religious learning may contain within themselves (or even be largely constituted by) recursive rules of self-correction; or they may limit themselves to the supply of procedural constraints rather than substantive ones. But it isn't my purpose to give a systematic analysis of kinds of pedagogical authority. I want only to note that the teaching of religious reading typically requires the explicit use of such authority, and that this will typically go with hierarchy. These (authority and hierarchy) are the first two properties characteristic of the institutional forms appropriate to the teaching of religious reading.

The other two are community and tradition. Religious readers do not read in isolation, either synchronically or diachronically. Their practices presuppose and engage with those who have already done what they are doing. Whence tradition. And they are directed at and responsive to a community of those now doing what they are also doing. Whence the communitarian nature of religious learning. These facts help to explain the typical products of religious reading-as-composition, products to be taken up at more length in subsequent chapters.

Communities with a past, a tradition of learning, require an institutional form. What this will look like depends mostly on whether the community as a whole values and has a place for virtuoso learners and teachers, those who devote all their time and labor to these things; and, in the case of communities that do have a place for such people, upon what proportion of the community as a whole is made up of them. There are many possibilities here. Some communities may not value virtuoso learning, while still practicing religious reading; others may have a few virtuosos, but not allow their number to make them more than a tiny proportion of the whole; while yet others may foster virtuoso learning in a fairly large proportion of their members. Institutional forms will vary accordingly. The examples to be considered in subsequent chapters will be from religious communities that value specialist religious reading—which I'll define provisionally as the kind of reading done by those who can articulate a significantly higher proportion of the information implied by their religious account than is usual. Specialist religious readers know, and can say a good deal about, what they do; nonspecialist ones are likely to know and be able to say less.

Communities that value the presence of specialist religious readers are going to need institutions that permit such people to devote the time and energy necessary to becoming specialists. This will usually mean institutions that permit specialists and would-be specialists to engage in no labor other than that required for specialized reading. The ideal setting for this, perhaps, is the monastery, for in monasteries distractions from religious reading may be minimized (even if in actual monasteries they rarely are). But this means that the institutional presence of communities of specialist religious readers requires a social order in which there are resources free for the support of materially unproductive people, and the will to use such resources for that purpose. And this is the most important institutional requirement for specialist religious reading: the existence of groups of leisured individuals, self-consciously communitarian and traditional, open about their constraint by authority, and committed to gaining the kind of moral relation to works produced by repetitive reading and memorization. Literacy in the narrow sense is unimportant by contrast and may very well be absent in some institutions devoted to training specialist religious readers.

Historically, the most obvious instances of a social order committed to providing such conditions have been medieval Europe, and Tibet from the fourteenth through the mid-twentieth century. In both of these some of the most powerful social institutions were the monasteries, in which at least some people were specialist religious readers; and in both (perhaps more important) the ideal of being such was taken seriously enough that there was little argument about the importance of devoting resources to this purpose. But Tibet is now an Autonomous Region (so-called) of the People's Republic of China; and the monasteries of Europe are either gone, casualties of the transformations in pedagogy produced by the shift of the intellectual center of gravity in Europe from the cloister to the *schola* in the twelfth and thirteenth centuries, and then later of the Reformation; or greatly reduced, casualties of the industrial revolution and the rise and incipient decay of consumerist capitalism. Where then to look?

Contemporary late capitalist cultures do see fit to devote a small part of their resources to the support of institutions in which specialist religious readers might flourish. These institutions are called universities, to use the most generic term; I mean those places in which the idea that some people ought to be supported in spending most of their time reading and writing is given institutional form. This is not, of course, the only function that universities have, or take themselves to have; but it is nonetheless a real one.

Western universities have their roots in eighth- and ninth-century Islamic institutional forms. They began to flourish in twelfth-century Europe (Bologna, Paris, and a little later Oxford and Cambridge); they were stimulated by the Renaissance, and given a final prod toward their present form by the development of the German research universities in the nineteenth century.[6] There are, perhaps, now a couple of hundred universities (in this sense) in the world, with the highest concentration to be found in Europe and North America. There is, in addition, a much larger number of institutions whose central reason for being is not to support people in reading and writing, but rather to train them in the performance of functions useful economically or practically to late capitalist societies—which is to say that they are there to create happy consumers and producers. These institutions, too, sometimes call themselves universities, but their emphasis is different. And there are many mixed cases in which it is difficult to be sure where the central emphasis lies. All these institutions are presently under more or less social and financial pressure to shift their emphasis away from supporting otherwise nonproductive readers and writers, and toward the training of individuals with skills useful for production and consumption. But it remains unclear what the results of these pressures will be, since there are equally strong pressures pointing in the other direction, encouraging traditionally vocational and teaching institutions to become more like universities.

That there are such institutions is a small sign of hope for those who might want to recover religious reading. It means that some of the institutional requirements for it can be met: there are places in which leisure and community are theoretically (and sometimes actually) available. From their foundation until the very recent past, the epistemology dominant in these institutions has made religious reading difficult; indeed, their rise has been one of the direct causes of the decline in such reading. Modernist theories of knowledge, of the person, and of reading, with all of which the university has been deeply implicated since the sixteenth century, are profoundly incompatible with the kind of learning at which religious reading aims. But the dominance of such modernist theories is waning. The effective demise, for instance, of epistemologies centered upon a putatively autonomous subject makes it no longer possible to mount a convincing and coherent theoretical argument against the desirability of religious reading solely on epistemological grounds; and that this is both the case and widely acknowledged to be the case suggests that one of the major obstacles to its recovery is no longer present.

The intentional recovery of religious reading by those working in western universities may therefore now be possible. But what, concretely, might this mean? First, recall that such reading requires that there be a tradition of such already in place before it can occur. And there are not many traditions of strong reading available within which religious learning might take place; perhaps no more than half a dozen, including at least Judaism, Buddhism, Islam, Christianity, Marxism, and perhaps a few others. These already have in place many of the institutional requirements I've been discussing: canon, index, community, tradition, and so forth. Some preserve vestigial houses of reading (monasteries, yeshivas, seminaries, and the like), but most have largely abdicated that function, or no longer have the resources effectively to maintain it. Universities might well provide a home for religious readers who are Jewish, Christian, Buddhist, and the like. To some extent they already do. But such readers in such a setting tend to lead a double life, cloaking their identity in the tattered garments of a *wissenschaftlich* modernity. There is no good theoretical reason to maintain such disguises, and many good theoretical and ethical reasons not to do so. Religious readers, actual or aspiring, can and should be public about their identity as such.

The difficulties for those who come out of the closet, as it were, are likely not to be strictly theoretical but rather broadly cultural. The culture of contemporary academia, to reiterate, is largely predicated upon an instrumentalist and consumerist attitude to what is read, upon a cult of individualism and novelty, and upon the uses of kinds of technology that make religious reading difficult or impossible. It also tends to assume without argument the validity and desirability of a particular and highly ideological version of liberalism: individualistic in both religion and politics, foundationalist and rationalist in philosophy, and rights-based and consequentialist in ethics. This tends to mean that universities reflect the suspicion of their ambient culture about public professions of religious faith that also involve claims as to how intellectual work ought be done, how pedagogy ought be practiced, and so forth. And, most of all, ideological liberalism tends to be suspicious of reference to authority as part of such claims. Insofar as such a liberalism attempts to maintain a foundationalist epistemology as the basis for a critique of religious reading, it will fail; and in fact such critiques are made less and less frequently. More common now is the attempt to rule such practice out of the public sphere by the exercise of legislative power, or by judicial interpretation of the Constitution or other legislation[7] (this trend prompted the passage of the Religious Freedom Restoration Act by Congress in 1993, the main purpose of which was to restore the requirement that there be a demonstrable compelling state interest in order to justify any state infringement upon free exercise of religion);[8] or to attempt to rule it out by ornate rhetorical expressions of puzzlement, dislike, or disgust, as Richard Rorty has recently done.[9]

These broadly cultural facts have a great deal of power, even if they cannot be given a coherent defense. It remains to be seen, as a result, to what extent (if at all) western universities will prove capable of providing a home for religious readers. That they would be the better for so doing is fairly clear. Religious reading, and the broader learning of which it is a part, is preferable, ethically and epistemologically, to the largely instrumentalist, consumerist, individualist, and in the end incoherent intellectual practices of the other two important players in the field: the earnest and unreconstructed modernist, and the dedicated and playful postmodernist (both of whom will tend to be ideological liberals in matters of public policy). But I am not optimistic that western universities will be able to muster the intellectual energy to acknowledge and support professed religious learners in their activities as such. And since the only other possibility (the houses of reading supported by and explicitly committed to religious institutions) seems even less likely to have the resources or the will, the outlook is not promising.

Epistemology

Religious reading implies an epistemology, a particular set of views about how knowledge is to be gained, maintained, and extended, and about what it is.[10] Any intellectual practice has such implications, so it is scarcely surprising that this one does. They are among the concomitants of religious reading. But what are these epistemological views? This question is usefully explored by using a distinction now standard in anglophone epistemology: that between internalist and externalist epistemologies.

Epistemological theories in general are interested in making distinctions between instances of belief that are not well grounded and that as a result have no claim to be called knowledge, on the one hand; and instances of belief that are well grounded and that therefore do have some such claim, on the other. For instance: I may believe that I can generate reliable beliefs about the course of future events by consulting the entrails of properly sacrificed goats. Most western academics (certainly most anglophone epistemologists) would say that beliefs about the course of future events generated in this way lack the property or properties that might give them claim to be called knowledge. By contrast: I may believe that I can generate reliable beliefs about what Boris Yeltsin said to Bill Clinton last night, even though he speaks no English and I no Russian, by consulting a report of the conversation in *The New York Times*. Many, perhaps most, anglophone epistemologists would be likely to think that beliefs generated in this way are of a kind such that they should be considered knowledge. The debate centers upon just what account to give of the property (or properties) that distinguishes beliefs of the first kind from beliefs of the second.

Internalist epistemologies typically claim that the property in question (it might be called 'warrant' or 'justification' or something similar) is internal to those who have the beliefs in question, something to which they have special access: they have had the proper experience, say, or have constructed or understood the proper argument, and to both of these facts they are better witnesses than anyone else. Internalism in epistemology goes nicely with deontology: I may be justified (warranted) in believing what I believe, on such views, if (and perhaps only if) I have fulfilled my epistemic obligations or duties. As Alvin Plantinga puts the point:

> [J]ustification, internalism, and epistemic deontology are properly seen as a closely related triumvirate: internalism flows from deontology and is unmotivated without it, and justification is at bottom and originally a deontological notion.[11]

For the internalist, then, what counts is whether we've fulfilled our epistemic duties; and we can tell whether we have by, paradigmatically, an act of introspection, one that will, if we're properly attentive, tell us whether, as John Locke puts it, we are like someone who "believes or disbelieves according as Reason directs him," or whether we are like someone who "transgresses against his own Light, and misuses those Faculties which were given him to no other end, but to search and follow the clearer Evidence."[12] Internalism in epistemology is, then, evidentialist, deontological, and (usually) radically individualist: you can tell whether you've fulfilled your epistemic duties simply by using your generically human intellectual equipment.

Externalist views are quite different. They claim that what makes a particular instance of believing justified (warranted) is something external to believers, typically some process or method of arriving at the belief in question that is not internal to them, and may not be known, understood, or controlled by them. Perhaps the most common kind of externalist epistemology is reliabilism, which is the view that you are warranted (justified) in believing something if and only if your belief has been produced by a reliable belief-forming practice or mechanism (sometimes called, in the trade, a doxastic practice). Externalist views allow (indeed, they require) a distinction between a belief's having been produced in the mentioned way and this fact being known to its believer. You may very well have beliefs that have been so produced, and that you are warranted in having as a result, and yet not know these facts about your beliefs; or if you do know them, you may not be able to give an account of just what it is about the doxastic practice in question that makes it reliable. And yet neither of these lacks prevents you from being justified in believing what you believe: you are warranted just because the belief was produced in the right way, whether you know this or not, and whether or not you can explain wherein the rightness of the way consists.

It may be (though it is not) the case that consulting the entrails of properly sacrificed goats is a reliable way of arriving at beliefs about the course of future events. Even if it were, an externalist would not need to require of those who might engage in such a practice that they should know it to be reliable, much less that they should know why it is, in order for it to produce largely true beliefs for them.

Externalist epistemologies, then, are typically nonevidentialist, antideontological (if being deontological means not just that you've fulfilled your epistemic duties but that part of fulfilling them includes knowing and being able to show that you've done so—as for Locke), and nonindividualist (since individuals need not be, and usually will not be, the final court of appeal on the question of whether and why particular beliefs are justified or warranted).

Religious readers will typically be externalist in epistemology. It should be obvious why. They will, explicitly or implicitly, hold the view that proper religious reading is among the belief-forming practices that usually produce true beliefs—and perhaps that it is an indispensable such practice. They will also typically think that the patterns of reading they practice and advocate are constitutively and necessarily tradition-specific; that engaging in them is best likened to the performance of a complex skill; and that, concomitantly, the idea that some particular set of patterns of reasoning or some particular set of claims to knowledge ought to be universally comprehensible to all humans just because we all possess some generically human intellectual equipment (a typical implication of internalist epistemologies) is as silly as the idea that the finer points of fugal composition ought to be comprehensible to all for this reason.

According to views like this, externalist views, knowledge is understood as available only to those who have troubled to learn the skills necessary for access to it, and many, perhaps most, such skills can be learned only within the bounds of tradition-based practices. These practices might be of many kinds: an obvious candidate would be exposure to the proper ways of reading or hearing the right works. And this, naturally, is where religious reading comes in, for it is likely to be the case that religious readers will see their modes of reading as at least a necessary condition for the development of proper understanding. If tradition-specific reading skills are not practiced, then much knowledge (and probably all the most important knowledge), they will say, remains unavailable. This is a typical pattern of epistemological reasoning implied by religious reading.

Postmodernist writers and religious readers are likely to have common ground here, and as a result may find themselves able to join forces against the remnants of modernity, much as radical feminists and conservative Christians find themselves able to join forces against purveyors of pornography. The reason is that internalist epistemologies fit well with neither postmodernist writing nor religious reading. Such epistemologies require a stability and givenness to the world that the former cannot grant; and they require an optimism about the generic untrained capacities of the person that is ruled out by the latter. This is one of the very few signs of hope for the recovery of religious reading in the contemporary western academy. Internalist epistemologies are no longer dominant there, largely because of the attacks of postmodernist critics; and once the individualism and foundationalism of internalism has been abandoned, there is at least conceptual room for the recovery of religious reading. This is one of several points of convergence between religious reading and postmodernist writing, a fact I am not alone in realizing. Fredric Jameson, once again, makes the same point, though inchoately, in a number of ways: he acknowledges that serious religious thinkers such as the Mennonite John Howard Yoder may properly be understood to have serious affinities with postmodernism. And Jameson sees the surface similarities between the literary and intellectual practices of postmodernist writers and (those I am calling) religious readers:

> Commentary indeed makes up the special field of postmodern linguistic practice generally, and its originality, at least with respect to the pretensions and illusions of philosophy in the preceding period, of 'bourgeois' philosophy, that with some secular pride and confidence set out to say what things really were after the long night of superstition and the sacred. Commentary, however, also—in that curious play of historical identity and difference mentioned above—now secures the kinship of the postmodern (at least in this respect) with other, hitherto more archaic, periods of thought and intellectual labor, as with the medieval copyists and scribes, or the endless exegesis of the great oriental philosophies and sacred texts.[13]

More laconically: postmodernism is an ersatz form of religious reading whose literary and intellectual practices make sense and provide nourishment only if they become religious. Recall Geoffrey Hartman's comments on Midrashic practice quoted in chapter 2. But, once again, it must be emphasized that what postmodernist writing and religious reading have in common is the rejection of internalist epistemology.

A final point on the epistemological concomitants of religious reading. Religious readers have usually seen quite clearly that their reading practices require rejection of the demand that these practices be justified with arguments that don't already assume their reliability and desirability. You can't show that it's epistemically good to read the Qur'ān religiously (that doing so is usually productive of knowledge) without already assuming that it is. Indeed, as Augustine pointed out long ago,[14] without submission to authoritative direction in religious reading you won't even be able to comprehend what the epistemic and ethical benefits of such reading are, much less provide a justification of them. This is the epistemological version of the points made earlier in this chapter about institutional authority; and it is an entirely proper one. No interesting and complex belief-forming practice proves capable of justifying its own reliability without already assuming that reliability. This is true of elementary logic: you can't show that *modus ponens* (*if p then q; p; therefore q*) is valid without using it in the argument that purports to show its validity; it is true of sensory perception: you can't show that this is generally reliable as a means of producing true beliefs without assuming that it is; and it is also true of every particular instance of religious reading: an attempt to show that it is reliable as a producer of true beliefs will already assume that it is, or it will fail. That religious reading already implies this epistemic stance is therefore a profound advantage rather than a damaging drawback.

4

The Fundamental Genres of Religious Reading

The Significance of Commentary

Religious readers have composed more commentaries than any other kind of work. If there is a single genre most characteristic of them, it is the commentary. Other genres (the epic narrative, the genealogy, the list, the law code, the hortatory sermon, the liturgical handbook, the spell collection) are insignificant beside it. A huge proportion of the literature composed in the handful of premodern literary languages of empire (Latin, Sanskrit, and Chinese are the most obvious examples) is commentarial, and most of it was composed by religious readers for other religious readers. The commentary is the principal means by which communities of religious readers have expressed themselves discursively.[1]

All this is obvious. To say it is certainly to say nothing new. And yet, there have been few systematic efforts by those who study religion and religious phenomena to explore the nature of commentaries and their composition, to ask whether and for what it might be useful to set their composition off from that of other genres as a distinctive discursive practice, and to offer a characterization or typology of commentarial acts and their products. There have, naturally, been many tradition-specific studies of particular kinds of commentary (Jewish, Confucian, Buddhist, Christian, Islamic, jurisprudential, and so forth); but most of these either pay no particular attention to the fascinating theoretical questions surrounding the very idea of commentary or use only the vocabulary indigenous to the particular tradition studied to do so.

The single partial exception to this generalization concerns work done within the ambit of contemporary biblical scholarship.[2] Here, the recent discussion of commentary seems to have been occasioned by doubts about its value as a means of advancing or communicating knowledge in biblical studies, as well as by theoretical uncertainty about the very nature of commentary. These uncertainties, in turn, are part of what seems to be a growing lack of assurance that the historical-critical method, whose sanctity is usually assumed by contemporary biblical commentators, will in fact yield what the student of the Bible ought to want. This leads to a desire for clarity about what a commentary is, both in its literary form and in its goals and purposes. Some of this work is useful and has informed what follows. But outside this, and some scattered remarks in works by scholars treating particular instances of commentarial activity, there is a striking lack of attention by western scholars to the nature of commentary and its significance for religious communities.

By contrast, there has been an enormous amount of theoretical attention paid by students of religion in recent decades to narrative, mythopoiesis, ritual, and the like. Jonathan Z. Smith has, for more than two decades, been drawing attention to the need for more work by scholars of religion on exegesis and commentary. In words first published in 1978 he said: "I expect that scholars of religion in the future will shift from the present Romantic hermeneutics of symbol and poetic speech to that of legal-exegetical discourse."[3] But what he expected has not yet happened. Bernhard Anderson, in his analysis of the state of play among the writers of biblical commentaries, was, in 1982, unable to find any serious historical study of the nature of development of commentary: "The biography of the genre," he wrote, "has not yet been written."[4] I want to go some way toward writing it, and in so doing to help in correcting the mixture of rationalist and romantic biases that still infect the study of religion.

What, then, is a commentary, and what is it to comment? In thinking about these deceptively simple-looking questions, it's helpful to keep in mind a distinction between commentary as an act (what commentators do) and commentary as a product (the works produced by commenting); the English language often uses the same word for both, and as a result confusion sometimes occurs. Both act and product are distinct from the object of commentary, that toward which the act of commentary is turned, or upon which it is performed. To take an easy example, when Spinoza provides, in his *Ethica*, an explication of one of his own axioms, the commentarial act is the act of explication; the object is the axiom being explained; and the artifact is the (in this case written) explication.

Acts of commentary, like other acts of religious reading, are usually performed within a tradition, and this suggests that those who engage in them will often have thought about what they are doing and why, about what can and what cannot be a proper commentarial object, and about what properties a commentarial work should have. Therefore it will often, though not always, be possible for the student of acts of commentary to find explicit statements by those who perform them about these matters. Religious readers in both medieval India and medieval Europe classified commentaries into kinds, typically by paying attention to the properties of such works, to the methods by which they should be composed, and to their proper purposes and uses. The same is true for contemporary western jurists and practitioners of the arts of biblical commentary. These classificatory and analytical attempts by practitioners of commentary ought to be of considerable help in the much-needed enterprise of arriving at a descriptive characterization of acts of commentary and their products that will usefully mark off these phenomena from others. But these resources, too, have scarcely yet been tapped.

The study of commentary should also make a contribution to the epistemological questions already raised in my discussion of the concomitants of religious reading. These are questions of central importance not only for those who want to study religion but also for those who want to practice seriously as a member of some community of religious readers. The central epistemological question I have in mind is that of how religious knowledge (the knowledge that communities of religious readers present in their comprehensive, unsurpassable, and central accounts) ought to be constituted, transmitted, and understood.

One possible view about this, a broadly externalist view in the terms of chapter 3, is that patterns of reasoning and the knowledge produced by them are constitutively and necessarily tradition-specific, and that using them is best likened to the performance of a complex skill. According to such a view, religious knowledge is understood as available only to those who have troubled to learn the skills necessary for access to it, and such skills can be learned only within the bounds of a set of tradition-based practices. These practices might include proper catechetical instruction, proper ritual practice, and (of primary interest here) exposure to the proper ways of reading the right works. This last, naturally, is where commentary comes in, for it is likely to be the case that on such views as these exposure to the products of commentarial activity will be seen as a necessary condition for proper reading or hearing, and so also for proper understanding. If tradition-specific commentarial skills are not at least understood (and at best practiced), it might be said, then religious knowledge will be simply unavailable. On such a view, commentary assumes an enormous epistemic importance: it becomes one among the guarantors of religious knowledge, one among the gatekeepers of heaven. Commentarial works, on an extreme version of this view, englobe and absorb the world, constituting for their skilled users (and composers) all, or all the religiously significant, parameters within which thought and experience can occur.

But there are other views. Some (internalists, usually) think that there are means of access to religious knowledge that are totally, or almost totally, independent of tradition-specific patterns of reasoning, and so also independent of tradition-specific commentarial acts, objects, and artifacts. For instance, it might be argued that everything of conceptual importance to the attainment of salvation (to the attainment of whatever end some community takes to be ultimately desirable for its members) can be arrived at by a priori reasoning, reasoning that can be practiced without training in any particular tradition of commentarial practice. An extreme (and extremely implausible) version of this view is that you could come to offer some religious community's account simply by sitting down in a quiet place and working it out for yourself. If this view is taken, then the epistemic importance of commentary will be minimal. The products of commentary will be seen as illustrative of truths already known or instantiations of principles already argued to rather than things exposure to which is constitutive of both the possibility and the actuality of salvific knowledge; and the use of them will then be far from necessary for the attainment of salvation.

Still others appear to think that salvific knowledge is attainable not by a priori reasoning, nor by the use of commentaries and other tradition-specific products, but rather through some universally available experience or experiences whose occurrence is not dependent upon tradition-specific variables such as commentarial practice. On this view, too, commentary will not have much epistemic significance; the best you might say for it is that it could be an instrument of contingent importance to the occurrence of whatever experience is taken to constitute the possibility of salvation.

Mixed positions are of course possible and are more likely to be met than any of these extreme views. But the sheer predominance of commentarial works within the literary output of religious communities suggests strongly that it is typically given a high epistemic evaluation by them, and that they are therefore more likely to approach the first of the positions just sketched (the one that affirms the importance of tradition-specific practices). And this fits well with the fact that religious readers tend to be epistemological externalists. For them, the composition and use of commentaries will likely be seen as one among the practices that, if rightly done, will produce knowledge—even if those who perform the practices can't say why this is so.

Commentary Defined

There is a broad and fairly uninteresting sense in which all human activity is commentarial. All of it presupposes and bases itself upon previous activity of a similar kind, and either explicitly or implicitly makes reference to it. Activity thus entails commentarial activity: the latter is intrinsic to the former. Consider the utterance of a simple sentence in any language. Suppose (what is unlikely) that the sentence is one never before uttered. The act of uttering it consists, in part, in commentary upon all earlier uses of the words in which it consists, for the semantic range of any word in any natural language is a function of (though not identical with) the sum of all previous uses of that word. A new use, then, gets its sense by presupposing and extending, and so commenting upon, all these earlier uses. And if the sentence in question is one that has been uttered before—as is the case with my writing (and your reading) the sentence that is the seventh proposition of the second book of Spinoza's *Ethica* (*Ordo et connexio idearum idem est ac ordo et connexio rerum*)—then a new utterance comments upon (presupposes, extends, gives exegesis of) the earlier utterances. Similar things can be said about more extended discursive acts, like the composition of a *ṭikā*, a Sanskrit exegetical work. Such a work can be understood as presupposing and extending the individual words and semantic units (sentences and so forth) in which it consists, as well as those of the work whose exegesis it overtly undertakes.

This applies to more than the use of words. When architects draw up plans for a new church and agonize over where to put the baptismal font, they are, in a sense, commenting upon all previous instances of the activity of font placing. When musicians play a phrase on the piano, or composers write notes on a stave, the same is true. Sometimes the commentarial or exegetical relationship of these acts to earlier acts of the same kind is obvious and explicit (think of Vaughan Williams's "Fantasia on a Theme by Thomas Tallis"); but even where it is not, the commentarial relation is still present. This is true even when a particular act self-consciously attempts the rejection of all previous acts of its kind; or when, to put this slightly differently, those who perform it think of themselves as undertaking something radically new, an unprecedented discursive act (consider Schoenberg's rejection of traditional tonal music in his composition of twelve-tone pieces from the late 1920s onward).

But this broad understanding of commentary takes in too much to be of any conceptual use. It makes commentary coextensive with exegesis. While it is no doubt true, and even mildly interesting, to say that all human activity is commentarial in this sense, this will not identify the commentarial as a distinctive practice. So a narrower understanding is needed, one that will have some bite.

Suppose we begin with a consideration of how to differentiate commentaries as works that have been composed, displayed, and (perhaps) stored from other kinds of works. Commentaries, like other works, are products of human activity. They may take many forms (for example, shaped stone; paint on canvas; vibrations in the air; symbols scratched on palm leaves; ordered patterns of light on the surface of a cathode-ray tube), but for the sake of conceptual ease I shall limit my analysis to those products of human activity that consist largely or entirely in words, either spoken (sung, chanted) or written (scratched, inscribed, typed, word-processed). Much of what follows can be applied to other kinds of work, but doing so will introduce some extra complications that I don't want to pursue.

With the investigation limited in this way to verbal works, what features must such a work possess in order to be usefully classified as a commentary? I distinguish three; their conjoint presence in some work will suffice to make it a commentary. The first is that there be apparent in it a direct relation to some other work, which is to say that some other work be overtly present in it. A commentarial work must be, in this sense, a metawork. The second is that these signs of being a metawork should dominate, either quantitatively or qualitatively. And the third is that its structure, the order in which material occurs in it, should be given to it by the work to which it is a metawork. I'll treat these in order.

First, as to being a metawork. This is a requirement that the metawork have in it overt signs of the presence in it of another work, the work to which it is a metawork. Direct quotation, paraphrase, and summary will be the three most common modes of such presence. Any work that lacks any one of these modes of relating itself to another work is not the product of a commentarial act. So, for example, the echoes of biblical narratives found throughout C. S. Lewis's children's stories will not suffice to make those stories biblical commentaries; neither will the threads of *Orlando Furioso* present in *Much Ado About Nothing* suffice to make the latter a commentary on the former. In neither case is there a sufficiently close relation between the work in question and that other work whose traces are found in it: there is no direct quotation; and there is no other evidence of, as Michael Fishbane puts it, "multiple and sustained lexical linkages"[5] between the one and the other. There is, in plenty, the reappearance and reworking of themes and motifs of various kinds, but this is not enough to make it proper to consider Lewis a biblical commentator (not, anyway, in his children's stories), or Shakespeare a commentator upon Ariosto. This points to an important requirement: formally speaking, there must be a close verbal relation between one work and another in order for there to be a commentarial relation between them. The presence of similar or identical plotlines, mythemes, structures, or other bits and pieces, will not suffice, since such similarities may not be evidence of the direct dependence of one work upon another at all, but rather evidence of the dependence of both upon some third, or upon some common stream of tradition.

But a vast body of works survives these exclusions. John of Damascus, in the 101st chapter of his compendium of heresies, composed in the seventh century, quotes the Qur'ān in order to refute it (he appears to have been the first Christian thinker to do this). Is John commenting upon the Qur'ān? In 1979, a punk-rock group called the Sex Pistols release a parodic cover of the 1950s rock-and-roll song "Rock Around the Clock," first made famous by Bill Haley and the Comets. Are the Sex Pistols commenting on Bill Haley? Tom Stoppard, in *Rosencrantz and Guildenstern Are Dead*, quotes *Hamlet* extensively as frame and springboard for his own dramatic creation. Is his play a commentary upon *Hamlet*? A good proportion of the New Testament is summary, direct quotation, or digest, of portions of the Old; is the former in part or in whole a commentary upon the latter? All these putative commentaries meet the first criterion: they are metaworks with significant traces of other works present in them.

But even if a work does exhibit overt signs of quotation, paraphrase, or summary, this will not suffice to make it a commentary. A further requirement is that such signs should outweigh other elements in it. They may do this either quantitatively (such signs would then simply have to comprise a majority of the work) or qualitatively, in that such signs provide the structure, organization, and purpose of the work, even when they do not predominate quantitatively. And, naturally, both modes of predominance may be present at once. To put this requirement rather differently: overt signs of quotation, summary, or paraphrase predominate in a work if and only if their removal would make the work incomprehensible, which is to say if and only if a reader/hearer cannot use the work without also using the work whose traces are significantly present in it. The fact that some work is a metawork must be essential and intrinsic to it in order for it to be properly called a commentary.

This requirement is intended to rule out, as commentaries, those works in which quotation, paraphrase, or summary are occasional or incidental elements, as well as those in which these things are extrinsic to the main purposes of the work, as far as these can be ascertained. For example, in the sixth chapter of *Bleak House* Charles Dickens puts a half-ironical paraphrase of some lines from the third act of *Antony and Cleopatra* into the mouth of Harold Skimpole, his Leigh Hunt parody. But it would be very odd to consider *Bleak House* a commentary upon *Antony and Cleopatra*. Dickens's use of these lines is merely illustrative, and not intrinsic to his work. What he writes can perfectly well (though incompletely) be understood without reference to Shakespeare's play. A slightly different kind of example is George Eliot's use of epigraphs to each chapter of *Middlemarch*: she quotes Spenser at the head of chapter 37, Shakespeare at the head of chapter 42, and so on. This epigraphical use of quotation, once a standard literary device in both fiction and nonfiction, is, again, a commentarial usage that by definition does not predominate, quantitatively or qualitatively, in the works in which it occurs, and as a result does not suffice to make them commentaries. There will be some overlap between what is ruled out by this criterion, and what is ruled out by the criterion of absence of direct quotation, paraphrase, or summary: works in which there are only allusions to, echoes of, and half-remembered references to other texts are also likely to be those in which these things do not predominate.

This question of quantitative or qualitative predominance is made more difficult by conceptual problems involved with the individuation of works. It is extremely difficult to give a satisfactory analysis of the relational property 'being a proper part of' as this pertains to works or work fragments; and this means, in turn, that it is equally difficult to give a satisfactory analysis of how to recognize the boundaries of a work. The intuitive notions that I have about this (and that you probably share) are closely bound up with my experience as both producer and consumer of the products of print technology, and with what I know of the ramifications of copyright law. And all this, naturally, is based on recent technological and cultural change, and is hardly a sufficient basis for a philosophical account of the mereology of works. But I shall not go further into this here, and in what follows shall treat questions of this kind on an ad hoc basis. So, for example, it might be perfectly reasonable for some purposes to take the paragraphs in which Dickens presents Harold Skimpole's ironic half-quotation of *Antony and Cleopatra* precisely as a commentary upon a part of (a few lines from) that play, and thus to treat it as a self-contained commentary that does meet the formal criteria so far mentioned.

The third criterion is that in order for there to be a commentarial relation between one work and another, one (the object of commentary) must provide the other (the commentary proper) with its structure, content, and order. The content and order of the latter must follow those of the former. Steven Fraade puts a stronger version of this point:

> [A]ll commentaries . . . can be said to exhibit the following structural traits: they begin with an extended base-text, of which they designate successive subunits for exegetical attention, to each of which they attach a comment or chain of comments, which nevertheless remain distinct from the base-text, to which the commentary sooner or later returns (that is, advances) to take up the next selected subunit in sequence.[6]

In an extreme case, that of the translation or word-by-word gloss, the order in which matter is presented in the work commented upon may be the only factor governing the order in which matter is presented in the commentary. Fraade seems to intend something like this. But I do not intend the requirement to be so rigid. The commentary may have systematic, theoretical, or practical interests of its own that require or make desirable interpolations, excursuses, asides, and so forth. Most obviously, if the commentary is taking a whole work as its object (subject to the remarks just made about the difficulties involved in individuating works, and so also in saying just what 'a whole work' might mean), it may offer elucidation of, or aids to the understanding of, matters that have to do with the work as a whole rather than with any particular part of it. Examples of these include tables of contents, analytical indices, and glossaries. The location of such aids in the commentary cannot, obviously, be determined by anything in the work commented upon, and their presence should not be taken to disqualify the work in which they are found from being called a commentary. This criterion is intended to disqualify as commentaries works that meet the preceding criteria (works, that is, with overt signs of quotation, summary, or paraphrase; and in which such signs predominate, quantitatively or qualitatively) but whose structure and order is not given them by the work or works they quote, summarize, or paraphrase.

For example, a judicial opinion might contain many quotations of, or paraphrases from, a statute, and these might dominate it, both quantitatively and qualitatively. That is, it might be reasonable to think of the opinion as being concerned very largely with exegesis of the statute, and material depending on, or taken directly from, the statute, might be, statistically speaking, the larger part of the opinion. But the opinion might use its quotations from or paraphrases of the statute in the service of its own argument as to whether, and how, the statute applies in some particular case, and the order and structure of this argument might not be given it by the order and structure of the statute. In such a case it's proper to think of the opinion as interpreting, or doing exegesis of, the statute; but not to call the former a commentary upon the latter. Similarly for a preacher whose text is, say, the first chapter of Paul's letter to the Romans, but whose interpretation and application of the text does not follow the order of the original, but rather chooses and recombines units of the original for the preacher's own hortatory purposes.

This is not to say that judicial opinions or sermons are never commentaries; only that it's necessary to look at the relations between particular instances of them and the works on which they might be thought to be commenting in order to decide whether they are or are not best so thought of. Once again, there are difficult marginal cases in which it isn't obvious whether to say that the structure of some work follows, for the most part and on the whole, that of another, and as a result can properly be called a commentary. But the criterion is an important one to bear in mind, since its omission broadens the scope of the term commentary to the point where it has very little analytical usefulness. If this criterion were omitted, it would follow that almost all current scholarly work in the humanities would have to be classified as commentarial; and while it is certainly true that most of it is exegetical, most of it is not commentarial in the formal sense indicated by the three criteria mentioned so far. It's an interesting corollary of all this that in most of those cases where current work in the humanities is properly commentarial (most obviously in the case of biblical studies) it is so incoherently, in that its professed goals cannot easily stand with its method. Hence the uneasiness among biblical scholars about commentary as a mode of constituting and communicating knowledge.

To summarize: if a work is a metawork in which there are overt signs of the presence of another work, by quotation, summary, or paraphrase; if these signs outweigh, either quantitatively or qualitatively, other elements in the work; and if the structure and order of the work is largely given to it by those of the other work whose presence is evident in it—then the work in question is a commentary.

This third criterion has another interesting implication. It requires that there will usually be a one-to-one relation between commentary and work commented upon. A commentary can have as its object only one work, not many (though it is of course possible for one work to have many different metaworks, whether commentarial or other), since its structure and order must be given to it by those of the work upon which it comments. This means that those works whose objects are many (chrestomathies, florilegia, catenae, and the like) cannot, by these criteria, be considered commentaries (though parts of them may be). The only exception to the one-one relation between commentary and object (and it's an interesting and prevalent one) is the case of subcommentaries and sub-subcommentaries. Consider, for instance, Yaśomitra's *vyākhyā* on Vasubandhu's *bhāṣya* on the verses of the *Abhidharmakośa*: the last-named is a medieval Indian work in verse upon which both of the first two comment directly. The first-named comments directly not only upon the last-named, but also upon the intermediate one, the *bhāṣya*.[7] It is proper to think of Yaśomitra's work, the *vyākhyā*, as having two objects to comment upon because all three criteria are met in its relation to both. This can only happen, though, in the case of nested subcommentaries and sub-subcommentaries like these: only then can there be a one-many relation between commentary and works commented upon.

Application of these three criteria will not divide the world of verbal works neatly into commentaries and noncommentaries. There will be marginal cases in which it is difficult to decide whether a particular work has or does not have overt signs of quotation, summary, or paraphrase; whether these signs do or do not predominate in it, quantitatively or qualitatively; or whether its structure and order is largely given to it by its object. But this is not a disabling weakness, or at any rate no more disabling than those attending upon the use of other genre-terms. 'Commentary' may not pick out a natural kind; but it certainly picks out an artifactual one whose contours are at least as well delineated as those picked out by terms like 'epic' or 'novel'.

Commentaries as Metaworks

I've said that one work may be related commentarially to another principally by direct quotation, by summary, or by paraphrase. But each of these formal relations may be given a more precise analysis. Commentaries whose objects are present in them principally by direct quotation I call either interpretations or reproductions. And those whose objects are evident in them principally by summary or paraphrase I call digests. Each kind is recognizable by its formal properties.

Interpretive commentaries are characterized by, first, overt and direct quotation of matter from the work being commented upon; and, second, by the explication of some parts of that matter in words not used by the object. An extreme case is that in which every word of the work being commented upon appears in the commentary, either singly or in groups, in the order in which they occur in the former; and in which every word or word group from the former is given an explanation in the latter. This is close to what medieval Europeans called *glossa*. Such a method requires some technical device for separating elements of the work being commented upon from those of the commentary (written English uses quotation marks; Sanskrit uses the particle *iti*). Such works were common in medieval Europe and in medieval India; they survive in contemporary western humanistic scholarship only in commentaries upon biblical works and some Greek and Latin works. But interpretive commentaries need not be such that every word of the work on which they comment is present in them; this is merely the extreme case of a much broader category.

Digests are different from interpretations. While the latter represent the work upon which they comment principally by direct quotation, the former do so by summary or paraphrase, and they typically have no (or minimal) explication. A good contemporary example of the digest may be seen in those sections of the *Cliff's Notes* series (these are pamphlets designed as crib-sheets for students of particular works in literature or philosophy—*Wuthering Heights* or the *Symposium*, for example) that contain a summary of the work studied. A more interesting instance of the digest may be found in the habit of eighteenth- and nineteenth-century writers in English of constructing long, discursive, chapter titles in which the content of the chapter in question is stated in summary form. For example, the title to the eighth chapter of Henry Fielding's *Joseph Andrews* reads:

> In which, after some very fine Writing, the History goes on, and relates the Interview between the Lady and Joseph; where the latter hath set an Example, which we despair of seeing followed by his Sex, in this vicious Age.

The abandonment of this elegant and witty habit is sad. Writers of philosophy, theology, and economics during this period used the device as often as novelists, and its contribution to clarity and to the aesthetic pleasure to be gained from reading their works is significant. Such chapter heads I would categorize as examples of autodigest, related commentarially to the chapter at whose head they stand. As with all digests, they do not quote directly, nor do they explain in any way other than by summary; but they do follow the structure and order of their objects, and evidence of the commentarial relation does predominate in them, both quantitatively and qualitatively. The nearest contemporary analogue to these autodigests, so far as I can tell, is the practice evident in some journals, both scholarly and popular, of providing a brief abstract at the head of every essay published.

Reproductions are different from both interpretations and digests. They are commentaries that consist entirely of a passage or passages quoted directly from some work other than themselves; or of a complete and verbatim reproduction of that work. Recall that the most familiar literary forms in which reproduction occurs (florilegium, chrestomathy, anthology) do not consist entirely in such reproduction; parts of them might be considered reproductive commentaries, but as a whole they are typically not such. When and why is a reproductive act usefully considered a commentarial act? Most usefully when the reproductive act uses a different medium, since then the semantic content and possible use of the work (or work fragment) reproduced is radically altered.

Examples are easy to find. The text of the Veda for instance, a primarily aural/oral object in India, was first printed in the second half of the nineteenth century (Max Müller's edition appeared between 1849 and 1874). Reproducing an oral text in bound, printed form is an act of reproductive commentary. A similar account should be given of more recent reproductions, such as the creation of electronic textual databases: the act of reading Plutarch from a CD-ROM whose content is displayed on a cathode-ray tube is a significantly different act, semantically and in other ways, from those of hearing Plutarch recited, reading his work written on a vellum page, or leafing through a bilingual printed edition in the Loeb Classics series (and each of these acts differs similarly from the others). In Japan you can buy handkerchiefs with the entire text of the *Prajñāpāramitāhṛdayasūtra* (in Chinese) on them. This, too, is best understood as an act of commentary-by-reproduction (though I'm not sure whether people actually blow their noses on these handkerchiefs).

Each of these reproductions is related commentarially to that which it reproduces because of the change in medium. By contrast, particular copies of a printed book are best thought of not as instances of commentary-by-reproduction, but rather as instances of the manufacture of multiple tokens of a single type. The same is true of reproductions of an oral artifact in similar settings: each time I recite the Nicene Creed, for instance, in a eucharistic setting, I don't think of myself as commenting upon other instances of such recital, but rather as producing yet another token of a well-known type. Again, there will be difficult marginal cases in which it is not quite clear which analysis to give. But it will be clear for most instances of reproduction whether a change in medium is involved or not; if it is, we are dealing with commentary; if it is not, we are probably not.

Translations of a work from one language to another provide some special difficulties. If, by courtesy, as it were, the words of the translation are taken to be semantically identical with the words of the original, then the translation will have to be seen as an instance of commentary-by-reproduction. If this is the view taken, then the act of translation will be one that involves reproduction in a new medium, somewhat like the printing of a manuscript. This seems the best view to take. But another possibility is to classify a translation as a digest, a kind of extended paraphrase of the original. On this view, the words of the translation are not semantically the same as the words of the work translated, which means that the latter is nowhere quoted in the former. Which classificatory option is followed depends upon the decision of some delicate issues in translation theory that are beyond the scope of this work.

These different modes by which one work can be present in another may of course be combined one with another. A commentary that is predominantly reproductive may also contain elements of interpretation: consider a contemporary collection of verbatim extracts from some author's work (*The Portable Emerson*, say) with explanatory notes at the foot of the page or the end of the book. And a work that is principally a digest may also be, in part, a reproduction or an interpretation. Although these terms neither pick out mutually exclusive genres nor state criteria by which all marginal and mixed cases can easily be categorized (there won't always be an obvious answer to questions like 'Is this an interpretation or a digest?'), they do nonetheless provide useful heuristic devices, Weberian ideal types that will give a useful avenue into the set of problems stated above; and they also do provide an exhaustive analysis of the principal modes in which one work can be present in another.

A broadly corresponding (though much briefer) analysis can be given of works commented upon, works that can be the object of commentary. Almost anything can, in theory, be such an object: an ordered set of actions or utterances, such as a performance of a play, an opera, or a liturgical act; a written or spoken work; a wordless physical object, such as a painting or a statue; a person's character; a mathematical proof; a set of institutional arrangements, such as the means by which the United States of America determines who has citizenship in it—and so on. Each of these phenomena possesses order and structure, and is therefore capable of dictating the order and structure of an artifact produced by commentarial activity directed toward it (which was the third criterion mentioned); many of them use words, and these words are capable of the various modes of presence in a commentary (quotation, summary, paraphrase) already discussed (this was the second formal criterion). There are more complications with objects of commentarial activity that possess no words, for these, it seems, cannot be quoted in a verbal commentary. What you think about this depends upon your views as to the possibilities of translation from the nonverbal to the verbal; or, to put the same point differently, upon what you think about the kinds of semantic content capable of being possessed by nonverbal objects. I am inclined to a case-by-case analysis here (for example, it seems to me that a different account should be offered of the semantic content of visual symbols than of mathematical formulae); but I shall not offer any such analysis here and shall rather arbitrarily restrict the domain of what can be an object of commentary to things that have words. But any such thing may be an object of commentary.

Commentary's Purposes

Given this understanding of what commentaries are, why would people compose them? What purposes might they have, and, especially, what purposes might religious readers have in composing them? The purpose or purposes you have in composing a commentary, in undertaking some particular commentarial act, will govern which elements of the work you're commenting upon you pay attention to, and how you treat them; and this means that purpose can often be discerned by looking at these things. Six commentarial purposes may usefully be distinguished: explanation, application, justification, refutation, absorption (or replacement), and the fulfillment of extratextual needs (a miscellaneous category, this last).

Explanation is probably the most common among these. Commentaries are often composed with the goal of explaining some feature or features of the work commented upon. Explanation is itself a complex phenomenon, of course; its kinds are many. The following are of principal interest when considering commentaries. First, causal explanation, understood as explanation of why, causally, something is as it is. This amounts, usually, to telling some causal story. Second, semantic explanation, undertaken in order to clarify what something means, to make it intelligible. Both causal and semantic explanation may be directed to the work commented upon as a whole (How did this work come to be as it is? What does it, as a whole, mean?), or to some feature or aspect of it.

There are many things common to causal and semantic explanation. Both may require or provoke controversial engagement with opposing views about the proper causal story to tell, or about the proper meaning (but exploring these aspects will trespass upon the domain of the third and fourth commentarial purposes—justification and refutation—so I'll leave them aside for now). Both will also often require the provision of items of information not explicitly present in the work commented upon; the commentary may then be seen, in Edward Hobbs's words, as a "filing cabinet of possibly helpful clues to the reader."[8] But the different purposes implicated with these different kinds of explanation will usually mean that different sorts of information will be considered relevant. Both kinds of explanation, also, may be directed at features of the work commented upon that have no (or minimal) semantic content: at, that is to say, a work's formal features. But when semantic explanation is so directed, it will, because of its interests, typically treat these features in terms of their possible semantic implications, while causal explanation will not. And finally, both kinds of explanation may be directed at semantic features of the work commented upon, although when causal explanation is so directed it will, naturally, tend not to focus upon these semantic features as such, but rather to tell some causal story about how they came to be what they are.

Some examples may help at this point. I take the nonsemantic features of a work to be those that do not directly contribute to its semantic content. It is probably true that any feature of a work might, in some circumstances, have semantic content. So the examples that follow shouldn't be taken as features that are in principle nonsemantic, only as features that will, under the circumstances in which a work is designed to be used, normally be so. For instance: that a printed book in English is set in Garamond rather than Helvetica is an interesting fact about it, and one certainly amenable to causal explanation. But it is not one that, for most readers of the book, contributes directly to its semantic content. Offering a semantic explanation of it will therefore require some ingenuity. Similarly, that a verse of a Sanskrit metrical work is prima facie capable of being read in two equally plausible but mutually incompatible ways is amenable to causal explanation—perhaps in terms of the demands of meter. Such causal explanation will usually not have semantic implications by itself; it may, of course, be coupled with a semantic explanation that recommends one way of reading the verse over another, but then the explanation is no longer entirely causal. Features of a work that are prima facie semantic (words, sentences, and so forth) will often attract semantic explanation: a word may be glossed with another; facts about the structure and organization of the work commented upon may be explained in such a way as to enhance the user's understanding of that work's parts; and so forth. But such semantic features, too, can be given causal explanation: the structure of a work may be explained causally in terms of the precedents and literary conventions that it follows, rather than in terms of the semantic implications it has.

So much, briefly, for explanation (causal and semantic). What about application, the second commentarial purpose? A commentator might be interested principally not in explanation, either causal or semantic (perhaps the features of the work commented upon are thought not to need explanation or have already elsewhere been exhaustively explained), but rather to offer suggestions or recommendations as to how the work commented upon might be used, applied, or deployed. Commentarial acts motivated by the need to apply will most often issue in exhortation or recommendation. For most contemporary speakers of English, the most culturally familiar forms of commentary in which application dominates are probably the sermon and the judicial opinion. Explanation may often be present in both of these, but exhortation (in the former case) and apodictic ruling (in the latter) always is.

Commentarial application may also have to do with patterns of action whose focus is the work commented upon rather than what that work suggests ought to be done in some other arena. It may tell you, that is, how to use the work commented upon rather than how to use what it tells you. Consider Jeremy Taylor's work *Holy Living*. In the fourth chapter of this work are given, as in virtually all manuals of Christian ascetical theology, rules for the proper reading of the Bible. Taylor explains how to read (or hear), when to read (or hear), in what frame of mind to read (or hear), and much else. Similarly, some Buddhist commentaries recommend that certain things be done with the works upon which they comment: that they be enshrined in stupas, circumambulated, and the like. And many Hindu discussions of and comments upon the Veda have to do not with what the Veda means, but with how to use it, what to do with it. Recommendations of this sort are commentarial in that, like the more familiar paraenesis of sermons or the apodictic rulings of judicial opinions, they point to what is supposed to follow, behaviorally, from the work commented upon. The difference is that sermonic paraenesis and legal judgment typically have to do with patterns of behavior whose object is other than the work commented upon (social behavior, ritual behavior, and so on), while those I'm talking about here are concerned with the use of the object itself. Extra layers of complication and interest are added when a work that is commented upon itself contains recommendations as to its own use.

The third and fourth purposes that might motivate a commentator are justification and refutation. Both are normative. Commentators motivated to justify will typically offer arguments in their commentaries to show why what is said by, or implied in, the work being commented upon is true or right; or why certain explanations (causal or semantic) of the work commented upon are to be preferred to competitors. Contrariwise for refutation. This is to say that commentaries will very often have controversial matter in them: different views about the truth or rightness of a particular view of what the work commented upon means may be canvassed and discriminated among, and one argued for over the others. Similarly for claims made on the basis of other kinds of commentarial activity.

It's important to notice a distinction here between two types of controversy, both of which may occasion and be implicated in commentarial acts. One will have as its topic the truth or rightness of what the work commented upon claims, or the significance of that work; the other will have as its topic the question of whether some particular causal or semantic explanation of the work is better than some other, or whether some particular mode of application of the work is better than another. For example, in the early nineteenth century Dayanand Sarasvati, a Hindu apologist and polemicist, commented extensively on the New Testament.[9] His comments were motivated by a desire to explain and then to refute: he wanted to show both that the work he was commenting upon had a certain meaning and that the claims made by the work were to be rejected, root and branch. It would be possible, naturally, to agree with Dayānanda that the New Testament has the meaning he attributes to it, and yet disagree with him that it, thus interpreted, is a farrago of nonsense and ethical depravity.

A distinction of this kind is important, because it shows that commentarial acts may be motivated largely or entirely by the desire to discredit or remove authority from the works they comment upon, as well as by a desire to explain or apply them. This intent to refute not just some particular reading of the work commented upon, or some particular causal story about its formation, but rather the truth of what it claims, the rightness of what it recommends, and any claim it makes to authority, need not be pursued only by argument. It may also be pursued (and often more effectively) by parody, by a mocking paraphrase whose intent is to discredit its object, or all objects of its kind. Consider, for example, Dickens's parody of evangelical Christian piety in the nineteenth chapter of *Bleak House*: Mr. Chadband, a man "in the ministry" but "attached to no particular denomination," has as followers mostly working-class women with middle-class pretensions who like to have their religion "rather sharp." Throughout much of the chapter, Dickens gives a precisely observed and hilarious parody of evangelical sermonizing. It's best understood as a commentarial act whose object is a genre rather than a particular work; but the technique is also common in relation to particular works, where its logical goal is the reductio ad absurdum and its method the mockery of rhetorical overkill.

There are many other examples of parodic commentary. A notable one is the treatment of the eighth Psalm in the seventh and fifteenth chapters of the Book of Job; this, it seems to me, is a fairly successful parody. Much less successful is Jacques Derrida's attempt to parody, commentarially, an essay by John Searle—although reading both Searle's essay and Derrida's parodic commentary provides considerable insight into the goals of two different strands of contemporary western philosophical thinking.[10]

Consider, by way of contrast, the second kind of refutation or justification, which has as its topic some causal story about a feature or features of the work commented upon, or one about some semantic interpretation of it. This differs from the first kind in that it is not concerned with the truth or rightness of what the work commented upon is agreed to claim; rather, the controversy is about what the work should be understood to say, or about what story should be told to account, causally, for how it says what it says. For example, scholars who study the New Testament are (still!) not agreed as to whether the proper causal account to offer of some features of Matthew and Luke is in terms of their common use of an independent sayings-source. In their commentaries on these works they will often engage in justification of their own view as to this question and refutation of opposing views. Such controversies, obviously, may be carried on within the context of broad agreement as to what the work (or some portion of it) may mean, and as to whether what it means is true or right (though these latter questions are typically systematically avoided by New Testament scholars).

Finally, the desire to justify or to refute, in any of the senses just distinguished, sits very well with the doxographical impulse. If you want to show that your reading of a work is the best in the field, or that your causal story about how some work came to be as it is defeats all other contenders, a very likely method will be the listing and categorizing of all other actual and possible opinions on the matter, with arguments for the superiority of the chosen ones. The Indo-Tibetan Buddhist commentarial traditions developed this doxographic method to a high pitch of perfection, but it is evident also in many other areas of modern western scholarship.

The fifth purpose that might inform commentarial acts is absorption/replacement. A commentator might, in composing a commentary on some work, intend to absorb that work into the commentary, and by so doing remove any reason for its continued independent existence. If the commentator is successful, the work commented upon will continue to exist only as part of the commentary—and it may also be the case that users of the commentary will not know that they are using a commentary, that there was once an independent work that has now been absorbed and replaced by the commentary. Perhaps, if some scholars of the New Testament are correct that there was a sayings-source used by both Matthew and Luke in the composition of their gospels, and that the order of at least some of the material in these gospels is determined by that of the matter in the hypothetical source, then the acts by which Matthew and Luke appropriated (expropriated) the matter of the source could be seen as commentarial acts motivated by the desire to absorb and replace. For neither Matthew nor Luke indicate their use of such a source explicitly, and both appear to have thought (if the hypothesis is correct) that they could absorb and present the source in such a way as to make further independent use of it unnecessary. This is typical of commentators who want to absorb and replace: they judge that they can do all that the work commented upon does, and do it better. The absorbed work therefore need not continue to exist.

The sixth and final kind of purpose that might inform the composition of a commentary is one that has little or nothing to do with the particulars of the work being commented upon. It is controlled by considerations outside the work. This means that in such cases commentators are not concerned primarily to explain, apply, justify, refute, or absorb the work upon which they comment. They are instead constrained and motivated by such things as institutional requirements (perhaps a commentary has to be composed in order to be granted a license to teach, but it doesn't matter what it says or whether anyone ever reads it), or ritual needs (perhaps a work, together with a commentary upon it, needs to be enshrined in a stupa, and for this purpose it may matter not at all what the commentary says or how it says it), or other needs that belong to the religious account from within which the commentator is working (perhaps the act of composing a commentary, like memorizing a work, brings merit). In cases like these, there will likely be indications within the commentary itself that it was not motivated by any of the other purposes: perhaps it is impossible to imagine any explanatory or other use that the commentary might have, in which case it might well be reasonable to assume that the commentator was motivated by extratextual needs.

So much, then, for the purposes that might inform commentarial activity. One final topic needs attention, and that is the question of the range and kinds of significance that a commentarial act (and its corresponding product) might attribute to the work upon which it comments. It may be the case that canon implies commentary, as Jonathan Z. Smith claims.[11] But it is certainly not the case that commentarial activity implies the canonicity of the work being commented upon. Such activity implies only that, in some context and for some reason, someone decided that the work in question required comment. Often, no doubt, the reason will be that the work is taken to have authority, religious or otherwise: it may be a sacred and canonical work, or it may be a legal statute with binding force. But, almost equally often, commentators treat the works upon which they comment with something quite far from reverence—as objects for refutation, parody, sarcasm, and so on. And, of course, there is a broad spectrum of other attitudes between homage and opposition that may be present in any particular act of commentary. This is an obvious point, but it is worth emphasizing in order to counter the common tendency to think of commentarial acts as always attitudinally subservient to their objects, as always and only concerned with explication of the inexhaustible semantic riches found in these objects. Michel Foucault sometimes seems to think this:

> For the moment I want to restrict myself to saying that, in what is most generally called a commentary [*dans ce qu'on appelle globalement un commentaire*], the difference between the primary and the secondary text plays two complementary roles. On the one hand, it permits (and indefinitely) the construction of new discourse: the excess weight of the first text [*le surplomb du texte premier*], its permanence, its condition of being discourse always reactualizable [*son statut de discours toujours réactualisable*], the multiple or hidden senses of which it is considered a container [*le sense multiple ou caché dont il passe pour être detenteur*], the reticence and the essential riches attributed to it—all this grounds an open possibility of speech [*tout cela fonde une possibilité ouverte de parler*].[12]

This is no doubt often true, and especially characteristic of commentarial acts that belong to religious communities. But it is certainly not true of commentaries as a whole. Commentators sometimes take the semantic content of the works upon which they comment to be not rich but boring; not worthy of reverence but of passionate opposition; not a permanent possibility of new interpretations but susceptible only to a single and final interpretation; not a work whose truth and rightness are salvific, but one whose falsity and wrongness are apparent and demonstrable.

Religious readers find the commentary a natural and proper genre in which to compose principally because it exhibits by its nature a deep seriousness about reading. It stays very close to the work upon which it comments, and just this kind of seriousness is the most important feature of religious reading. Not all commentaries are produced by religious readers, of course. Many of those written by contemporary biblical scholars are not. And a commentary whose principal goal is to refute or demonstrate the worthlessness and undesirability of the work upon which it comments will typically not exhibit the attitudes of a religious reader. But even in such cases, and most especially when the commentary has something to say about every or almost every feature of the work upon which it comments, there will inevitably be traces of the devotional and detailed rereading of works characteristic of the religious reader. It's scarcely possible to read a work with the closeness, clarity, and care required of a commentator without having it enter your soul—even if this is not your intention.

Commentary's Formal Features and Ideal Readers

Hints as to how a particular commentary is meant to be used (as to what its ideal reader or hearer is like) can often be found in its formal features, as well as in what (if anything) it says about its own purposes. Three formal features are especially important. First: How does the commentary signal the distinction between matter that belongs to it and matter that belongs to the work it comments upon? Second: How large is the typical unit of matter given treatment by the commentary? And third: Is the commentary usable and comprehensible by itself, or does it presuppose and assume knowledge of matter not explicitly present in it?

The first feature is significant because it can be informative both about the commentary's attitude to the work commented upon and about what the ideal reader of the commentary is expected to know. Suppose, to take an extreme case, a commentary does not explicitly signal in any way the distinction between its matter and that of the work commented upon, but that it nonetheless fulfills all the conditions set out earlier for being a commentary. Suppose, that is to say, it weaves its own matter together with that of its object in such a way that no joins or seams are evident. Sometimes the prose of Augustine or Barth is like this: they write upon a topic treated also in some biblical work, following the order of the treatment there and weaving references to and quotations of the biblical work into their own prose, but without explicit signal. The result is, formally speaking, sometimes a commentary; but the reader who knows nothing of the original will not realize this because of the lack of explicit evidence of it. Such a lack of signals will most often indicate an assumption on the part of the commentator that the work commented upon will be known intimately to the ideal readers of the commentary—known as a religious reader knows. But it may conceivably also suggest that the commentator intends to subsume the work commented upon into his own, and to make the commentarial object of no further independent significance. There will usually be other hints in the commentary as to which of these states of affairs should be assumed.

Most often, a commentary will explicitly signal the distinction between its matter and that of the work commented upon. This may be done by giving the commentary's words a diction, style, or form that differs from those of the work commented upon; perhaps the latter is in verse or some other metrical form, and the former is in prose; or perhaps the former is in elegant Ciceronian periods and the latter in demotic commentarial Latin with no pretensions to elegance. All these modes of signaling difference will be equally evident whether the commentary is read or heard; but there are some signals exclusive to one mode of display or the other (voice tone or volume for the former; manuscript layout or typographic devices for the latter). If signals of this latter type are used, it may indicate something about the way in which the commentary was composed, stored, or displayed.

If clear signals of the difference between the matter of the commentary and that of its objects are given, this will suggest something about the ideal readers of the commentary. Perhaps it will suggest that they are not expected to know the work commented upon intimately; or that signaling the difference between the two works is meant to provide a cue for some action to occur when the commentary is read or heard—perhaps you bow your head (or prostrate yourself or cross yourself) when the original work is heard or read; or that signaling the difference is required of the composer of the commentary in order to show reverence to the work commented upon. Once again, there will usually be other indications in the commentary as to which of these interpretations is on the right track.

The second formal matter to which it is useful to pay attention in thinking about the ideal reader of a commentary is the amount of the work that the commentary chooses to comment upon at a time. For instance, imagine a long work in verse such as Asaṅga's *Mahāyānasūtrālaṅkāra*, a Buddhist work composed in India in (perhaps) the fourth century. This work contains 805 verses divided into twenty-one chapters.[13] A commentator upon it might choose the half-verse (sixteen syllables per half-verse is the most common metrical form) as the unit for comment, and might treat each half-verse as an isolated unit, without attention to what goes before and after. In such a case, a commentary would consist in 1,630 effectively separate commentarial discussions, put together like beads on a string, no one bead betraying knowledge of any of the others. Or the commentary might choose to expound larger units, perhaps five or ten verses at a time, though with the same separateness in its discussion of each unit. In this case, the beads would be larger, but would remain effectively separated from one another on the commentarial string. Or, at the other extreme, the commentator might proceed through the *Mahāyānasūtrālaṅkāra* verse by verse or word by word, but treat no verse and no word as anything other than a part of the whole. In this case, every comment would assume knowledge of the whole of the work commented upon, and would be principally concerned to show how the verse or word being expounded is part of the tapestry of the whole.

Most commentaries will fall somewhere between these extremes. But considering how a particular commentary relates the parts to the whole of the work being commented upon, and doing so by looking at the size of its typical expository unit, may suggest things of interest about its ideal readers. Suppose it adopts some version of the beads-on-a-string approach. This may suggest (and, again, there will likely be other clues in the commentary) that its ideal reader uses and knows (perhaps has memorized) the work commented upon as a collection of gobbets rather than as a whole—much as we use a dictionary of quotations, though with the fillip of memorization. And the other extreme, in which every part has significance only as an element of the whole, will suggest just the opposite: that the ideal reader uses and knows the whole of the work commented upon, as a whole.

Third, it will be helpful to ask whether the commentary is capable of being understood by itself, or whether it presupposes that its readers have available to them matter from the work commented upon that it does not contain itself. It's common for Sanskrit commentaries upon verse works to identify a verse being commented upon by quoting only its opening word or phrase, and then to proceed with the discussion as though all of the verse (not just the tag quoted) were available. If you don't know the verse referred to, or you don't have the work being commented upon in front of you, the discussion makes little sense. The ideal reader is in this case not expected to use the commentary by itself. By contrast, it is often the ambition of contemporary commentators on the Bible to provide all the materials necessary for reading their work inside the covers of the book that contains it. So the biblical work being expounded is given in full, sometimes in multiple versions. In a case like this, ideal readers are expected to need to open no other book than that which contains the commentary. Here too, then, a good deal can be learned about the pedagogical situation in which a particular commentary is used by paying attention to its formal properties.

So much for the significance, nature, and uses of commentary for religious readers. Although this is a genre of fundamental significance for such readers, it is not alone in being so. Anthology is another.

Anthology Defined

Religious readers are in search of flowers. They find them, naturally enough, in the works they read, the gardens they work: these gardens are full of fragrant blooms to be culled, carefully pruned, and rearranged into new bouquets. Making such bouquets often requires the composition and use of one of the most characteristically religious genres, some of the names of which are anthology, florilegium, enchiridion, chrestomathy, and *samuccaya*. But what exactly is this genre? What are its characteristics, its likely uses, and the institutional settings and pedagogical practices that make the composition and use of instances of it possible and desirable?[14]

Samuel Johnson's dictionary defines 'anthology' to mean 'collection of flowers'. This is not the meaning that most twentieth-century users of English would naturally give to the word, but, etymologically, Johnson was right. 'Anthology' is derived from Greek words meaning exactly that, and 'florilegium' is its Latin translation, bearing the same literal meaning, though it appears to be a modern coinage, not clearly instanced before the seventeenth century. It is derived from *flos* ('flower') plus *legere* ('to cull, gather, pluck'—though the same verb means 'to read' and may be involved, etymologically, in the word 'religion'). Even though 'florilegium' comes into use so late, closely connected terms go back at least to Ovid, and the tropes of flower culling, flower smelling, and flower reading are found everywhere in classical and medieval Latin literature. Such images are the olfactory and visual equivalent of the gobbet-chewing, ruminatory imagery already discussed. The Greek term 'anthology' has stayed alive in English (though with some significant changes in meaning and the effective loss of its etymological resonances), while its Latin cousin has not.

In addition to 'florilegium' and 'anthology', the pedagogical traditions of the West have used a number of other genre terms that overlap significantly. Prominent among these are 'chrestomathy' (collection of material useful for learning); 'testimonia' (collection of authoritative sayings); 'enchiridion' (manual of instruction); and 'commonplace book' (written collection of edifying extracts). Indian Buddhist pedagogues have also used works of this kind and have labeled the genre in various ways. The principal term of importance in that context was *samuccaya*, though there are other overlapping terms. In my discussion of the genre I'll use the term 'anthology', though with regret that 'florilegium' has not remained alive in current English.

Formally speaking, an anthology is a work all (or almost all) of whose words are taken from another work or works; it contains a number (typically quite a large number) of extracts or excerpts, each of which has been taken verbatim (or almost so) from some other work; and it uses some device to mark the boundaries of these excerpts. Any work that meets these conditions is an anthology.

The person who composes one of these is best thought of as a compiler rather than an author. Bonaventure, in his analysis of the four ways of making a book, makes this point by distinguishing a compiler from a scribe, a commentator, or an author.[15] A scribe simply writes out someone else's matter, adding and changing nothing; a commentator writes out matter both his own and someone else's, but joins his own words to those of others for clarificatory purposes (*ad evidentiam*); and an author writes out matter both his own and someone else's, but his own words form the greater part of his work, and those of the other are attached for support or confirmation (*ad confirmationem*). A compiler differs from all three: his work is made by writing out the words of others accumulated from various places, but not joining to them any of his own (*aliquis scribit aliena addendo sed non de suo*). Among the kinds of works compilers in Bonaventure's sense might produce are anthologies. Following him, I shall reserve the term compiler for those who assemble anthologies, and I shall call the parts of such works excerpts.

Anthology's Formal Features

This brief definition leaves quite a lot of room for maneuver and raises a range of formal questions that will have to be asked of every particular anthology. It places no exact limit, for instance, on the proportion of an anthology's words that are not taken from another work or works—the proportion, that is to say, that does not consist of excerpts. If less than three-quarters of some work consists of excerpts, it is unlikely to be reasonable to categorize it as an anthology. But it is very likely that at least some of every anthology's words will not be excerpted from elsewhere. An anthology may tell its users where its excerpts come from; it may contain an introductory explanation of its (or its compiler's) purpose, or a justification of its principles of selection and ordering; it may provide sectional divisions, explanatory matter, and other ancillary material. But most of its contents will be excerpted, and its principal reason for being will be the provision of the excerpts in which it consists.

The definition also leaves unspecified the number or length of an anthology's excerpts. If a work contains fewer than (say) six excerpts it will sound odd to call it an anthology; it will at least be a rather small bunch of flowers. There seems to be no upper limit, though. An anthology might very well comprise hundreds or thousands of excerpts. The length of excerpts is likewise not specified: they may be as short as a few words, or as long as many thousands, though as I shall argue later, the length of an average excerpt in a particular anthology provides some useful clues as to how it was composed, displayed, stored, and used. An individual bloom is a small thing, capable of being taken in by the senses at a glance (and a smell); while it may be beautiful enough, sufficiently full of aesthetic, intellectual, or moral complexity, to repay frequent and close examination, it is unlikely to be sufficiently large that it cannot effectively be contemplated all at once. A biblical verse or a Sanskrit *śloka* is a flower; the Psalter or the *Mūlamadhyamakakārikā* is a garden. If we are guided by etymology, then, as well as by the demands of memorization, an anthology's excerpts are likely to be short.

Also unspecified in the definition given are principles of organization. There are many possibilities here. Some are purely formal. The excerpts may be arranged by length, or by kinds of meter (if the excerpts are in verse), or acrostically, or by language (if the anthology contains excerpts in different languages), or alphabetically (perhaps under an excerpt's first word). Such formal principles of sorting need have nothing to do with either the content or the source of the excerpts; they might be of use in recalling or using the excerpts, or they might give aesthetic pleasure, or, conceivably, they might communicate some message additional to any found in the excerpts considered severally. For instance, something complex and interesting might be spelled out by the initial letters or syllables of an anthology containing several thousand excerpts.

But more common than such formal principles of organization are substantive ones. Excerpts might be arranged by topic, for instance, so that all those on money or meditation or marriage might be kept together. Or they might be arranged by source: if an anthology's excerpts come from more than one source (more than one of the church fathers, or more than one sutra, for example), all those from the same source might be kept together. Or, perhaps, excerpts might be arranged according to some pedagogical scheme in which those to be studied and learned in the first year of work are kept together, followed by those to be studied and learned in the second, and so on. Such an arrangement might overlap with a topicwise structure, but need not be identical with it.

The tradition of thinking about commonplaces (*koinoi topoi* in Greek; *loci communes* in Latin) is relevant to this question of how to arrange the excerpts in an anthology. From Cicero onward, the term 'commonplace' was used to denote a theme or topic or subject that could be illustrated by many particular instances. The foolishness of lovers or the benefits of religion are examples of commonplaces in this sense: there is an infinite number of examples of each in actuality, and also many examples of witty phrases or finely tuned observations about each in literature. The commonplaces or topics (in the Aristotelian sense) are, as W. D. Ross (borrowing from Cicero) puts it, "the pigeon-holes from which dialectical reasoning is to draw its arguments."[16] That is to say, the commonplaces provide the concepts or categories by which individual bits of information (individual blooms) are stored or arranged.

There is a connection here with the kind of memorial storage discussed in chapter 2. The *topoi* or *loci*, the 'places', are also (or can be) the locations in the imagined memory-palace used to place bits of information or bits of text. The difference is that now they are ideas, categories, concepts (Aristotelian topics) by which items of knowledge in the mind are articulated with other items of knowledge. They are the forerunners of the categories we use to organize and store books in libraries. The Library of Congress's subject categories are a functional equivalent of Cicero's *loci communes*. The organizing categories of an anthology (if it has any) may reasonably be called its commonplaces.

Still at the formal level, there is a question of number and kind of sources. Most often, perhaps, an anthology will have many sources—both many works and many authors. But this need not be so. The Christian tradition preserves many anthologies whose only source is the Bible (though it can reasonably be asked whether this is one or many sources), as it also does those whose only source is a particular author (Augustine, say, or Aquinas, or Barth), even if also different works by that author. An anthology may also limit itself to sources of a particular genre—Buddhist sutras, for instance (though 'sutra' is not really a genre term for Buddhists), or Greek dramas, or epic poems. It is also possible that an anthology might limit its sources to works that deal with a particular topic: someone might construct an Arthurian anthology, drawing only from works about the Arthur myth cycle, for instance. There are other possibilities, but it will in any case be important to ask about an anthology's rationale for drawing upon this body of sources rather than that. Sometimes this will be obvious: anyone using a Plato anthology will reasonably infer that it was part of the compiler's intent to draw only upon works by Plato. But sometimes the purpose will be neither obvious nor stated, and will have to be inferred from the anthology's content and what is known about its context.

The last purely formal matter that needs to be addressed here is the question of quotation.[17] In the definition given above I said that most of an anthology's words are taken from another work or works, and that the excerpts in which it largely consists have each been taken verbatim (or mostly so) from some other work. But this way of putting things leaves a lot of questions unanswered, mostly because the idea of quotation, or verbatim reproduction, is a murky one. Consider first the question of translation; when I quote Wittgenstein as saying: "What is your goal in philosophy? To show the fly the way out of the fly-bottle," am I really quoting him? Should I not rather have quoted him as saying, "Was ist dem Ziel in der Philosophie?—Der Fliege den Ausweg aus dem Fliegenglas zeigen"?[18] Decisions about this, as also decisions about whether, and, if so, how, to classify a translation of a work as a commentary upon that work, require difficult decisions in the area of translation theory.

But even when translation is not at issue, there are deep questions about just what verbatim reproduction means. Must it mean just and always exact reproduction of some word string found in the source? Or can it extend to include representations of the gist of what the word string says? We (contemporary writers of English) tend to make a fairly rigid distinction between *oratio recta* and *oratio obliqua*, and (in written English) to use the device of quotation marks to enclose just and only a word string from the source being quoted (though it is worth noting that standard U.S. English conventions not only permit but require placing in quotation marks matter not found in the word string being quoted—I mean punctuation marks that belong not to the word string being quoted but to the work in which the word string is being newly deployed). But it need not be the case that every anthology must follow just these conventions. Indeed, since these conventions are largely dependent upon print technology, it is in principle unlikely that they will be followed where that technology is absent. It will be important to ask of any particular anthology, then, just what quotational conventions are being used. How are the boundaries of excerpts (their beginnings and ends) marked? And what is the relation between the word strings found inside these boundary markers, whatever they turn out to be, and those found in the work from which the excerpt was taken?

As an example of how loose these relations can be, consider this: Pliny wrote in one of his letters: *Iam undique silvae et solitudo ipsumque illud silentium quod venationi datur magna cogitationis incitamenta sunt* (now the selfsame silence that one finds in hunting as a result of the sylvan solitude all around provides great stimuli for thought). In the *Florilegium Angelicum*, compiled in Orléans in the twelfth century, this becomes: *Silentium maximum cogitationis incitamentum* (silence is the greatest stimulus for thought).[19] All the specifics of Pliny's letter have been smoothed out, leaving something that, according to the conventions of contemporary English, isn't a quotation at all.

Anthology's Purposes

Quotation, whatever the conventions governing it in a particular case, has most fundamentally the purpose of superimposing the past upon the present, or of representing the past to the present. This, which is now being quoted, was said before and is now being said again. Such superimposition or representation may be done for many reasons: to provide evidence for some set of claims or states of affairs, as in a court of law or in much exegetical work done by contemporary western scholars; to provide material for a critical engagement with the past; to parody the past; to show how stupid and reprehensible were those who once said things like this; to provide matter for the delectation, rumination, instruction, and transformation of those in the present for whom the past is being quotationally represented, and so on. This last range of purposes will be typical of the anthology intended for use by religious readers. The excerpts found in a religious anthology will be used in the formation and nurturing of a properly religious account (an unsurpassable, comprehensive, and central account, recall). The principles of organization of a religious anthology will typically reflect this broad purpose, and it will be important in every particular case to ask just how they do so.

Once again, George Steiner is useful here. Commenting on the depiction of reading in Jean-Baptiste-Siméon Chardin's painting "Le philosophe lisant" (completed in 1734), he says:

> With his quill *le philosophe lisant* will transcribe from the book he is reading. The excerpts he makes can vary from the briefest of quotations to voluminous transcriptions. The multiplication and dissemination of written material after Gutenberg in fact increases the extent and variousness of personal transcriptions. The sixteenth- or seventeenth-century clerk or gentleman takes down in his hornbook, commonplace book, personal florilegium or breviary the maxims, 'taffeta phrases', sententiae, exemplary turns of elocution and tropes from classical and contemporary masters. . . . Such recopying had manifold purposes: the improvement of one's own style, the deliberate storage in the mind of ready examples of argument or persuasion, the buttressing of exact memory (a cardinal issue). But, above all, transcription comports a full engagement with the text, a dynamic reciprocity between reader and book.[20]

Notice the connection that Steiner makes between the impulse to gather flowers and to preserve them in an album, as I am calling it, and the "buttressing of exact memory." Notice, too, the kind of engagement with a literary work that the impulse to copy parts of it suggests to Steiner. It is (though he does not call it so) a religious engagement.

In addition to asking about the principles of organization of a particular anthology, it will also be important to ask about the importance placed by it upon the display of quotation as such. At one extreme, no importance at all may be given to this. An anthology of this type may not signal that its excerpts are excerpts. It may present them as flowers new-bloomed, even if they have in fact been culled from a garden planted hundreds or even thousands of years before. Compilers of such anthologies may conceal their function as such, or may at least regard the fact that their excerpts are excerpts as much less important than the nutritional value or aesthetic pleasure to be derived from their contemplation.

An eighteenth-century English gentleman copying into his commonplace book bons mots from Samuel Johnson or Henry Fielding might very well do so without indicating their source, and might later lard his own conversation or writing with them without indicating that they had a source other than his own imagination. This is not plagiarism in the late twentieth-century sense (itself a concept that implies views of the individual, of rights, and of authorship that are for the most part deeply incompatible with religious learning); it is instead an instance of an attitude to the quotable riches of the past that judges open acknowledgment of the origin of those riches to be about as important as open acknowledgment of the seed wholesaler is to hungry people as they begin to eat their rice at dinner. An anthology that exhibits this attitude to its excerpts is likely to signal them as such either minimally or not at all; and the absence of such signals will suggest (though it will not guarantee) an attitude to the blooms of the past something like the one sketched in this paragraph. Such an attitude comports well with religious reading, so it will be important for my purposes to ask what importance a particular anthology places upon the display of quotation as such. The answer may indicate that the compiler and the ideal reader are both religious readers—or it may at least increase the likelihood of that being the case.

Compilers may find it useful to display their excerpts as such because they think that a good part of their authority or efficacy is given them by the fact that they are, and are known to be, re-presentations of the past, by the fact that they are excerpts. In such a case it will typically suffice to gesture vaguely at the status of an excerpt as such, as a re-presentation of the authoritative past. So, for instance, medieval Indian Buddhist works often signal excerpts by such devices as *sūtrokta* ("it is said in a sutra"), or *ity eke* ("some say"), without further specifying the sutra or the some. It is enough to show that the past is being re-presented; the precise part of the past in question is less important. Similarly, Latin Christian anthologies (at least until the twelfth century, when developments in manuscript technology and changes in institutional setting began to have effects) tend to signal their excerpts by such devices as *origenes dixit* ("Origen said"), with no indication of where and when.

Both these attitudes to the importance of displaying quotation as such (not displaying it at all and doing so only minimally) are broadly compatible with the inculcation of religious reading; and both suggest that compilers who exhibit them do not think of the anthology they are compiling as suggesting to its users that it would be a good thing to trace the excerpts to their original source and consult the blooms in the garden from which they were originally culled. The point of anthologies that exhibit these attitudes to the blooms of the past is principally to produce a sweet-smelling bouquet for the present, not to encourage a return to the past. As a result, insufficient information is given to make such a return easy, even if a reader wants to make it—which explains the frustration that late twentieth-century users of anthologies of these kinds often feel, for we typically do want to make such a return, or at least to feel that we could; and this means that we are not ideal readers of these anthologies. Conversely, when compilers do provide detailed source information for their excerpts (not just "someone said" but "Nāgārjuna said in the fourth verse of the twenty-first chapter of the *Mūlamadhyamakakārikā*"; not just "Augustine said," but "Augustine said in the fifteenth book of the *De Trinitate*"), this will suggest that the actual or possible return to the original gardens is a matter of some importance. Consider the source apparatus of an anthology like the *Oxford Dictionary of Quotations* as a case in point.

In coming to understand the attitudes to reading implied by any particular anthology, then, it will be very important to pay attention to the significance placed upon the display of quotation as such. This will reveal something of importance about its ideal reader. There are, in addition, other questions to be asked about the formal properties of anthologies, questions that can be answered without appeal to anything but the work itself. These too, like those just discussed, will show something of importance about the attitude to learning implied by the work, which is to say about its ideal reader.

The first of these has to do with the nature of the excerpts in which the anthology consists. How many and how long are these? Their length severally, and the length of the anthology as a whole, may suggest something about the ways in which the work is likely to have been composed, stored, and displayed. If the excerpts are short, gobbet-sized, this may indicate that the anthology is intended for use as a tool of memorization (recall the earlier discussion of mnemotechnique in my analysis of religious reading). If they are long and very many, this may indicate that the ideal reader is not intended to memorize them, but to use the anthology as a work of reference, much as we use anthologies or dictionaries of quotations.

Then there are questions about the anthology as a whole. What is the nature of those parts of it that do not consist in excerpts? Does the compiler explain the purpose of the compilation? Are there helps like subject or topic heads, indices, tables of contents, explanations of difficult material, source notes? The presence or absence of these things will also suggest a great deal about the composition and implied use of any anthology, as well as about its ideal reader. The greater the number and kind of such helps, the greater the likelihood that the anthology is a work of reference rather than one to be memorized and chewed over. Its ideal readers are likely to keep it on the shelf and take it down when they need some specific information.

Questions whose answers require information not found in the anthology itself need also to be asked, though it will often be difficult to answer them. One range of such questions has to do with the use made by the compiler of the sources from which the excerpts are taken: are these sources quoted verbatim? If not, what sorts of changes are made, and why? (Recall the example of the *Florilegium Angelicum*'s fairly drastic alterations in its 'quotation' from Pliny.) Such questions are usually difficult because of a lack of information about just what the source used by a compiler contained. Even when we know and have access to the source, the version of it that we read may not have been the version read or recalled by the compiler. But sometimes it is possible to arrive at some useful conclusions about these matters, and when it is we can often thereby discern something of a compiler's quotational practices, and this in turn can be of great use in understanding the attitudes to the past implied by the work.

Finally, there are always important extratextual questions to be asked about material culture: what were the methods of text storage and text display current when this anthology was first composed and displayed? What were the salient institutional forms and pedagogical practices? Knowing something about these, when possible, can provide essential information about a particular anthology's use in the transmission and preservation of a comprehensive, unsurpassable, and central account—a properly religious account.

Consider an ideal type: an anthology the source of whose excerpts isn't indicated; whose excerpts are gobbet-sized; whose principles of organization are not discernible; and whose mode of display and storage involves writing only incidentally. This is likely to be an anthology whose main use lies in the provision of especially juicy gobbets to chew on with the mandibles of the mind, especially delightful blooms to be arranged and rearranged into a bouquet that is part of a religious account. The extreme form of this would be an anthology that is never displayed, that exists virtually, only in the memory of the individual who created it. The corporeal equivalent would be a commonplace book belonging to someone who doesn't intend that it should circulate, and who gives no indication of the sources used in its compilation.

Another ideal type: an anthology the sources of whose excerpts are carefully and precisely indicated, together with information on how to find them; whose gobbets are of widely varying length; whose method of quotation is only and exactly verbatim; whose method of organization appears designed for repeated use and reference rather than for memorial storage (perhaps it contains indices, subject headings, and the like); and whose method of display and storage involves corporeal objects at every stage. This is likely to be an object for consumerist reading, plundered for particular purposes, kept on the shelf for repeated use. Its blooms are not likely to be used in the formation and nutrition of a religious account. They are, instead, designed for practical purposes, to be cited and quoted as ornaments to their ideal readers' own compositions.

Commonplace Books

The history of the commonplace book illustrates many of these points about anthologies.[21] In Renaissance Europe, readers often made their own anthologies by copying out choice excerpts from what they read. This copying appears to have been a standard part of the reading process, as widely used then as the luminous yellow highlighter and the photocopying machine are by college students now. Leisured and cultivated readers then would have felt their reading to be lacking in some fundamental way if it had not involved the copying of excerpts. Sometimes the excerpts copied were organized with care under some system of categories or commonplaces; and sometimes they were simply copied and preserved one after another, as they were encountered, with no attempt at organization. In the former case, as Thomas Fuller put it in 1642, the copying reader would have to hand a commonplace book full of "Notions in garrison, whence the owner may draw out an army into the field on competent warning."[22] In the latter case, the reader would have a series of excerpts that would be nourishing or useful for composition only when committed to memory by some articulated system of the kind described in chapter 2.

The seventeenth century also saw an increase in self-consciousness about these excerpting practices. People began to write about them, to offer theories as to what they were and as to how they might be done better. It's usually the case that when a practice becomes the object of theoretical attention on any scale, its reason for being is no longer (or is not yet) obvious to those who engage in it. The flood of publications in the English-speaking world in the late 1980s and early 1990s on the compositional use of computer technology, and on the uses of reading printed matter, provides contemporary illustration: in the former case, new users of computers for composition need a theory about what they are beginning to do and some recommendations as to how to do it better; in the latter case, those who continue to read printed matter need reassurance that this is still a good thing to do, and perhaps some theory as to why. Practices that are not yet problems to those who perform them don't usually attract much theoretical attention. The same is mostly true of practices that are no longer engaged in.

In seventeenth-century Europe, the practice of making anthologies by excerpting was becoming problematic for many reasons, among which two stand out. The first was the vast increase in the quantity of things that could be read, due mostly to printing. If you read many books of many kinds, and industriously excerpt passages from them all as you go, you will very soon have in your commonplace book a mass of material of a diversity and range that in the fourteenth century would have been unthinkable. It will not be obvious how to control and order this material; nor will it be obvious how to decide what to excerpt, and from what to excerpt. The seventeenth and eighteenth centuries saw the wide distribution for the first time of ephemeral literature (broadsheets, newspapers, occasional polemical tracts, novels): what is the industriously excerptive reader to do with all this?

In addition to these problems of selection and ordering, there was the associated problem of the gradual loss of interest in the mnemotechnical practices that had been central to the anthologizing work of readers in pre-Reformation Europe. Anthologies from the seventeenth century onward seem less and less to have been collections of gobbets to be stored in the memory for chewing over, and more and more to have been designed for writerly purposes, as collections of matter that might be referred to and used in composition. This is what Thomas Fuller meant by his military metaphor: the anthologist's excerpts are foot soldiers to be deployed in the bloodless combat of literary polemics. They are to be called up and arrayed on the field of print wherever they can inflict the most damage on opponents and provide the most strategic support for the writer's argument. But if this is what they are for, and they have not been memorized and placed in an articulated system of memorial storage, then they must be stored on the page in such a way that they can be easily found and used when needed. Achieving this provided some theoretical problems to which attention needed to be paid.

A final problem for Renaissance and post-Renaissance anthologists was the development of historicist intellectual tastes. These tastes, evident in Erasmus and in Luther (though in very different ways), led anthologizing readers and polemical writers to be increasingly interested in sources, origins, and the recovery of the past. "Augustine said" was, by the late seventeenth or early eighteenth century, scarcely enough to provide a useful foot soldier for the literary engagements of that time: reference to page and column of the printed editions then being produced was thought necessary. This need for precise reference in a world of multiplying printed editions created special difficulties for those who wanted a commonplace book whose excerpts were identified with sufficient precision to make useful troops of them.

All these issues are evident, explicitly or implicitly, in John Locke's essay on the commonplace book, probably written in the late 1670s when Locke was in France (he was then in his middle forties).[23] The English title of this piece ("A New Method of a Commonplace Book") suggests that Locke wanted to present a new and better way of organizing and keeping a commonplace book, while the French title ("Méthode nouvelle de dresser des recueils") suggests that he offered a new and better way of organizing excerpts. Both are in fact the case. He spends most of his space in the essay on three closely associated questions. First, how to enter excerpts into a commonplace book in such a way that those on a particular topic may most easily be kept together. Second, how to construct an index that will permit excerpts on a particular topic easily to be found. Third, how to provide a reference for each excerpt so that it can easily be found again in the work from which it was copied, even if the edition originally used is no longer to hand. Each of these concerns is characteristic of its time: if you're faced with an increasing volume of works from which to make excerpts, and an increasing number of topics (commonplaces) under which to order them, you're going to need good methods of entry and indexing; and if you want, in a world where multiple printed editions of the same work are suddenly becoming available, to ensure that you can make the return from your excerpt to its source (in any edition), you'll need a good system of reference. None of these needs would have been apparent to a compiler in medieval India or medieval Europe; they were pressing for Locke. Locke's solutions to these problems are elegant and still useful. They found sufficiently wide acceptance that blank commonplace books "prepared according to Mr. Locke's system" were manufactured for sale in England until the beginning of the twentieth century.

For the entry of excerpts Locke recommends that the compiler first "find out a head" (i.e., a subject heading, or a *topos*, or a commonplace) under which it should be categorized. This head should be "some important and essential word to the matter in hand"; Locke gives as an example "Adversariorum Methodus" (method for commonplace books), which is the subject head he gives to his own essay on the topic (Locke preferred to use Latin for his heads, even if that was not the language of the work from which he was taking an excerpt). The matter of the excerpt should then, he says, be written under the head, beginning always on the verso and continuing as long as needed—to the recto, and the subsequent verso, and so on. The next excerpt to be entered will likely require a different head, and the same method should be followed for it, beginning on the first blank verso. Each excerpt may therefore be of any length, from a few words to many pages. When you want to enter an excerpt under a head already present in your commonplace book, you begin to copy it immediately following the end of the last excerpt to have been entered under that head. If, as is likely, your new excerpt extends beyond the page upon which you began it, you continue it on the first blank verso, which may be many pages distant. A notation is put at the foot of the page on which the excerpt began to indicate the number of the page on which it continues. All the excerpts under a single head can thus easily be read seriatim, even when they're widely scattered through the commonplace book.

Retrieval of excerpts under a particular head requires an index. Locke's preferred form requires, as he boasts, only two pages (verso/recto), no matter how large the commonplace book and how many subject-heads and excerpts it might contain. The two index pages are divided first into twenty sections following the order of the alphabet (omitting or amalgamating the six least common letters by a method and with a rationale whose details it would be tedious to explain). Each of these twenty divisions is then further subdivided into five, one for each vowel. This yields 100 divisions (A/a, A/e, and so on). The page number upon which the excerpts belonging to a particular subject head begin is then entered in the division corresponding to its first two vowels. For example, the page number upon which the excerpts having to do with commonplace books (for which Locke's head, recall, is "Adversariorum Methodus") begin would be entered under A/e ('a' being the first vowel and 'e' the second). No additional page numbers need be entered, for once the first page of excerpts belonging to this head has been found, the rest will follow either immediately, or by attending to the notations at the foot of the page. Space is saved by not having to write the subject heads in full on the index pages; this is what permits Locke to limit his index to two pages.

There remains the question of reference: how to indicate the source of an excerpt in such a way that it can be retraced to the original, even in a different edition. Locke recommends that the source of every excerpt be indicated by author, "the title of the treatise, the size of the volume, the time and place of its edition, and (what ought never to be omitted) the number of pages that the whole book contains."[24] This last is important because, when this information is combined with the specific page from which the excerpt is taken, an application of the rule of three will yield the place (or very close to it) where the excerpt is to be found in a different edition. For example, if you copy an excerpt from page 300 of a 700-page edition of Locke's *Essay*, and you later want to find your excerpt in a 1,400-page large-print edition, you'll easily be able to do so by dividing 700 into 1,400 and multiplying the result by 300 (which is an instance of the application of the rule of three).

There are further refinements and details to Locke's method of a commonplace book, but what I've given are the fundamentals of the system. A number of points are worth noting. First, a Lockean anthology assumes printed editions as the norm. Second, it shows no interest in mnemotechnique. Third, it's designed to deal with volume, in number of excerpts and subject heads, as well as in possible length of particular excerpts. And fourth, it has as a central concern the kind of accuracy in source citation that makes possible a retracing of the excerptor's journey, a relocation of the culled bloom in its original garden. In all these respects it serves writerly rather than readerly concerns, and is significantly at odds with the anthologizing interests of the religious readers at whose anthologies I'll be looking in the next two chapters. Lockean anthologies have their notions well garrisoned: they are ready for battle. It's not so clear that the blooms they contain are ready to be lingered over, savored, sniffed and smelled at leisure.

5

Commentary and Anthology in Buddhist India

Buddhist Literature in India During the First Millennium

Indian Buddhists composed, stored, displayed, and redisplayed an enormous quantity and variety of literary works in the first millennium of the Christian era.[1] This literature included many narratives (*avadāna*); devotional works (*stotra*); some plays and poetry (*kāvya*); a good deal of systematic theoretical work in philosophy, jurisprudence, and liturgy; law codes; ritual handbooks; commentaries; digests; anthologies; and collections of spells, chants, and charms. It's very difficult to arrive at an assessment of the relative quantities of these various kinds of works produced during this period. This is partly because most of this literature does not survive in the Indian language (most often Sanskrit) in which it was composed (much of it does survive in either Tibetan or Chinese or both); but it is also because of its sheer bulk. There is vastly more than any one person can read, no matter what their linguistic virtuosity—and certainly I have not read enough to be able to make well-grounded generalizations. But a few observations can be made on the basis of the catalogues and indices to the collections of Buddhist works translated into Tibetan from Sanskrit.

The *Catalogue-Index of the Tibetan Buddhist Canons*, made by Japanese scholars in the 1920s and 1930s at the Tōhoku Imperial University, lists every work contained in the edition of the Tibetan Buddhist canon made from woodblocks carved at the Derge (sde dge) monastery in Khams in North-East Tibet. There are 4,569 such works, ranging in length from very short (one or two folios) to very long (more than 1,000 folios). The vast majority were translated from Indian originals, but some few were made from Central Asian or Chinese works. The collection does not contain indigenous Tibetan compositions (there are some disputed cases, but the generalization is supportable for my purposes), and since most of the works in it were composed in India, it seems reasonable to use it as the basis for some very general comments about the range and kinds of Indian Buddhist literature.

The entire collection is divided into two large divisions: *Bka'-'gyur* (*Kanjur* in the phonetic representation, meaning "collection of Buddha's words"), and *Bstan-'gyur* (*Tanjur*, "collection of treatises").[2] The first division has many fewer works than the second (1,108 to 3,461), and is also shorter, perhaps one-quarter as long. Very few of the works in this first division are either commentaries or anthologies. About one-third of them are discourses attributed to the Buddha of our world and age (Gautama Śākyamuni); some of these treat doctrinal matters, and some legal or ritual ones; some are systematic/didactic in form, and some are narratives. But none, or almost none, has the form of a commentary or an anthology. Almost two-thirds of the works in this division are collections of incantations (*dhāraṇī/mantra*), or works generically called tantra; most of the latter contain descriptions of rituals, of the paraphernalia used in them, and of the *maṇḍalas*, or sacred enclosures, by means of which the ritual space (and in the end the whole cosmos) is delimited and defined. None of these (at least, none of the few that I've read) is either a commentary or an anthology; there are in fact no more than one or two possible commentaries in the entire *Kanjur*.[3]

Among the 3,461 works in the second major division, the *Tanjur*, a very large number are commentaries in the formal sense I've given to that term.[4] Virtually all are exegetical in some way, but by no means all are commentaries. There are, for instance, many devotional hymns to deities and bodhisattvas (perhaps 100 or so), and collections of instructions for ritual and meditative practice (about 1,700 of these). But the vast majority of the remaining 1,600 or so works almost certainly are commentaries in my sense—probably as many as 1,300. Obviously, I haven't read all of these; I base my judgment upon the fact that works amounting to something like this number use genre terms for commentary in their title (*'grel pa*, *'grel bshad*, *don bsdus pa*, *rgya cher 'grel pa*, and so on)—and works that I have read with these terms in their title do meet my criteria for being commentaries. Of the few hundred works in the *Tanjur* not accounted for as hymns, manuals for practice, and commentaries, most are either anthologies, or freestanding systematic presentations of theoretical thought in some area of discourse or another.

A little more statistical precision may be gained by looking a bit more closely at two divisions of the *Tanjur*. In the division containing *yogācāra* (*sems tsam*) works, there are sixty-six works, among which forty-seven are, judging by their titles and what I know of their content (and in this case I've read the whole or parts of between twenty and thirty of them, so my judgment is based upon more than titles) commentaries. The other nineteen are freestanding digests, summaries, or anthologies. And in the division containing *abhidharma* (*mngon pa*) works, there are eighteen works, among which twelve are commentaries and six are freestanding digests or treatises. In these divisions, then, the ratio of commentaries to noncommentaries runs at two to one or better.

The upshot of these preliminary and very sketchy observations on the kinds of Indian Buddhist works preserved in the Tibetan canonical collections is that commentaries are very well represented: almost certainly more than a thousand are found there, more than any other single genre with the exception of manuals for meditational and ritual practice (and this is not so much a genre as a categorization by content). Other genres (narratives, spell and chant collections, law codes) are less well represented. It's much harder to say how many anthologies (according to my definition) the Tibetan canonical collections contain; I suspect not more than 100 or so at most, but titles don't always make it clear whether a particular work is an anthology, since no single Sanskrit or Tibetan genre term picks them out with precision.

This is not surprising. My definitions are constructed for my specific purposes, and it would be very odd indeed if the purposes of Indian theorists should turn out to overlap to any significant extent with mine. There are, however, some terms commonly affixed to works that do, formally speaking, meet my definitions. For anthologies, the most common word is *samuccaya*; both the Buddhist anthologies that I'll discuss later in this chapter use this word in their title. Etymologically, the word means something like 'a piling up of extracts', or 'an assemblage of excerpts'. But it isn't always applied to works that I would call anthologies. Sometimes, as in the *Abhidharmasamuccaya* [Compendium of Abhidharma], a work composed possibly in the fourth century in India, it means something like 'compendium': this is a work that provides a brief but systematic conspectus of the technical terms of *abhidharma* thought. What it 'piles up' or 'assembles' are precisely these technical terms, not excerpts from other works. Or there is the *Ṣaḍdarśanasamuccaya* [Compendium of the Six Philosophical Systems], a digest possibly from the eighth century, again not an anthology strictly speaking but rather a summary overview of the tenets of these schools. Once again, the term *samuccaya* in this case is best translated 'compendium' rather than 'anthology'. But the term's semantic range certainly includes (what I mean by) anthologies, even if it also goes beyond them. I have not been able to find in Sanskrit works from the first millennium of the Christian era any extended discussion of the term *samuccaya*, or of a genre that might overlap significantly with what I mean by anthology.

There's a bit more to be said about Sanskrit terms for works that fall wholly within my definition of commentary, or that overlap significantly with it. The first thing is that Buddhists composing in Sanskrit during the first millennium use a very large number of terms for commentarial works. Those that come to mind most easily are *bhāṣya*, *vṛtti*, *vyākhyā*, *upanibandhana*, *paddhati*, *vārttika*, and *pañjikā*. These terms do not, however, appear to describe genres that can be sharply differentiated one from another. If there are differences in genre between Candrakīrti's *Prasannapadā* [Clear-Worded] (which is called a *vṛtti*) and Vasubandhu's *bhāṣya* to the *Mahāyānasaṅgraha* [Digest of the Great Vehicle], or between either and Yaśomitra's *Sphūṭārthā* [Plain-Meaning] (which is called a *vyākhyā*), then I cannot tell what they are and the works in question do not discuss the matter.

In spite of this vagueness, there are perhaps some generalizations that can be made for Buddhist works: a *vṛtti* seems never to be a subcommentary, but always a work that comments directly upon another work, and upon one only; a *vyākhyā*, by contrast, appears always to be a subcommentary. But this is differentiation not strictly by genre but by the nature of the work(s) commented upon. Once that difference has been established, the methods of commentary used may be identical. This is not to say that Buddhist *bhāṣyas* and the rest always use the same methods of commentary. They do not. Some provide word-by-word comments, making sure to explain every jot and tittle; others treat only matters of special interest, saying nothing about considerable portions of the work they treat; yet others mix these methods, occasionally providing digressions amounting to many pages that have nothing directly to do with the work being commented upon—and so on. But it is to say that differences in commentarial method are not marked, or at least not consistently marked, by difference in the terms used to label commentaries.

I have not been able to find in Buddhist works from the first millennium any explicit address to the question of kinds of commentary and the proper terms to be used to describe different kinds. Buddhist literature is an ocean, of course, and it may be that such discussions are present; but the earliest explicit address to this question that I've been able to find in any Sanskrit work from the period comes almost at the end of it, in an encyclopedia of poetics called *Kāvyamīmāṃsā* [Investigation of Poetry] by Rājaśekhara, composed perhaps during the first two decades of the tenth century. Rājaśekhara's goal in this work is systematically to state the scope, nature, goals, and methods of the practice of poetic composition, of what poets do (*kāvyakrīyā*), and of the theory that informs it. In the second chapter he describes the intellectual background that poets need before they can compose. An important part of this background is study of the *śāstras*, the technical treatises, which together with the *kāvyas*, the poems, Rājaśekhara takes to comprise the whole of literature. And it's also in the second chapter, whose title is *śāstranirdeśa* (description of the technical treatises), that he gives the defining characteristics of the various kinds of these treatises, among which are included various types of commentary.[5] The whole chapter is of interest, but of special concern to me are his definitions of kinds of commentary, and of their relations to sutras, which Rājaśekhara takes to be the core of all *śāstras*.

For Rājaśekhara, a sutra is a short and unambiguous work, precise, with universal scope, and without metrical insertions and redundancies (*alpākṣaram asandigdhaṃ sāravad viśvato mukham astobham anavadyañ ca sūtraṃ sūtrakṛto vidūḥ*). It is, that is to say, a work ideally suited for religious readers, since both its brevity and its depth cry out for close, repetitive reading, memorization, and, of course, the composition of commentaries that bring to light the inexhaustible meanings hidden in the sutra. And so Rājaśekhara at once turns to the kinds of commentary that a sutra might provoke and without which it would remain somnolent, as Paul Dundas has nicely put it in his study of Jaina commentaries.[6]

Rājaśekhara begins with *vṛtti*: this, he says, opens up the entire extent or course of the sutra upon which it comments (*sūtrānāṃ sakalasāravivaraṇaṃ vṛttiḥ*). A *paddhati*, by contrast, is a subcommentary: it explicates analytically both a sutra and a *vṛtti* (*sūtravṛttivivecanaṃ paddhati*). A *bhāṣya*, different from both, is a polemical commentary: it says what it has to say after canvassing and rejecting wrong views on particular parts of the commentary. A *ṭīkā* provides occasional elucidation of the meaning of terms in the work upon which it comments, skipping from one place to another without commenting upon everything. A *pañjikā* analyzes difficult words (*viṣamapadabhañjikā pañjikā*—notice the alliteration), acting as a kind of grammatical and semantic gloss. And, finally, a *vārttika* treats "topics that have been stated, not stated, and badly stated" (*uktānuktaduruktacintā vārttikam iti*), which rather puzzling statement a twentieth-century commentator on Rājaśekhara's work interprets as meaning that a *vārttika* gives close consideration to those places in the work upon which it comments where error or carelessness might have caused the composer of the sutra to say something susceptible of misinterpretation.

This set of definitions certainly indicates some of the functions that a commentary may have (word-by-word elucidation, polemical engagement with misinterpretations, exegesis of obscure words or difficult passages), and in that respect it is quite like the analysis I gave in chapter 4. But I doubt that Rājaśekhara's attempt to link these functions to particular genre terms is descriptive of the ways in which these terms were used in India, even in the tenth century. It is better thought of as a normative set of definitions, an attempt to prescribe how these terms should be used, to what sorts of works they should be affixed. And it would be interesting to know whether Rājaśekhara's work had any influence upon the ways in which these terms were used after the tenth century. But at the very least, this passage from the *Kāvyamīmāṃsā* sheds some light upon the way in which one Indian theorist, at the end of the period that interests me, and in a thought world not too dramatically different from that of the Buddhist composers whose works I treat, thought about commentaries and their functions.

This glance at the range and assortment of works composed by Buddhists in India during the first millennium shows that among Indian Buddhists during this period, there were specialist readers who did little but cultivate their capacity to understand, comment upon, and compose works in particular genres, some of which are, both formally and substantively, of great complexity and technicality. How did they learn their skills, and what skills were involved? Were these specialist readers close to the ideal type of the religious reader, or to that of the consumerist reader? How, to put this question sanskritically, did *śāstragrahaṇa* occur?[7] Literally, this means 'getting the treatise'; more elegantly, 'receiving precise and technical textual instruction'. The question about *śāstragrahaṇa* is another version of my question about the ideal readers of literary works: if we can come to an understanding of who were the ideal readers of the products of Indian Buddhist learning, then we will also have come to an understanding of how they received and gave precise and technical textual instruction. The first task is to say what can be said about the pedagogical methods and textual technologies of Buddhist India.

Teaching and Learning Literary Works in Buddhist India

For the first five hundred years or so of Buddhism in India, Buddhists (lay and monastic) got their literary works by ear, stored them in their heads, and displayed them with their tongues and vocal chords. Moreover, they did so almost entirely in local institutions: in the village, at the feet of a reciter and expounder; or in the local monastery, in the one-on-one teaching relation prescribed in the monastic code for the induction of novices into the community. There were, until the Christian era, no translocal educational institutions in Buddhist India; and, as the comments in chapter 2 on the uses of writing in ancient India have already suggested, writing was either altogether absent as a tool for the composition and display of literary works, or at least insignificant for those purposes. It follows that it was also insignificant for pedagogy, for the transmission and appropriation of literary works—for, that is to say, *śāstragrahaṇa*.[8]

The *Vinaya*, the monastic rule, prescribes for monks the duty of teaching (orally) the doctrine of Buddhism to those encountered on the daily begging rounds, and Buddhist works are full of stories about monks (and nuns) preaching before kings and other possessors of wealth and power. All this, of course, was both local and aural: monks and nuns speak to those they meet as they walk around the village; or the locals visit the monastery for teaching; or a discourse is given to the local potentate. The complex skill of being a Buddhist monk was also transmitted in this local fashion: each novice was allotted a preceptor upon whom he attended each day, and from this preceptor he learned how to behave as a monk behaves (how to wear the robe, how to sit, how to eat, how to walk) and to know what a monk needs to know. The preceptor-novice relation (at least in its ideal type) is intimate: the standard metaphor is that the preceptor is a benevolent parent and the novice an obedient child. And, it's important to note, becoming a monk as it's presented in the *Vinaya* is mostly a matter of learning skills, of amassing knowledge how (to revert once again to Gilbert Ryle's terms).[9]

Knowing literary works is much less important than possessing monastic skills, and even when it is essential (every monk, for instance should know the disciplinary code [227 rules] contained in the *Prātimokṣa* sufficiently well to be able to recite it at the monthly meeting of the whole monastic community), more emphasis is placed by the rule upon the know-how of reciting it, and of avoiding the offenses proscribed by it, than upon simple knowledge that these are the relevant offenses; still less stress is placed upon the complex theoretical knowledge involved in explaining why just these are the offenses that count, and what it is about each that makes it an offense. *Śāstragrahaṇa* was not a centrally important part of becoming a monk for most of those who did so, both in the early period (until the time of Kaniṣka, perhaps around AD 100), and in the classical period of Buddhism's institutional and intellectual flourishing in India (from Kaniṣka until the end of the first millennium).

In spite of its relative lack of significance in early Buddhist monastic education, the storage and redisplay of verbal works did, of course, have some importance to local Buddhist communities during both the early and the classical periods, and there are some indications in works produced in that time as to how these things were done. Most of these indications focus upon display-by-recitation, which, in turn, presupposes (though very little is explicitly said about it) storage in memory. Some monks were given the title *bhāṇaka* (reciter), and were classified according to the bodies of work they were able to recite: some were called *dīrghabhāṇaka* (reciter of the long collection), some *madhyamabhāṇaka* (reciter of the intermediate collection), and so forth.[10] And Buddhist histories give considerable attention to the so-called councils, gatherings of monks at which large bodies of work were recited, in part as a way of authorizing them as *buddhavacana* (Buddha's word), and therefore as bearing canonical status for the community. The accounts of these gatherings for recitation make them sound translocal: as if the entire *bhikṣusaṅgha*, the entire monastic community from all over India (or at least representatives of it), were present. It's not clear how much historical credence should be given to these accounts; but they do at least indicate that by the time they began to be composed, perhaps two or three centuries after the death of the Buddha (just before the beginning of the Christian era), Buddhists were beginning to think in terms of the desirability of translocal institutions, even if as yet there were none.[11]

It's beyond dispute that Buddhists composed their works mentally or with the use of speech, displayed them aurally, and then stored them memorially well into the classical period. I've already quoted (in chapter 2) the verses about the use of writing for storing the Buddhist canon, and I noted then that writing seems to have been understood in those verses exclusively as a tool for storage rather than one for composition or display. This, if it's right, coheres very well with the standard vocabulary for composition and display found in Buddhist works throughout the classical period. This vocabulary says nothing about writing; for composition it almost always uses verbs of making (*kṛ*-, etc.), and for display verbs of showing (causatives of *dṛś*-, etc.). So someone whom we (or Bonaventure—see chapter 4) might call the 'author' or 'writer' of a work is standardly called its 'maker' (*kartṛ*) or its 'shower' (*darśayitṛ*).

A good example of these usages is to hand in a Buddhist philosophical work composed in about the fourth century of the Christian era together with two of its commentaries. The work in question is called *Madhyāntavibhāga* [Discrimination Between Middle and Extremes]; it is a work in verse attributed by the tradition to Maitreya, the Buddha-to-be who is separated from Buddhahood by just one birth. The first commentary to this work, called a *bhāṣya*, is attributed to Vasubandhu; and the second commentary, a subcommentary that expounds both the verses of the *Madhyāntavibhāga* and the prose of the *bhāṣya*, is attributed to Sthiramati (it is called a *ṭīkā*). There are, then, three layers in this corpus. But, according to Sthiramati in the *ṭīkā*,[12] four persons had to do with the composition and display of these three layers. Maitreya composed the verses and spoke them in private to Asaṅga while the latter was visiting him in a heavenly realm; Asaṅga then learned them and made them public by speaking them; Vasubandhu elucidated their meaning; and then finally Sthiramati explained Vasubandhu's meaning. Maitreya, whom we might call the author of the verses, is said by both Vasubandhu and Sthiramati to be their *praṇetṛ*, their 'promulgator'—one who gives them, in my terms, their first display. Sthiramati further explains that *praṇetṛ* means *kartṛ*, 'maker', 'agent of production'. Asaṅga, by contrast, is the speaker (*vaktṛ*) of the verses; they are stored in his head and retrieved therefrom for their second and subsequent displays. He has no authorial or compositional functions, and is required only because Maitreya is not usually available here in our world-realm to display and redisplay his own composition. Vasubandhu and Sthiramati then explain their own function in producing this corpus of works with various terms suggesting explication and elucidation (*arthavivecana* and so forth).

The *Madhyāntavibhāga* corpus, then, has a composer; it has people who store it (memorially) and display it (aurally); and it has people who hear, ponder, and expound it. But it has, in the narrow sense, no writers and no readers; and if it is stored by being written on palm leaves, this is not a fact of interest to its composers and users. In all these respects it is entirely typical of Indian Buddhist literature.

The vocabulary of writing (*likh-*) and of books as physical objects (*grantha, pustaka, pattra*) is likewise almost entirely absent from the literary output of this period. When works want to refer to themselves they almost always use the appropriate genre term (*śāstra, kāvya*) or the work's title, rather than any terms that suggest material objects. Likewise, the vocabulary of reading, of running the eyes over scratch marks on palm leaves or pieces of birch bark, is absent: instead, one is said to hear a work recited by someone else, or to cause others to hear a work. Or one repeatedly studies (*svādhyāyaṃ kṛ-*) or ponders (gives *cintā* or *bhāvanā* to) a work. There is no vocabulary in classical Sanskrit to indicate what English means by 'reading to yourself'; and while some of the verbs occasionally translated 'to read' (e.g., *paṭh-*) may certainly include looking at marks scratched on leaves or bark and vocalizing them while thinking about their meaning, there is no verb that specifically denotes such an activity. *Paṭh-*, for example, most often means not to read to oneself but to recite or to study; and the work studied may well be consulted only in the memory.

This picture of Buddhist *śāstragrahaṇa* is confirmed by the highly idealized sketch of the Brahmanical and Buddhist educational systems given in the *Milindapañha* [Milinda's Questions],[13] a work whose date and place of composition remain uncertain, but which certainly reflects some assumptions about study and learning that were current in Buddhist circles at the beginning of the Christian era. This work tells the story of Nāgasena, a young Brahmin who becomes a Buddhist. Near the beginning of the work, Nāgasena's education is described. His father hires a Brahmin teacher to instruct Nāgasena in the Veda; instruction proceeds aurally until he has the entire Vedic corpus by heart, along with the works that teach some of their ancillary disciplines: grammar, prosody, debate, and so forth. Nāgasena learns by hearing and reviews what he has learned mentally. The idealized nature of the account is evident mostly in the amazing speed with which he is said to learn; but that learning is done in this way is simply assumed. The same methods are assumed in the account of Nāgasena's Buddhist learning: he is given instruction in Buddhist metaphysics (*abhidharma*) aurally; and in short order he is able to recite verbatim the entire corpus of works dealing with this topic.

In the early period, then, *śāstragrahaṇa* for Indian Buddhists was mostly local. This began to change, though slowly, with the increasing prominence of "a new juridical person, the monastery, which possessed estates and moveable goods."[14] The monastic rule places strict restraints upon the portable property that an individual monk may own, and on most interpretations the possession (and even the handling) of money is strictly forbidden to monks. But no such restriction was ever understood to apply to the Sangha (the monastic order understood collectively), or to particular groups of monks living in a specific place. Even in the earliest times, such groups were gifted with land and other material goods by local potentates; Buddhist works describe some of these gifts as having been made to the Buddha, to Gautama Śākyamuni himself. Whatever the likelihood of this, it is certain that such endowments were common by the time of Aśoka, and standard by the beginning of the classical period. A couple of examples will illustrate how these endowments were made and what they might mean.

Faxian, a Chinese Buddhist monk and scholar, traveled in India and Sri Lanka between 399 and 414, principally to find more reliable manuscripts of the Vinaya than those available to him in China. He made the outward trip by land via Khotan, and the return trip by sea from Sri Lanka via the straits between Sumatra and Java. He left an account of his travels, in which there is much detail about particular Buddhist monasteries, some general impressions of the fabric of life in them, and a description of his difficulties in finding the manuscripts he'd come in search of. In this travelogue there are several passages relevant to this question of the endowment of Buddhist monasteries. This one is typical:

> After Buddha attained to pari-nirvana the kings of various countries . . . built viharas for the priests and endowed them with fields, houses, gardens, and orchards, along with the resident populations and their cattle, the grants being engraved on plates of metal, so that afterwards they were handed down from king to king, without anyone daring to annul them, and they remain even to the present time.[15]

According to this account, local potentates grant, in perpetuity, land and local populations to work it so that the monks may be supported without having to engage in agricultural labor for themselves.

Some examples: Tibetan sources provide some details about the royal endowment of the first monastic foundation in Tibet, at Bsam-yas in the 770s.[16] This endowment provides 150 families who are to be responsible for the support of the monastery and its inhabitants; specific quantities of barley, rice, butter, salt, horses, materials for writing, and so forth, are allotted to each monastic grade. Bsam-yas was, of course, not an Indian foundation but a Tibetan one; but since it had very close connections with Indian monastic institutions (specifically with Nālandā, on which more below), it's likely that its organization was closely modeled upon that of its Indian ancestors. Further, both inscriptional and textual records remain of the gifts given by Gopala I (who flourished in the second half of the eighth century) to various monasteries, including Nālandā. He is said to have given gardens to the monastic order, as well as residential buildings, statues (one statue of Vāgīśvarī unearthed at Nālandā mentions Gopala in an inscription on its base; he may have been its donor), and reservoirs.[17]

It's clear, then, that monasteries could own property, including land, buildings, livestock, and the labor of human beings. These facts made possible the development in Buddhist India of properly translocal institutions for the training of religious readers; and from the third or fourth century onward, such institutions did indeed begin to develop. I'll make a few comments about one of them, Nālandā.[18]

Nālandā, some of the ruins of which have been excavated and preserved during the last 150 years, was located at about 25° north, 85° east. This is in contemporary Bihar (the name of which, interestingly, is derived from *vihāra*—'monastic building'; the region was so named because of the large number of monasteries that once graced it), about thirty-five miles southeast of Patna (ancient Pātaliputra), and about seventeen miles northeast of Rajgir (ancient Rājagṛha). The first hard evidence of its existence is in another travelogue by a visiting Chinese monk, in this case Xuanzang, who was in India between 629 and 645 in search of manuscripts and teachings relevant to the Yogācāra school of Buddhism.

Xuanzang's time in India overlapped with Harṣa's reign (606–647), and while this was a period of relative prosperity and stability, he was robbed twice by bandits and almost sacrificed to Durga by river pirates. Harṣa appears to have been relatively sympathetic to Buddhism and its institutions, especially toward the end of his long reign (which was roughly when Xuanzang was in Bihar). But Xuanzang's account nonetheless shows that many once-flourishing monasteries were moribund at this time—though this does not appear to have been the case for Nālandā, of which he gives a full and useful account.

The permanent monastic population of Nālandā was, according to Xuanzang, in the thousands, reaching ten thousand if visitors are counted. He records his admiration for the learning of the monks and their faithful observance of the monastic rule; and he makes passing comments about curricula, public disputation on doctrinal matters, and the composition of treatises by particular monks. But his chief interest is in telling stories connecting various architectural and iconographic features of the place with events from Śākyamuni's life, or with other significant events from the history of Buddhism in India. There is mention of the presence of specific relics of Śākyamuni (hair clippings and nail parings), of stupas, and of statues of Avalokiteśvara, Tārā, and Śākyamuni. The largest of these last is said to be eighty feet in height.

Xuanzang and his biographer also give details about the size of particular buildings within the monastic complex. Most of the residential buildings are said to be four stories high; the whole complex is surrounded by a wall; and (an especially interesting feature) there is a *vihāra* or residential building under construction. This may suggest that Nālandā was expanding in the 640s. Monastic diet is also described: the daily ration for each monk included rice, butter, nutmeg, areca nuts, and camphor (this last presumably not to eat but to repel mosquitoes?). And finally, Xuanzang's biographer mentions the endowment of the place:

> The king gave more than a hundred villages for their [sc. the monks at Nālandā's] sustenance. Each village had two hundred families who daily provided several hundred *shi* of polished nonglutinous rice, butter, and milk. Thus the students could enjoy sufficient supplies of the four requisites without the trouble of going to beg for them. It was because of this effort of their supporters that the scholars could gain achievements in learning.[19]

Nālandā was, according to Xuanzang and his biographer, clearly a translocal institution in size and in the area from which it drew people who wanted the training it could give. His own presence there shows that Nālandā was international in its clientele. Xuanzang's impression of it is largely confirmed by what another Chinese pilgrim, Yijing, has to say.

Yijing, a Buddhist monk with special interests in finding and studying manuscripts containing the monastic rule, left the east coast of China in November 671 and sailed south to Sumatra, where he stayed for eight months, studying Sanskrit grammar, monastic discipline, and ritual. He then went by ship from Sumatra to Bengal, arriving there in February 673; he spent most of the next twelve years studying at Nālandā. In 689 he made landfall in China once again, having left in Sumatra the manuscripts he had collected in India. In the same year he returned to Sumatra, and spent the next five years there copying and translating the works he had brought back from India. Later still, after his final return to China in 695, Yijing translated many more works of various kinds. He wrote a brief account of his travels and of Buddhist doctrine and practice in India and Sumatra while he was in Sumatra from 690 to 692. Most of this work is given over to an analysis of questions about monastic discipline, but there are also some brief observations about Nālandā—for example, that its monks follow the discipline of the Sarvāstivāda, that they number more than 3,000, that they live in eight *vihāras* containing 300 apartments each, and that the monastery is supported by more than 200 villages.[20]

The next account we have of Nālandā from an outsider is by a Tibetan scholar-monk by the name of Chos rje dpal (which in Sanskrit is Dharmasvāmin; he is most often referred to by this Sanskrit name), who traveled in Nepal and India from 1226 to 1236. He later dictated an account of his travels to a disciple, Chos dpal dar dpyang, who wrote a brief biography of his master incorporating it. Among the places visited by Dharmasvāmin was Nālandā. He was there from 1234 to 1236, and his account of what he saw gives a useful snapshot of Nālandā at that time. Bihar was then in political chaos. Muslim forces had destroyed some of the major Buddhist monastic establishments (Vikramaśilā had been razed in 1206, and Bodhgaya was almost deserted), but there was as yet no stable Muslim state and the Sena monarchs retained some remnants of political power. Dharmasvāmin apparently met with Buddhasena, king of Magadha, in 1234. But his account of this event and of almost all his travels in Bihar is shot through with mentions of the threat or presence of *gar log* (*turuṣka*, or Muslim) soldiers. His description of Nālandā mentions damage done by these soldiers, but also suggests that many of the buildings were left standing, and that some were occupied. He describes seven pinnacles (*śikhara*) at the center of the complex, and fourteen to the north; he also mentions a total of eighty-four small *vihāras* made of brick, of which two were in a condition to be lived in. Details are given about surviving images of Mañjuśrī, Avalokiteśvara, and Tārā. Seventy monks, led by Rahulaśrībhadra, were in residence, and Dharmasvāmin appears to have been impressed by their knowledge of Sanskrit grammar, and to have studied this under their tutelage.[21]

These accounts by non-Indians can be supplemented (and are largely confirmed) by the mass of archaeological and epigraphical evidence that has come from the excavations at Nālandā.[22] This evidence strongly suggests that there was no significant building on the site before the early fifth century (probably in the reign of Kumāragupta I between 413 and 455) and that Nālandā received regular royal patronage (and sometimes massive donations) from the time of the Gupta monarchs until that of the Pālas (that is, from the fifth to the twelfth century). There is also epigraphical evidence of sponsorship from non-Indian monarchs. An inscription on copper plate records that in the thirty-ninth regnal year of Devapāla I (probably 854), some villages were granted by that king for the support of a monastic residence donated by Balaputradeva, king of Suvarṇadvīpa (i.e., Java/Sumatra, part of what is now Indonesia). There are also inscriptions in Chinese found in the approximate neighborhood of Nālandā; these too indicate strong international connections.[23] Many seals found on the site describe Nālandā as belonging to the monastic assembly of the four quarters (*caturdiśāryabhikṣusaṅgha*), which phrase (a traditional Buddhist one) indicates the universal monastic assembly, the notional collection of all the monks there are, anywhere in the world (an idea much like the Christian notion of the Church Catholic as the Body of Christ). The use of this phrase very strongly suggests that those in charge of Nālandā thought of the institution as translocal. This is to say that the institution's self-perception at the level of theory cohered well with its reality.

Xuanzang's biographer provides some details about pedagogical arrangements at Nālandā. He says that about one hundred separate classes were given each day, and that a class consisted of a discourse delivered by a teacher from a raised platform.[24] This statement suggests at least that the main tool of instruction was something like what we call a lecture, a spoken discourse; and that the number of students attending each class was not enormous—assuming equal distribution, about thirty at each class if we follow Yijing's estimate of monastic population, and perhaps as many as eighty if we follow Xuanzang's. But since the estimates of both are likely to be too generous rather than too modest, and since it is not likely that all the people they count were at Nālandā to study, these numbers should probably be reduced. Classes, then, were relatively small: they consisted of a small group of students sitting at the feet of a teacher, listening to a discourse on some work or some topic.

As can be seen from the excavated ruins at Nālandā, the monastic complex contained a number of large, square courtyards, open in the center and with monastic cells running around the edge. The courtyards vary somewhat in size, and it is not clear whether the cells were built to a single storey in height, or whether (as Xuanzang suggests) they extended higher, perhaps to four storeys. But however this was, a typical arrangement seems to have been a courtyard with seven or eight cells on a side, yielding an open space in the center of a courtyard about eighty feet square. It was in these open courtyards, almost certainly, that the daily classes took place.

Xuanzang's biographer and Yijing's travelogue both mention the use of 'pulpits' by teachers. It's not quite clear what these were or what they were for. If, as seems likely, they were something like a lectern or a raised platform in front of the (probably seated) teacher, they may have been used to hold a manuscript of the work being expounded, or possibly to hold some other ritual paraphernalia. Wooden holders for palm-leaf manuscripts can still be found in India (they are sometimes called *vyāsāsana*), and they are meant to support a manuscript at the right height for a seated reader. But even if this is what Xuanzang and Yijing mean, it doesn't necessarily follow that a teacher would read from or consult a manuscript supported in this way. In my own hearing of teaching from Tibetan Buddhist monks I've often seen a teacher sitting on a raised platform giving teaching with a blockprint work in front of him. But he rarely consults it. He usually quotes the work from memory, and then gives oral exposition. What counts about the physical object (the manuscript) is not its capacity to be read, but rather its presence. Perhaps it was like that at Nālandā.

It's very clear from the scattered comments on these matters made by the Chinese and Tibetan visitors to Nālandā that the dominant mode of display was aural: most learning took place through the ears, and competence in learning was exhibited with the mouth. Xuanzang's biographer, for instance, explains that scholarly achievement is ranked according to the number of works that someone is capable of explaining—and he seems to mean oral explanation, without book.[25] Yijing is a bit more precise and detailed. He says that after full ordination to the monastic order (*upasasampadā*), the precepts contained in the *Prātimokṣa* are learned, and then:

> the candidate begins to read the larger Vinaya-pitaka; he reads it day after day, and is examined every morning, for if he does not keep to it constantly he will lose intellectual power. When he has read the Vinaya-pitaka, he begins to learn the Sutras and Sastras. Such is the way in which a teacher instructs in India. Although it is a long period since the days of the Sage, yet such a custom still exists unimpaired.[26]

Yijing also mentions the learning by heart of two hymns by Matṛceta, of Aśvaghoṣa's *Buddhacarita*, Nāgārjuna's *Suhṛllekha*, the *Jātakamālā* by Āryaśūra, and some other works, as well as the daily "reading over" of the *Ratnakūṭasūtra*.

These statements mix the vocabulary of reading with that of learning by heart in such a way that, while it is fairly clear that Yijing wants to distinguish between the two, it is not so clear whether, or to what extent, he intends 'reading' to mean the perusal of a manuscript. There are some indications that this is what he means. For instance, in his description of the methods used to teach Sanskrit, he uses language that does seem to suggest the handling of a material object:

> If men of China go to India for study, they have first of all to learn this (grammatical) work [he means the *Kāśikavṛtti*], then other subjects; if not, their labour will be thrown away. All these books should be learnt by heart [Yijing appears

here to include the *Aṣṭādhyāyī* and perhaps also the *Dhātupāṭha*, as well as the *Kāśikavṛtti*]. But this, as a rule, applies only to men of high talent, while for those of medium or little ability a different measure (method) must be taken according to their wishes. They should study hard day and night, without letting a moment pass for idle repose. They should be like the Father K'ung (i.e., Confucius), by whose hard study the leather binding of his Yi-king was three times worn away; or imitate Sui-shih, who used to read a book a hundred times.[27]

The appeal to Confucius' reading habits certainly implies the handling of a material object. But it's worth noting that even here the repeated handling of manuscripts is said to be what people of lesser ability do; those of greater ability or talent memorize them and then reread by consulting the pages of the memory. And this trope—that the élite, the virtuosos, the specialist readers, memorize easily and compose spontaneously—is found throughout Xuanzang's and Yijing's works, as indeed it is throughout much of Chinese literature. Consider this example, from Yijing:

These men could compose a work on the spot [on] whatever subject was required. . . . [T]he Indian teachers are able to compose verses at once. . . . [S]uch men could commit to memory the contents even of two volumes having heard them only once. What, then, was the need to them of reading a book a hundred times? . . . In India there are two traditional ways by which one can attain to great intellectual power. Firstly, by repeatedly committing to memory the intellect is developed; secondly, the alphabet fixes one's ideas. By this way, after a practice of ten days or a month, a student feels his thoughts rise like a fountain, and can commit to memory whatever he has once heard [not requiring to be told twice]. This is far from being a myth, for I myself have met such men.[28]

This passage is interesting not only for its praise of memorial capacity as the paradigm of good learning, but also for its mention of the alphabet as a means of fixing one's ideas. This may be nothing more than the Chinese speaker's fascination with the unfamiliar device of an alphabet; but it may perhaps also indicate the use of the letters of the Sanskrit alphabet as tags for a random-access memorization and retrieval system. As I said in chapter 2, the use of alphabetical tagging systems as mnemotechnical devices was common in medieval Europe, and those who used it preferred an alphabet belonging to an unknown language such as Hebrew or Akkadian to the familiar Latin one, for in the case of an unknown language, the letters can have pure mnemonic function, unburdened by other associations. The Sanskrit letters would have had something of this function for a native user of Chinese, especially since Chinese is not an alphabetic language. So perhaps Yijing is speaking about mnemotechnique here; and even if he is not, he clearly gives great importance to the achievement of memorization.

Dharmasvāmin's comments on the methods of teaching and learning in use in the much-reduced Nālandā of his time strongly reinforce the impression of predominantly aural display and memorial learning given by the Chinese pilgrims. When Dharmasvāmin arrives at Nālandā and begins to study under Rahulaśrībhadra he doubts that he needs to hear again the *Gurupañcaśikha* (a grammatical work being expounded by his teacher) because he has already memorized it; but Rahulaśrībhadra persuades him that he does indeed need to hear a Sanskrit commentary to the work so that he might become fully skilled in it.[29]

In Nālandā at the time of its flourishing (and indeed at all the times about which we have information), then, *śāstragrahaṇa* happened from ear to mouth to memory. Once the work had been apprehended (heard and learned), expertise in it was displayed with the mouth once again, both by recitation (verbatim quotation) and oral commentary—as in the teaching situations described by the Chinese pilgrims. None of this is to say that there were no manuscripts at Nālandā, or at the other translocal institutions of virtuoso reading in Buddhist India. All of the Chinese accounts make mention of the libraries they see on their travels, and all of them had the collection of manuscripts as one of the purposes of their visits to India. Also, numerous inscriptions all over Buddhist India, including many found at Nālandā, mention the merit-making activity of copying (or, more often, copy-sponsoring, causing to have copied) Buddhist works. But it is to suggest that manuscripts and the libraries that stored them were not of prime pedagogical importance.

Even apart from the paucity of mentions of the use of manuscripts as tools for teaching, there are reasons for thinking that manuscripts are unlikely to have been of much pedagogical importance in translocal institutions of learning in Buddhist India. Most prominent among these is the expense and material difficulty of producing the huge number of copies that would have had to have been made were such objects to have been of central importance for teaching in an institution having several thousand students.

All this evidence suggests the following imaginative picture of the ideal-typical teaching situation at Nālandā at the time of Devapāla I. You're sitting on the ground with thirty or so other monks in an open courtyard under the shade of a coconut palm. In front of you on a raised wooden platform is the teacher; before him, on a small lectern, is a large bundle of palm leaves, bound together with a cord threaded through a hole in the center of each leaf, and protected by an intricately carved and brightly painted wooden cover at the top and bottom of the manuscript pile. The pile of leaves is a manuscript of Śāntideva's *Bodhicaryāvatāra*,[30] a work composed about a century before your time, perhaps in the very institution in which you find yourself. The teacher doesn't unwrap the manuscript bundle or consult it in any way; instead, he chants the portion of the work he's going to expound that day, beginning *śikṣāṃ rakṣitukāmena cittaṃ rakṣyaṃ prayatnataḥ* (one who wants to protect his training should protect his mind with great diligence). You've memorized this section (the opening of the fifth chapter), and you move your lips and bob your head rhythmically as the teacher's chant goes on. After ten verses or so the teacher stops chanting; his tone and attitude change; he begins the work of exposition, using now his own words. You feel sleepy after a few minutes, and the echoes of your teacher's words in the resonant manifold of your memory begin to die away, to become fainter . . . you have no manuscript in your lap; you have nothing to write with and nothing to write on. Communication and learning are by sound, gesture, and thought.

This picture is a speculative fantasy, a thought-experiment of the "this is how it might have been" variety. But it does fit with what we know of what went on at Nālandā and places like it in the classical period of Buddhism in India—and it fits better than would any other (equally fantastical) reconstruction I can come up with. It certainly fits better than a picture in which each of the students in the courtyard has a palm-leaf manuscript of the *Bodhicaryāvatāra* in his lap, and is industriously scribbling notes with a *lekhani*, a reed pen, on a prepared pile of palm leaves. But more needs to be said about the physical properties of manuscripts in India in order to ground this claim.[31]

Tools for Writing in Buddhist India

People who wrote (in the narrow sense) at Nālandā (or Vikramaśilā or any other translocal Buddhist institution in India) between the time of Harṣa and the later Pāla kings would most likely have written on the leaves of *corypha umbraculifera*, which in Sanskrit is *tālī*, and in English is sometimes called 'talipot' or 'taliphat' (from *tālī*-plus-*pattra* [leaf]). This is a kind of palm. Jeremiah Losty describes, in his study of bookmaking in India, the preparation necessary in order to make these leaves ready for writing:

> The leaves of the talipot in its natural state are arranged like a fan and are about 1.3 m long and 15 cm wide at their broadest, tapering off to both ends, being divided by a central rib round which the leaf naturally folds. Each fold is cut from the rib, and fashioned into its finished shape, about 6.5–9 cm broad by up to a metre in length, and then subjected to several processes of boiling, drying, and rubbing. The finished leaf is a smooth and flexible, light-brown surface.[32]

The *corypha* grows naturally only in the south of India, beneath the fourteenth parallel (i.e., a little north of Madras/Chennai, and 300 miles or so south of Bombay/Mumbai). It can be cultivated a little further north than this, but not much. It may have been the *corypha* that Xuanzang's biographer meant when he wrote:

> To the north of the city [an unidentified city somewhere in South India, perhaps near Konkanapura] was a wood of Tala trees more than thirty *li* [i.e., about ten miles] in circumference. The leaves of these trees were oblong with a glossy color, and they were the best material used for writing in various countries.[33]

If Xuanzang did mean the *corypha*, and if the city he mentions really was near Konkanapura, then he was somewhere near the sixteenth parallel, considerably to the north of the tree's usual range. It may be that Xuanzang was shown a stand of *corypha* here, so far north, as a curiosity.[34]

The *corypha*'s leaves were not the only surfaces used for writing in India, of course. Leaving aside the more permanent epigraphical surfaces (stone, metal), other materials known to have been used for manuscript writing in India include the leaves of the palmyra (*borassus flabellifer*, called *tāla* in Sanskrit); various barks, including that of the birch (*betula utilis*, *bhoja* or *bhūrja* in Sanskrit) and that of the aloe (*aquilaria agallocha, sāñci* in Sanskrit); cotton; and paper. A few words on each of these.

The palmyra (*borassus*) is also a species of palm. Its leaves are smaller than those of corypha: the longest reach about twenty inches, and the broadest about two. This difference in size gives a useful way to tell which leaves a particular manuscript is written on, for apart from size it's difficult to tell the prepared leaves of the two species apart. *Borassus* is apparently not native to India (it may have been introduced from Africa), and it grows happily much further north than *corypha*—at least to the twenty-seventh parallel, not far south of Delhi.

On the basis of direct examination of 130 manuscripts in the 1890s (and on the basis of assumptions about the material of many others not directly seen, assumptions based mostly upon their reported dimensions) A. F. R. Hoernle drew the following conclusions about the geographical and temporal distribution of the use of these two kinds of leaf for writing. First, in North India (north of the twentieth parallel) virtually all manuscripts before 1675 are *corypha;* none that can reliably be dated before 1600 has been shown to be *borassus*. He concludes that *borassus* leaves were not used at all for book writing in northern India before the end of the sixteenth century, and were not widely used before 1675. Even when palmyra leaves did begin to be used, it was only in Bengal, Bihar, and parts of Orissa, that is to say in the northeastern parts of India, after 1600. The use of *borassus* almost completely superseded *corypha* in these parts of India until paper became the dominant material after the end of the eighteenth century. By contrast, in western India only *corypha* leaves were ever used for book writing until the appearance of paper in the thirteenth century.

On birch bark, Alberuni, the Muslim ethnographer and observer of Indian manners, had this to say in the eleventh century:

> In Central and Northern India people use the bark of the tuz tree, one kind of which is used as a cover for bows. It is called bhurja. They take a piece one yard long and as broad as the outstretched fingers of the hand, or somewhat less, and prepare it in various ways. They oil and polish it so as to make it hard and smooth, and then they write on it. The proper order of the single leaves is marked by numbers. The whole book is wrapped up in a piece of cloth and fastened between two tablets of the same size.[35]

It's not quite clear what Alberuni means by "Central and Northern India," but it's probable that the area he intended would have included Nālandā. It's rather less likely that birch bark would have been used as a significant medium for manuscript preparation there after the time of Harṣa, or indeed that it was ever so used for the writing of lengthy manuscripts. It's more difficult to prepare than either *borassus* or *corypha* leaves, and much more difficult to write upon. Wherever palm leaves of either type were known and available, they supplanted barks quickly and completely. After the eighth century or thereabouts, only in extreme northerly areas like Kashmir was birch bark still used for writing manuscripts.

Cotton (*paṭa*), suitably stiffened with paste, was also used in some areas, though apparently not widely. There are relatively few surviving instances, the earliest from the eighth century. Paper making was learned from the Chinese by Arabs after the conquest of Samarkand in 751 (Alberuni gives an account of this), though it was known and paper was used for writing much earlier than this in Central Asia. Paper manuscripts have been found at various sites there, the earliest of which may be second or third century; and the cache of paper manuscripts found at Gilgit certainly shows that it was being used in the Himalayan regions by the sixth century. But there is no evidence at all for its use anywhere on the Indian subcontinent until the eleventh century, and no substantial evidence for its use in Central or South India until colonial times. Palm leaves were still being used for writing manuscripts in places as widely separated as Bihar and Tamil Nadu in the late nineteenth century; and the Sanskrit word for paper (*kāgada*) is a modern coinage, derived from the Persian *kaghaz*.

Palm leaves, then, were the main medium. There are two methods of writing on them. The first uses a reed pen (*lekhani*) with ink (*maṣī*) to write directly on the surface of the palm (hence the use of verbs derived from *likh-* for writing). The second uses an iron stylus (*lohakaṇṭaka*) to incise letters into the surface of the leaf; the incised leaf is then brushed with ink and cleaned with sand, leaving ink only in the incisions. The former method works better with the *corypha*, which takes ink well; the latter is easier with the *borassus*, which accepts ink directly onto its surface less easily even after curing and preparation. Writing with *lekhani* and *maṣī* on a *corypha* leaf doesn't produce much absorption of ink, so it's possible to wash a leaf that's been written on and then to write something new on it. This gives rise to the possibility of palimpsests. All *corypha* manuscripts from North India are written with pen and ink; but those from South India (both *corypha* and *borassus*) are much more commonly written with incision. Once written, a manuscript's leaves usually had a hole bored through the middle and were strung on a cord (*sūtra* or *naḍi*) and protected by wooden covers placed at top and bottom of the pile. The term *pustaka* (Hindi *pothi*) is used for the whole object—leaves plus cord plus cover.

All this strongly suggests that those who wrote manuscripts for storage in the libraries of Nālandā and Vikramaśilā, or for enshrining in stupas or placing inside statues, would have used pens and ink to write on prepared leaves of *corypha umbraculifera*; that once written, the leaves would have been strung together and protected by some covering; and (given where Nālandā was) that the unprepared *corypha* leaves would have been brought there from several hundred miles to the south.

Rājaśekhara, in the *Kāvyamīmāṃsā* (composed, recall, most probably in the tenth century), provides an interesting list of materials that poets should have to hand when they compose.[36] They need, he says, a board suitable for being written upon with chalk (*samputikā saphalakakhaṭikā*); palm leaves or birch bark suitable for being written upon with ink (*salekhanīkamaṣībhājanāni taḍipatrāṇi bhūrjatvaco vā*); palm leaves prepared for being incised with a metal stylus (*salohakaṇṭakāni tāladalāni*); and well-cleaned flat surfaces (*susaṃsṛṣṭā bhittayaḥ*, perhaps smooth walls) capable of being written upon. This confirms what is known from surviving manuscripts, a summary of which I've just given; but it adds, interestingly, the use of chalkboards—perhaps for trying out some lines of thought or phrases before recording them more permanently on one of the other media? It's not surprising, of course, that no examples of such jottings survive. It's interesting, too, that Rājaśekhara seems to imagine that a poet-composer would also be a writer, not that (as some other evidence suggests) a member of the scribal caste (*kayasthā*) would have done the business of writing to the poet's dictation.[37] Perhaps practice on this varied.

The ideal writer's workshop described by Rājaśekhara is probably not very different from that of a writer at Nālandā under Harṣa or the Pālas. It remains now only to ask what helps for the reader a typical manuscript prepared in North or Central India between the eighth and the eleventh century might have had. Would it have had features of layout or punctuation or organization that suggest ease of use for reference or private (and silent) reading?

Different scripts were used in different parts of India; I'll say nothing about the complicated set of questions surrounding those issues since they're not relevant to my interests here. What is relevant is the practices standardly used to represent Sanskrit words when ink and palm leaf are the media for such representation, and about these some useful generalizations can be made. First, there is almost no white space (or, given the color of a prepared corypha leaf, light brown space). Margins are small; there is space left for a binding hole, which is most often in the leaf's center; and that is all. There are no spaces, typically, between words: letters are written in a single unbroken string until a mark of punctuation stops their march, which may not be for as much as two lines, and this on a palm leaf where the length of a line may be twenty-five to thirty inches. When marks of punctuation are used (which is far from always), they are typically limited to the single *daṇḍa*, a vertical line somewhat similar in function to the period in written English. There are usually no devices used to show emphasis: no change in size of letters, no underlining, no distinction between upper and lower case. The typical palm leaf, then, contains an almost unbroken mass of black letters: even for someone at home with the script used and the scribal hand in which it is presented, these are not objects to scan. They cannot be read quickly (neither could a page of typeset English with no word breaks, no paragraph markers, no variations in type size, and only the occasional period). The most natural way of reading them, if they are read at all, is by vocalizing: sounding the phonemes as their written forms come before your eyes, so that you can understand where the words break, and as a result can begin to get the sense.

Changes in these conventions developed only very slowly. Substantially the same methods of display are evident even in paper manuscripts from the seventeenth century and later.[38] Not all palm leaf manuscripts show this lack of visual aids for the reader; some, for instance, are heavily illustrated.[39] But my impression is (and since almost all palm-leaf manuscripts from the first millennium no longer exist, no one will ever know for sure) that the conventions I've described were dominant.

My imaginative sketch of the ideal-typical pedagogical situation at Nālandā under the Pālas is supported by this summary investigation into the material culture of bookmaking in a number of ways. First, the material conditions under which copies of manuscripts were made guarantee that they would have been expensive and scarce. The raw material (*corypha* leaves) wasn't local and had to be imported; and, of course, the enterprise of copying is very labor-intensive. These factors would have been offset to some extent by the fact that sponsoring the copying of manuscripts was seen as a meritorious act, and this would have encouraged at least some wealthy lay people to pay for it (though, of course, not necessarily to read what they had paid to have made, nor to intend that anyone else should read it). But still, the sheer expense of producing copies makes it very unlikely that all thirty members of my imaginary class at Nālandā would have had a copy of the work being studied on their laps. But the second reason is probably still more important. The palm-leaf manuscripts that would have been available at Nālandā in the Pāla period (and indeed throughout its existence) weren't objects intended as tools of reference for private readers. Their physical characteristics preclude any such use. They may have been used as cues for vocalizing their content; but even then, given their appearance, they would have been much less effective as such cues than would matter written on the pages of the memory.

The principal significance of manuscripts at Nālandā (and throughout Buddhist India) had therefore not to do with their pegodagical use but with the significance of their presence. Whether stored in a library, enshrined in a stupa, or lying on the lap of a teacher, they represent the word of the Buddha by their presence. They are the *buddhavacana* that is also the *dharmakāya*, the body of doctrine: they are a mode of Buddha's presence, and so it matters that they be present, but not that they be read. The training of specialist religious readers at Nālandā did not occur by way of manuscripts, at least not principally: it occurred by hearing, memorizing, and pondering.

That this is the case is supported by the only study I know that treats the question of how Indian Buddhist scholastics quoted their sources—the question, that is, of what the use of devices that suggest quotation (*punaḥ sa evāha, ity uktam*, and so forth) actually implies about the relation of the words so signaled to words in the source quoted. The study is by Ernst Steinkellner, and it analyses Kamalaśīla's quotations of his Naiyāyika opponents (mostly Uddyotakara) in his commentary to Śāntarakṣita's *Tattvasaṅgraha* [Digest of Truth] (all these individuals were active in India between the sixth and the ninth centuries).[40] Steinkellner finds that Kamalaśīla sometimes quotes verbatim, but much more often his quotations represent the gist of the work he's representing, or a digest of its content, rather than its actual words. Steinkellner makes an attempt to discern why Kamalaśīla sometimes quotes verbatim and sometimes does not, but I am not interested in those suggestions so much as in the fact that it's not possible to tell from the presence of quotation markers whether the matter enclosed by them comes verbatim from its source. In many cases, perhaps the majority, it does not; I suspect that this is generally true of scholastic literature from the classical period of Buddhism in India, and it will be important to bear it in mind in reading the studies of particular Buddhist works to follow.

Steinkellner is not interested in questions about the material culture of bookmaking and book use in classical India. But in the case of Kamalaśīla's quotations of Uddyotakara's *Nyāyavārttika* [Nyāya Commentary] it's important to ask them.

The *Nyāyavārttika* is a long work; four or five hundred palm leaves at the least would be required for a complete copy, and, given what I've said about the conventions governing the representation of Sanskrit on palm leaves, these would have been without word divisions, largely without punctuation, and certainly without other place-finding aids. Kamalaśīla quotes (verbatim and otherwise) from widely separate parts of the work. Are we to imagine him turning over the palm leaves, trying to find his place? Or are we to imagine him consulting the pages of his memory? Neither scenario, perhaps, is free from difficulty; but if there is a balance of probability, it leans toward the latter rather than the former. If you think otherwise and want to offer arguments for your intuitions, you'll have to do so by showing how the material culture of bookmaking in classical India could have permitted, practically speaking, the use of a lengthy Sanskrit manuscript as a work of reference. This seems to me no easy task.

This broad picture of textual teaching and learning in Buddhist India and of the material culture of the book within which it occurred may be further illuminated by a close examination of some particular works. In what follows I shall take four works, two commentaries and two anthologies, and ask of them a series of formal questions based upon the genre analyses given in chapter 4. I am not in a position (perhaps no one is) to say how representative the works chosen are. I chose them because they meet the following rather simple (and entirely contingent) criteria: they were composed in India and in Sanskrit by Buddhists between (roughly) the first and the eleventh century of the Christian era; there are printed editions (I am no palaeographer); and these editions are available to me. I hope the works are representative; they will at least be illustrative.

The four works are *Sūtrasamuccaya* [Anthology of Sacred Works], *Śikṣāsamuccaya* [Anthology of Instruction], *Triṃśikābhāṣya* [Exegetical Commentary on the Thirty Verses], and *Sāratamā* [The Supreme Essence] (also known as the Commentary on the 8,000-Perfection-of-Wisdom, *Aṣṭasāhasrikāprajñāpāramitāpañjikā*). I'll say more about each of these in the proper place; for now it will do to say that the first two are anthologies and the last two commentaries. Initially I'll question these works solely as such, without reference to what is known (or speculated) about their situation. And I'll question them throughout with an eye to what they might tell us about their ideal readers, drawing upon the questions derived from the formal analysis of these genres given in chapter 4. The goal throughout is to say what can be said about the ideal readers of these works, and to assess to what extent they are religious readers—to what extent they are interested in presenting and developing an unsurpassable, comprehensive, and central account.

Sūtrasamuccaya [Anthology of Sacred Works]

The *Sūtrasamucaya* [Anthology of Sacred Works] (SS) was composed in Sanskrit, but does not survive in the original.[41] It was translated into both Tibetan and Chinese, and both these versions survive. They both say that the work was "made" (*kṛ-*, here meaning 'compiled') by Nāgārjuna, and this attribution is supported by later Buddhist scholastics in India. Modern scholarship, as usual, isn't happy with this traditional attribution,[42] but I see no pressing reason not to assume it, and I shall do so in what follows. If the attribution is correct, and if the usual dates for Nāgārjuna are correct, the SS may date from the first or second century after Christ, and may have been compiled in South India.

Since the work does not survive in the original Sanskrit, comments on its length and structural features must of necessity be based on the Tibetan version (I cannot read Chinese). The printed edition of this version takes up 208 pages, of which perhaps one-fifth is devoted to footnotes. In the Derge (sde-dge) xylographic edition, the work occupies sixty-seven double-sided folios; converting this by the proper formula into Sanskrit syllables, we arrive at about 70,000; converting this in turn into thirty-two-syllable verses (the standard meter) we arrive at about 2,200; and at a medium-fast recitation speed of nine verses to the minute it would take a little over four hours to recite the whole work.

Assessing the number and kind of excerpts in the SS is made easy by the work of Chr. Lindtner, who, beginning from earlier work by Anukul Banerjee, provides a complete list of all sources mentioned by name in the SS, and of the number of times they are mentioned.[43] Since Nāgārjuna never provides an excerpt without saying which work it comes from, and since he mentions the name of a work only when attributing an excerpt to it, totaling the number of times each source is mentioned gives the number of excerpts in the whole work. The upshot is that Nāgārjuna provides 167 excerpts, drawn from sixty-eight different named sources. Many of the sources are excerpted only once; the largest number of excerpts comes from the generically named *Prajñāpāramitā* (nine), the *Bodhisattvapiṭaka* (eight), the *Candragarbhaparivarta* and the *Vimalakīrtinirdeśa* (seven each), the *Gaṇḍavyūhasutra* and the *Ratnarāśisūtra* (six each). The majority of the excerpts in the SS are between eight and forty lines in length in Pāsādika's edition. There are perhaps ten very short excerpts (three lines or less), and a slightly larger number of relatively lengthy excerpts (three-four pages or seventy to 100 lines). And there are three very long excerpts of about 200 lines each (61–69, 113–120, 146–154). These three excerpts together comprise almost one-eighth of the entire work.

Almost all the words in the SS belong to the excerpts; very few are the compiler's own (less than 1 percent), and most often these words are little more than a brief introductory formula that includes the name of the work from which the immediately following excerpt is taken. For example, in introducing a brief excerpt, Nāgārjuna says simply: *zla ba'i snying po'i le'u las kyang* (89) ("and from the Candragarbha"). The excerpt follows, and concludes with the words "so it is said" (*zhes gsungs so*). This is the standard form. But sometimes there are longer passages in Nāgārjuna's own words, most often when a string of excerpts on a new topic is introduced. One of the longest is this:

> Nonetheless, the Tathāgatas undertake the teaching of the doctrine [*chos bstan pa*] in many universes, and they do so by means of many vehicles [*theg pa sna tshogs kyi sgo*], not just three. [They teach] both by way of the power of monastic discipline, and by way of the the great variety of meritorious actions done by living beings. (132)

There follows at once a lengthy excerpt from the *Gaṇḍavyūhasūtra*. But these more lengthy introductory or connecting statements are the exception: there are only about ten of them in the entire SS.

Nāgārjuna almost never identifies the location of his sources with any greater specificity than providing their name; the only possible exception is when he specifies a particular section of the *Gaṇḍavyūha* (132). Sometimes, indeed, it seems that he locates an excerpt with not even this degree of precision, but only by mentioning a type or category of literature—*avadāna*, say, or *prajñāpāramitā* (2, 27, 45, 112, etc.). In the latter case, Nāgārjuna seems to mean usually either the work that we call *Aṣṭasāhasrikāprajñāpāramitāsūtra* [The Sacred Work on the Perfection of Wisdom in 8,000 Lines], or that which we call *Pañcaviṃśatisāhasrikā* (that in 25,000 lines)—but even these he is not exactly quoting (to which point I shall shortly return). While he does want to tell the users of his anthology the names of the works from which he has taken his excerpts, he does not seem concerned to provide them with sufficient information to permit or to encourage locating the excerpts in their sources.

The boundaries of Nāgārjuna's excerpts are, then, marked with clarity and precision: each is provided with a clear beginning ("In X it is said," "In Y we find") and a clear end (*zhes gsungs so/ity uktam* = close of quotation). Nāgārjuna does not indicate that he has abbreviated his excerpts; neither does he indicate that he is offering a summary, a digest, or a paraphrase. In every case, it seems, the user of the SS is presented with a complete and perfect pearl of a quotation, immediately preceded and followed by another such. But this appearance is misleading. In at least some cases, Nāgārjuna was self-consciously abbreviating and summarizing his sources, without indicating that he had done so. For example, a passage quoted from the *Vajracchedikā* is in fact a digest of two separate passages from that work, with no indication that this is so (176–177);[44] most of the phrases given in the SS are also found in the *Vajracchedikā*, but not always in the same order, and often with many lines of matter omitted. A somewhat different kind of example is a long excerpt (73–76) from the *Vimalakīrti*. This follows the order and the substance of the original,[45] but with many differences in wording and turn of phrase. And, to take a final example, the sole excerpt from the *Saptaśatikāprajñāpāramitāsūtra* once again gives the gist of its original, but omits perhaps one-fifth of it, eliding repetitions and some connecting devices (156–157).[46]

These examples appear to be typical of Nāgārjuna's methods of quotation in the SS (Śāntideva is different, as the next section will show). It's difficult to be sure, of course, since a good number of the sources from which he draws his excerpts do not survive; and there is the added difficulty that Nāgārjuna's work itself does not survive in Sanskrit, the language of its composition. My generalizations about his methods of quotation are based upon a comparison of only a few of his 167 excerpts with the works from which they were taken. Nonetheless, and with due and proper tentativeness, I think it fair to say that the excerpts that make up the SS rarely or never contain verbatim quotation as this is understood by us. The appearance of pearls on a string, altered only by a change in setting, is misleading: these pearls have not only been reset, but reshaped, ground down, and altered in both shape and size.

The last formal question to be addressed about the SS has to do with the presence in it of helps to its users: structuring devices, topic markers, indices, and so forth. There is, in effect, only one such aid, and that is the division of the work as a whole into ten parts, each of which begins with an announcement of the topic of the excerpts in that part. The topic announcement usually consists of a sentence in the indicative, followed by a question, which sometimes repeats the content of the sentence in the indicative. For example, the first topic announcement reads: "The appearance of a Buddha [*sangs rgyas 'byung ba*] is very rare [*shin tu rnyed par dka' ste*]. If one says that the appearance of a Buddha is very rare, this is known because of what is found in many sutras" (1). A string of excerpts on this topic then follows. The ten parts are of very unequal length. The first six take up only thirty-two pages of the critical edition (a little more than one-seventh of the whole), while the last (on the rarity of beings whose aspiration is turned toward the single vehicle) takes up almost half the work. Apart from these ordering devices there is nothing: no statement of purpose or intended audience; and no argument about goals.

So much for formal matters. What do these things suggest about the ideal readers of Nāgārjuna's SS? First, and with a fair amount of confidence, that they were monks. Second, that it was important for them to know that the excerpts in the SS were from works that made it reasonable to think of them as *buddhavacana*, Buddha's speech, but not that it was necessary for them to have independent access to these works, or to retrace the excerpts to their sources. There is nothing in the character of Nāgārjuna's work to suggest that a full or proper understanding of it requires independent access to the sources it quotes (in this Śāntideva's *Śikṣāsamuccaya* differs, as the next section will show): the SS stands alone as a self-contained work. That its ideal readers were meant to use it as such is also suggested by the fact that Nāgārjuna almost certainly reshaped and summarized his quotations in accord with his own interests in compiling the SS. He was not much interested (and did not expect his readers to be) in reproducing the exact words of his sources. From which it follows with a reasonable degree of probability that the ideal readers of the SS were interested in it for the nourishment it could give their religious accounts of things. The excerpts of the work are matter to be heard, learned, thought about, and meditated upon. They are prime fodder for the ruminatory religious reader, and as such will be of little interest to the contemporary scholar, except for the philological and historical information that may be gleaned from them. An apt illustration of the difference between religious and consumerist uses of this text is given by Chr. Lindtner: in his foreword to Pāsādika's edition (vi) he makes explicit the importance of the SS for philological and historical reasons; but he shows no sign of being interested in it as a religious reader, nor any of seeing that it was used by religious readers. The response of a consumerist reader to a work like this is to make a critical edition of it; that of the religious reader is to learn it by heart.

Finally, there is little in the character of the SS to suggest whether its ideal readers were meant to have a palm-leaf manuscript of it before them, to consume it with the eye; or whether they were meant to hear it, to absorb it with the ear. But the comments already made about manuscript technology in India at this period, coupled with the probable early date of the work, strongly suggest the latter scenario.

Śikṣāsamuccaya [Anthology of Instruction]

The *Śikṣāsamuccaya* [Anthology of Intstruction] (SK) is attributed to Śāntideva, who was among the more influential Indian Buddhist scholastics and intellectuals.[47] As a result much hagiography accumulated around his name,[48] and it is no longer possible to separate from these stories information that a positivistically inclined historian might think of as being historically reliable.[49] All that matters for my purposes is that Śāntideva probably lived from the last quarter of the seventh century to early in the second half of the eighth, and that he probably did much of his work at Nālandā. The SK is in classical Sanskrit (except when the works from which it takes excerpts are not).

Counting by syllables and verses, the SK contains about 192,000 syllables (6,000 verses). At the standard recitation speed of nine verses to the minute, it would take about eleven hours to recite. Almost all of it consists of excerpts from other works: my estimate is that Śāntideva's own words comprise between 3 and 5 percent of the whole work. Most of these words are very brief phrases introducing an excerpt and giving the title of the work from which it was taken, just as with Nāgārjuna's SS. But there are places where Śāntideva says more, for instance in his introductory remarks at the beginning of the whole work (3–4), and sometimes when he introduces a new topic, summarizes one just dealt with, or indicates where to find more on a topic (41, 69–70, 146, 187). There are also a few places where he offers a digest or paraphrase of what is said in some other work or works rather than a direct quotation (11–12, 66, 81, 92, 147). But even counting all questionable cases, Śāntideva's own words, as *auctor* rather than *compilator* to recall Bonaventure's way of putting things, do not amount to more than 5 percent of the whole.

Now to the excerpts themselves. By my count there are 12 of these. The exact number is uncertain because it's unclear whether some passages should be understood as excerpts or digests—whether, that is, they are direct verbatim quotations or restatements in summary form of the gist of a passage. Śāntideva sometimes strings together a number of passages from the same work, connecting them with phrases like *atraiva ca* ("also just here") or *punar apy āha* ("and he also said"). In these cases it isn't always clear whether the passages so strung are contiguous in the original (and so best counted as a single excerpt), or not (and so best counted separately). I've taken the first of these options. If anything, then, the count of 312 should be revised upward rather than downward.

About half the excerpts are in prose and half in verse. The longest is a string of 172 verses (174–185), though there are a couple of others that approach this length (131–139, 156–164). The shortest excerpt is probably *dānaṃ hi bodhisattvasya bodhiḥ* (26)—"for giving is the bodhisattva's awakening." Between these extremes there are many (dozens) of short excerpts, between one and three lines long. Probably the largest number are between four and twelve lines; and while there are not many longer than that, the great length of the few there are makes them take up a very high proportion of the whole work.

Śāntideva provides a number of helps to his readers, including some tools to order his excerpts. The first of these is a division into chapters (*pariccheda*). There are nineteen of these, each given a title intended to state its topic, and each marked with a concluding formula, such as this: *āryaśikṣāsamuccaye vandanādyanuśaṃsā saptadaśaḥ paricchedaḥ samāptaḥ* (167)—"the seventeeth chapter in the revered Anthology of Instruction, on the advantages of such things as worship, has been completed." The nineteen chapters are not of uniform length. They range from twenty pages (chapter 1) to two (chapters 2 and 10).

The second structuring device is twenty-seven verses in *śloka* form. These are scattered at irregular intervals through the work, the first four being found in the long first chapter; the fifth and sixth in chapter 2; half of the seventh in chapter 3; the other half toward the end of chapter 5, and so on. Some chapters contain as many as four of these verses, while some have none. Neither are the verses distributed evenly through the work in terms of the amount of matter that separates each: as many as thirty-five pages pass without a verse, while in one sixteen-page stretch, nine verses are found. They are slightly more evenly distributed as far as the number of excerpts separating each goes: while the longest gap between verses extends to about 20 percent of the whole work, it comprises only about 15 percent of the number of excerpts—which is to say that the longer gaps between verses are accountable in part (but only in part) by the fact that these gaps contain longer excerpts.

A final point on these structuring verses. Śāntideva nowhere says that they are his matter, and they are not always clearly signaled as verses. That is, sometimes the verses are framed by devices that clearly show what they are, and sometimes they are not. As an example of the former, verse four is immediately preceded by *katamāni ca tāni marmasthānāni yāni hi sutrānteṣu mahāyānābhiratānām arthāyoktāni yad uta* . . . (14) (and what are those essential points stated in the sutras for the benefit of those who delight in the Mahāyāna? They are . . .). The verse follows, and then is itself immediately labeled as a summation of the restraining vows to be undertaken by a bodhisattva. In cases like this, a verse is immediately recognizable as such by its context and use, as well as by its meter. But, in contrast, consider the use of the last ten syllables of verse 25:

> So much for the treatment of the constant practice of confidence for the increase of merit [*evaṃ tāvac chraddhādīnāṃ sadābhyāsaḥ puṇyavṛddhaye*]. . . . What is FRIENDLINESS [*maitrī*]? . . . And what is RECOLLECTION OF BUDDHAS AND SO FORTH [*buddhādyanusmṛtiḥ*]? . . . [There follows a series of verses from the *Rāṣṭrapālasūtra*]. (169)

In a case like this there is no way for users of the SK to recognize the words in upper case as belonging to the structuring verses—not metrically, because not enough of them is quoted; and not by context, either. The only way to recognize these words as part of one of Śāntideva's *saṅgrahaślokāḥ* (structuring verses) is by already knowing (having in mind or to hand) these verses. More on this in a moment.

As to other helps to the reader: there is no table of contents or index of works cited. There are, though, a number of other kinds of help. The first is the occasional connecting or summary statements scattered through the work. These seem designed to remind the reader which topic is under discussion, or which has just been completed and which is just about to begin. A good example (among the more lengthy) is the following passage that opens the ninth chapter:

> Guarding in this way [i.e., in the way just described] against immoral behavior, which is full of anguish [*bahuduḥkha*] and conducive to lack of restraint [*aviratapravṛtta*], and removing the bonds of the obstacles that consist in action [*karmāvaraṇanibandha*], the practitioner should restrain himself so that his passions might be purified [*kleśaviśodhane prayateta*]. In this connection, he should begin by being PATIENT [*kṣameta*], for one who is not patient loses energy for such things as religious reading [*śrutādau vīryaṃ pratihanyate*] because he gets tired of it. And one who has not read religiously is aware neither of the means to attain concentration [*samādhyupāya*], nor of those to purify the passions. Therefore, one who is not tired of it SHOULD UNDERTAKE RELIGIOUS READING [*śrutam eṣeta*], for even for one who is aware [of the proper means], and yet lives in company, becoming concentrated is difficult. THEN HE SHOULD GO TO THE FOREST, and even there, since the mind of someone not deeply engaged in calming distraction [*vikṣepa-praśamanānabhiyukta*] is not concentrated, HE SHOULD ENGAGE HIMSELF WITH CONCENTRATION. And since concentration is not obtained otherwise than on the basis of the purification of passion, HE SHOULD DEVELOP MEDITATION ON THE IMPURE THINGS [*bhāvayed aśubhādikam*]. So much for these statements about the purification of passion. Now the exposition follows. (100)

A number of interesting things are going on in this passage. First, Śāntideva connects what is to come in the ninth chapter (at the opening of which this passage stands) with what has just been treated in the eighth, whose announced (and to some extent actual) topic was *pāpaśodhana*, purification from actions and attitudes that are not meritorious. In saying this, Śāntideva is providing an explanation of the order of matter in his work: a help to its readers. But he is also explaining, phrase by phrase (those words in upper case) his own summary verse as a way to make these connections, and indicating ("So much for these statements about the purification of passion") that he is doing so. More in a moment on what this suggests about the use of Śāntideva's verses by the SK's ideal readers.

Another kind of help that Śāntideva provides his readers is in his own introductory statement about the nature of his work. He begins by extolling the benefits of hearing the jewel of the doctrine (*dharmaratna*) and the dangers of not hearing it (which include the suffering of being burnt in the consuming fires of hell), and encouraging his hearers to pay close attention because today they can hear (religiously read) the jewel of the doctrine, which is very hard to get hold of. Then he says:

> After doing humble reverence to the Buddhas with their followers and their bodies of doctrine [*dharmakāya*], and to all those worthy of worship, without

> exception. I will state this introduction to the discipline of those who follow the Buddhas [*sugatātmajasamvarāvatāra*] using beneficial passages that have been excerpted [*samuccitārthavākya*). Here I say nothing that has not been said before [*na ca kiṃcid apūrvam atra vācyam*], and I have no skill in compilation [*samgrathanakauśala*). (3)

The formulaic rejection of the importance of novelty and even of the compiler's skill at compiling are part of the conventional wisdom of the religious reader. But it is striking to see them in such stark form here. Śāntideva presents his work as entirely unoriginal, and as all the better for it.

Yet another kind of help that Śāntideva provides his readers is evident in his identification of sources from which he has excerpted his *arthavākyas*, his meaningful and useful blooms. He identifies by name 104 of these, usually citing the name of the work from which an excerpt is taken immediately before the excerpt. Some sources are mentioned many times (e.g., the *Candrapradīpasūtra* gets twenty-five mentions), but the majority are mentioned and excerpted only once or twice. Śāntideva's ideal readers are, therefore, expected to need to know the source of any bloom with which they are presented. But identification of a source by name is usually as far as his help goes; only very occasionally does he mention a particular section or part of a work. For instance, he identifies one excerpt as coming from the *Jñānaparivarta* [Section on Awareness] (175), which (though he does not say so) is a part of the *Samādhirājasūtra*. But this level of specificity is very much the exception. Even when there was a standard division of a long work into parts or sections (as with the tenfold division of the *Daśabhūmikasūtra*), Śāntideva rarely cites it. There are, also, odd occasions when he doesn't provide even this relatively minimal help in identifying the source of an excerpt: sometimes he gives a verse or prose excerpt without saying where it is from (32, 66, 75, 145), even though it is signaled as a quotation. But this too is rare.

Śāntideva's general practice, then, is to identify the source of his excerpts, even if not with all the precision available to him, and to mark the boundaries of each excerpt with precision and clarity. But sometimes the SK's relationship to its sources is a bit more complicated than that evident in this standard and simple form. Consider the following passage:

> The ten paths of bad action are evil. In the *Saddharmasmṛtyupasthāna* it is evident that their fruition is bitter. From that work only a portion of the sacred work is set forth (*tataḥ kiṃciñ mātraṃ sūtram sūcyate*), beginning with the result of taking sentient life. On that he says . . . (42)

The excerpt that follows is long, but Śāntideva wants his readers to know that he is giving only a portion of it. Similarly, he sometimes tells his readers that there is more information on a topic in the source he has just excerpted, or that he has abbreviated a passage (66, 81). He also uses the standard Sanskrit device to signal matter omitted from a quotation (*peyyālam*, 12, 16, 29–30, 143).[50]

When the SK does quote directly (rather than summarizing or abbreviating) it generally does so verbatim. It's impossible to establish this finally and fully, of course, because many of the sources excerpted by Śāntideva either do not survive at all, or do not survive in the original. But where I have been able to check Śāntideva's quotations against printed editions of the sources he excerpts, there is always a verbatim correspondence (or very nearly so).

But Śāntideva represents his sources in other ways than by direct quotation. He provides digests, glancing references, and (as I've already shown) pointers to places where more information can be found. Consider the following passage:

> The teaching is just as already set forth. But teaching on one's own and others' nonmeritorious actions is found in the revered *Akṣayamatisūtra*, in the treatment of the accumulation of merit. Delight [is treated in] the *Bhadracaryāgāthā*, or in the section on delight in the *Candrapradīpa*. Eager seeking [is treated in] the same *Bhadracaryā*. The transformation [of merit] is completely treated in the same revered *Bhadracaryā*, or one might look [at the treatment] of [merit]-transformation in the *Vajradhvaja*. (153)

This is rather like a contemporary academic footnote beginning 'vide' or 'confer', and then giving a list of sources. There are other such passages (e.g., 100).

This is about as far as a formal analysis of the SK can take us. What now can be said on the basis of this analysis about its ideal readers? I'll begin with the obvious and work up to the more speculative. First, then, the work's ideal readers are monks, and monks who are at the relatively early stages of their training. Many of the excerpts require a monastic setting; and Śāntideva tells us himself that the SK is of special benefit for those beginning their training—for *śikṣārambhakas* (3).

Next, the ideal readers benefit not just from the matter given in the excerpts, tasty and nourishing though this is; they benefit also from knowing its source, the name of the work from which a particular excerpt is taken. Knowing that an excerpt is drawn from a sutra suffices to show that it is the Buddha's speech, and so evokes in its readers the proper attitude of reverence—in this the SK is like the SS. But an important difference is that Śāntideva's ideal readers are expected to have access to the works from which he has drawn his excerpts independently of their presence in the SK. Recall that Śāntideva sometimes abbreviates his excerpts and indicates that he has done so in such a way that suggests consultation of the original would be beneficial. Recall also that he sometimes indicates, without giving it, where further information on a topic may be found. This strongly suggests that independent access to these works is the ideal case, even if not the actual one. There were no such indications in the SS.

Next, the SK's ideal readers have memorized the twenty-seven verses that provide one of its ordering devices. And they have done this before they begin to read the whole work. If this is not the case, and the work is read from a printed page or a palm leaf without prior memorization, then the twenty-seven verses have no useful function: it's next to impossible even to recognize them for what they are, and they can serve only as a puzzlement and a distraction. They are separated out from the body of the work in the printed editions, of course, and indicated by various typographical devices. But none of this would have been the case in the palm-leaf manuscripts that were the only way to store the work in physical form for many centuries after its composition.

More can be said on this matter, though somewhat more speculatively. It's likely that the ideal readers of the SK heard it from the mouths of their teachers rather than pored over a manuscript. This would accord with the standard pedagogical practices of the time and place, so far as we can ascertain them; it accords, too, with the formal properties of the work. The SK's ideal readers, then, would first have learned the twenty-seven structuring verses, and then have received the rest of the work, bloom by bloom, from the mouths of their teachers, until each bloom was safely stored in memory for later rumination.

I've said that the ideal readers of the SK were expected to have independent access to the works excerpted in it. But how could they have had such access? There are only three possibilities: they could have memorized these works themselves; they could have had access to a teacher or teachers who had done so; or they could have had access to a library in which manuscripts of these works were stored. The first option can safely be ruled out. Those who already have in their heads the 104 sutras excerpted by Śāntideva do not need the SK. They might need a work that presents the practices of the path in the order given them in the SK; they might even need a work that points them to the relevant pieces of the works in their heads; but they do not need the excerpts in full, for they already have them. The third option (the library) is possible; but very few monasteries would have possessed such a library at the time, given the enormous expense of creating and preserving manuscripts. And this means that very few actual readers of the SK would have had access to one (though perhaps those at Nālandā did). The mode of reference that Śāntideva adopts also makes use of manuscripts to locate passages mentioned (but not quoted) in the SK unlikely. As I've said, he rarely provides even the degree of precision in locating an excerpt that would have been possible for him, and the task of finding a two- or three-line excerpt in its original context in a lengthy palm-leaf manuscript with no more information than that it's there somewhere would have been no easier for an eighth-century reader than for me—which is to say, exceedingly difficult. The most likely option, then, is the second, according to which ideal readers of the SK could have had independent access to the works excerpted therein through the memories and mouths of a teacher or teachers who had studied them and stored them in memory. This fits with what's known about the standard pedagogical practice of the time. It fits, also, with the cues in the SK itself, especially the location of excerpts by title alone. It is easier (still not easy, but easier) to locate a brief extract in a large work stored in memory by the kinds of random-access techniques described in chapter 2 than it is to locate it in a manuscript or a printed book. So the ideal-typical situation, I imagine, was one in which a reader of the SK who wanted to know what more is said in the *Candrapradīpa*, for example, on the perfection of patience, and who had not read this work, would consult a teacher whose lineage had entrusted the work to him, and who had it at memorial command.

Actual readers are often very far from ideal readers. And it's important to say that although the SK does strongly suggest that its ideal readers should have independent access to the works it excerpts, the vast bulk of it can be read with profit and understanding if this is not the case. It probably was not the case (as it is not now) for many readers of the work in classical India, and yet no doubt many of them profited, as religious readers, from their reading of it nonetheless.

It remains to ask whether the SK's ideal readers are religious readers. The answer must be an emphatic affirmative. This is not a bouquet of flowers for botanists or for Lockean writers; it is one for Buddhists who need flowers to smell, gobbets to chew over. It is self-consciously at the service of a particular religious account of things, and that account is not framed by historical or antiquarian or other positivist interests that require only its mention and not its use. Śāntideva uses the account he presents, and the fact that some of his interests (such as verbatim quotation and source reference) are evident also in anthologies intended for consumerist readers (like the *Oxford Dictionary of Quotations*) does not mean that the ideal readers of his works are consumerists. He is not interested in making possible a journey back into the past for antiquarians; neither does he want to enable the production of more of those works of the imagination that we call histories. The SK is the work of a religious reader and is designed for other religious readers; its fundamental goal is to make good Buddhists better.

Triṃśikābhāṣya [Exegetical Commentary on the Thirty Verses]

The *Triṃśikābhāṣya* [Exegetical Commentary on the Thirty Verses] (TBh) is exactly what its title suggests: a prose commentary upon a verse work.[51] The verse work, the *Triṃśikā*, is attributed by most Buddhist traditions to Vasubandhu, the great scholastic thinker and systematizer who may have lived in the fourth century. The commentary is attributed to Sthiramati, one of the more prolific composers of commentaries in Buddhist India. Buddhist historians in both China and Tibet connect him with Nālandā (among other places), and locate him in the seventh century, at the time of Harṣa (and Xuanzang).[52] Western scholars have tended, upon the basis of epigraphic evidence, to date him earlier, making him a contemporary of the monarch Guhasena, whose reign probably ended about AD 570.[53] The verses, together with their commentary, survive in Sanskrit.

What characteristics do these verses have? Saying something about this will be important in elucidating how the commentary achieves its goals. Each verse is in regular *śloka*-meter (eight syllables per quarter-verse), and in standard classical Sanskrit. Here is an English rendering of the first three verses, with the end of each half-verse marked with a slash (to represent the *daṇḍa*):

> There is a manifold metaphorical application of 'self' and 'things' [*ātmadharmopacāra*] / It has the transformation of consciousness [*vijñānapariṇāma*) as its locus, and this transformation is threefold / Maturation, what is called thinking [*manana*], and the representation of a domain [*vijñaptiviṣaya*) / Among these, maturation is that consciousness called store [*ālaya*]; it is the container of all seeds / This comprises representations of place and acts of appropriation that are not brought to awareness / It is always connected with contact, attention, knowledge, conceptualization, and intention. (13)

It should be fairly clear that the verses aren't meant to be read alone—not, anyway, if you want to understand them. While they make approximate grammatical and syntactical sense, meaning is usually far from clear. There are difficulties with pronoun-reference ("it" after the first stroke? "these" after the second?); there are obvious difficulties with technical terms ("transformation," "maturation," "representation," and so forth); and there is a complete and dramatic absence of helps to the reader—no announcement of topic, no overview of what's to come, no statement of goals. This isn't to say that the *Triṃśikā* is without meaning; it's only to say that the meaning it has does not lie close to the surface, and that this was perfectly evident to its composer (Vasubandhu, if it was he). The ideal reader of these verses needs to possess much knowledge and skill that is nowhere mentioned in them. Part of the required knowledge is found in the commentary, and I'll return to a consideration of how the ideal reader might have used the verses after taking a look at what the commentary does with them.

The commentary is in classical Sanskrit prose. In the edition I've used it extends to thirty pages with an average of twenty-nine lines to the page and about thirty syllables to the line. This comes to a total of about 26,000 syllables, equivalent to something over 800 verses; at the usual medium-fast recitation speed of nine verses to the minute, the whole work could be recited in about an hour and a half. It is, then, a relatively short work: about one-fifth the length of the SK, for instance. To put this another way: all the verses of the *Triṃśikā* are incorporated into the commentary in their proper order, which means that about one-eighth of the whole consists of the verses, and seven-eighths of prose exposition. But the expository prose is not distributed equally among the verses. Sometimes there are long stretches in which no verse is quoted (16–18, 30–33), and sometimes the prose of the commentary is interrupted every seven or eight lines by a verse or part of one (34–37). Every verse (and almost every word of every verse) is commented upon; but some comments are no more than brief word glosses, while others are relatively lengthy disquisitions.

In terms of the criteria of chapter 4, then, the TBh is clearly a commentary. It is a metawork whose order and structure are given to it by those of the work to which it is a metawork; and it represents all of the work around which it is structured by direct verbatim quotation.

Sthiramati does explain his own goals in composing his commentary, or at least he says what he hopes his analysis will achieve. He wants, proximately, to demonstrate the truth of a particular philosophical thesis (that there is no enduring principle of identity in persons or things, *pudgaladharmanairātmya*), and ultimately to remove the passions and attachments attendant upon holding views other than this (15). He does not say that he wants to explain the verses around which his commentary is constructed; he seems to have seen his goal in philosophical and soteriological terms rather than in commentarial ones, and so his remarks on this are not of much help in understanding how he saw his activity as a commentator.

Some examples will help to clarify Sthiramati's commentarial method. He does three sorts of things. First, he offers explanations of individual words from the verses, or of the syntax of a particular verse. Second, he offers explanations with a broader structural focus, showing why the author of the verses introduces a particular topic at just this point, and how the matter at hand relates to questions just treated, or to those about to come up. And third, he offers extensive discussion of some question raised by the verses (as he interprets them), sometimes engaging and offering arguments against opposing views on whatever the question is.

Here's an example of the first kind of comment, with some elements also of the second:

> The threefold transformation that was mentioned is not yet itself made clear. So in order to enumerate its divisions [Vasubandhu] said: "Maturation, what is called thinking, and the representation of a domain." This means that the three divisions of transformation are called, respectively, maturation, thinking, and the representation of a domain. Among these, maturation is the continuation of the results [of action] in accord with what issues from the power of the complete maturity of the tendencies; these in turn come from good or bad acts. The afflicted organ of thought is what is called thinking, because its nature is ceaselessly to think. The representation of a domain refers to consciousness in its six aspects, among which the first is the visual; this is because each of these appears as a sensory domain, among which the first is physical form. (18–19)

A full explanation of the substance of Sthiramati's comments would be lengthy and would divert attention from what's important at this stage of the investigation. So it will have to suffice to say that Sthiramati is dealing with some fairly technical parts of the philosophical psychology specific to Yogācāra Buddhism. Formally, though, matters are simpler. Sthiramati begins by explaining what the topic of the first half of the second verse of the *Triṃśikā* is (the enumeration of the three kinds of transformation), and why it needs to be introduced here (because it's necessary for a full understanding of the concept of transformation). These are broadly structural comments: they suggest the importance for the ideal reader of keeping the flow of the argument in mind, of thinking both back and forward through the whole work.

After quoting the half-verse, Sthiramati then takes up in due order the exegesis of each of the three phrases in it. Again, the substance of what he has to say lies outside my interest here; but formally, these are narrow word- and phrase-specific explanations that do not look beyond the immediate context.

These two kinds of explanation together make up the bulk of the TBh. There is, for example, a section of it that offers little more than definitional glosses upon a long list of terms for kinds of mental event that occur in the verses (25–33). But there are also many other instances of structural comments. For example:

> The transformation that is maturation, together with its detailed analysis [*savibhāga*], has been described. Now, he [Vasubandhu] speaks of the second transformation, "that which is called thinking" (v2b), beginning with the words "based upon that, it functions" (v5b). Here, although it is established that for the sensory consciousnesses (visual and the rest), the sense organs (the eye and the rest) are the basis, and the sense objects (physical form and the rest) are the objects, no bases and objects are established in the same way for the afflicted organ of thought. But since consciousness without objects and bases is not proper [*na ca*

> *vijñānam āśrayālambananirapekṣaṃ yujyate*], [Vasubandhu] said [what follows] in order to establish what is the basis and what the object of the afflicted organ of thought, and in order to establish its meaning. (22)

Prescinding once again from the substance of this passage, there are some interesting formal features. First, Sthiramati refers both forward and back, to a verse not yet discussed or quoted in his commentary (v5b in the translation just given), and to one long since quoted and discussed (v2b). This strongly suggests that Sthiramati assumes the ideal reader to have access to all thirty verses from the beginning of his commentary, and not just to the verse being quoted and discussed at the moment. Structural comments like the one just translated require, in order for them to make sense and be useful, that their readers have in mind the shape and order of the whole of the work commented upon—or at least that they can rapidly get access to the earlier and later parts of the work referred to. If I'm reading a commentary upon the Gospel of Mark, and upon reaching Peter's confession in chapter 8 I find that the commentator refers me both back to chapter 2 (where it has been foreshadowed) and forward to chapter 15 (where it will be recapitulated), I will, in order to find such a comment useful, need either already to know the whole Gospel, or to have a copy open before me. So also with Sthiramati's reference back to verse two and forward to verse five.

But there's still more implied in this passage. The quotation from verse two that I've enclosed in quotation marks in my translation is in fact not explicitly signaled as a quotation in the work; it is embedded in the sentence without the use of the usual particle (*iti*) that marks quotations. In this it differs from the quotation from verse five, which is so marked. But ideal readers are obviously meant to recognize the phrase from verse two as such; and since it is not marked, the only way they can do so is to have verse two in their memories. This strongly suggests that the kind of access to the thirty verses of the *Triṃśikā* presupposed by structural comments of the kind I've quoted is mnemonic. Ideal readers have learned the thirty verses before studying the commentary, and the Steinerian resonant manifold that is their mind vibrates in the proper manner when a phrase from one of the verses is quoted. They are not scanning a bundle of palm leaves, wondering whether what's just been said is scratched somewhere there.

In general, Sthiramati does mark his quotations from the verses as such, prefacing them with *āha* (he said), or some other verb of saying or showing, and ending them with *iti*. But he doesn't always do so. In addition to the example just mentioned, the last twenty-one syllables of the seventh verse (this is also one of the rare cases in which Sthiramati takes as his unit for exposition something other than the quarter-verse, the half-verse, or the whole verse) are simply incorporated into a sentence without being marked (24; compare 40–41, where verses 22–23 are quoted without mark). In this case it would be difficult for hearers of the commentary to know that a verse was being quoted unless they already had the verses memorized; and it would be even harder for a reader of palm-leaf manuscripts. So while Sthiramati's methods of quotation are generally compatible with the use of the commentary by readers who do not have independent access to the verses he is expounding, there are enough exceptions strongly to suggest that this is not the typical situation for the use of the TBh.

What, then, of this work's ideal readers? They are people (men almost certainly and monks very probably) being trained in a particular scholastic tradition whose topic (at least in this work) is fundamental ontology, by which I mean a detailed and precise analysis of the kinds of things there are in the world, of the properties they share, of those that individuate one from another, and of the lexicon of technical terms that enables discussion of these matters within the constraints of the relevant tradition. They have memorized the verses of the *Triṃśikā* before beginning the study of the commentary; and it is likely that they hear the commentary rather than read it from a bundle of palm leaves, and that they hear it within a frame of further oral exposition. All this coheres well with what is known about the mechanics of teaching and learning in Buddhist India. It is also probable (though there is no clear evidence either from within or without the work) that the commentary was composed and given its first display without the use of writing: that the written objects (palm-leaf manuscripts) that we use for making our printed editions were produced for storage rather than for display, and that they are products subsequent to and consequent upon Sthiramati's aural display of the work.

Were the ideal readers of the TBh religious readers? Certainly they were in terms of their reading practices as I've just sketched them: they have read and savored the juicy morsels of the *Triṃśikā*'s verses until these are stored memorially to be ruminated at will. As a result, they have furnished a resonant manifold for later religious reading of commentaries like the TBh. But I've also said that religious readers typically use their reading in the service of developing and nurturing a comprehensive, unsurpassable, and central account of things, and it's not so obviously or immediately the case that the ideal readers of the TBh were so using it. The work itself deals with ontology, and does so in scholastic mode; by itself it does not offer a religious account of things so much as a sketch of and a lexicon for an ontological system. But this system can very well be a part of a properly religious account; and if the TBh is put together with the other works that were most likely read by its readers, it is entirely reasonable to think of it in just this way: as containing part of a religious account.

Sāratamā [The Supreme Essence]

The *Sāratamā* [The Supreme Essence] (SU) calls itself a *pañjikā* (a word commentary, perhaps) on the *Āryāṣṭasāhasrikāprajñāpāramitāsūtra* [Sacred Work on the Perfection of Wisdom in 8,000 Lines, hereinafter simply '8,000'].[54] Both the surviving manuscripts attribute it to Ratnākaraśānti, an attribution that later Buddhist scholars and historians largely, though not unanimously, support. This man, if the tradition is to be relied upon (and there is no particular reason to doubt it), flourished in the first half of the eleventh century and was in charge of Vikramaśilā, a translocal institution of Buddhist learning in North-Central India not too different from Nālandā (though probably not so large). He may have been a disciple of Naropa and a contemporary of Prajñākaramati.[55] It's probable, then, that the SU was composed toward the end of the period in which the translocal (indeed, international, transcontinental) monastic institutions of Buddhist India were able to flourish.

The work was composed in classical Sanskrit. Using the measures already mentioned, it must originally have contained about 243,000 syllables, which is equivalent to about 7,600 verses; it would have taken about fourteen hours to chant at the usual nine-verse-per-minute rate. This means that it is about one-third as long again as the SK, about nine times as long as the TBh, and almost four times as long as the SS.

What of the work upon which the SU is a commentary? This is a little complex. As I've said, the work describes itself as a word commentary upon the 8,000; this is a long work (longer than the SU) that calls itself a sutra, and that is one among many works of different lengths that call themselves "Perfection of Wisdom" (*prajñāpāramitā*). The 8,000 version is divided into thirty-two chapters; so also is the SU: the structure and order of the latter is therefore provided by the former, and in this sense the latter is a metawork to the former. This relation is evident also in the fact that parts of the former are quoted verbatim in the latter and given exposition there (although only a small proportion of the 8,000's matter is so quoted, as is obvious by the fact that the 8,000 is longer than the SU; I'll return to this question in a moment). So it is proper to call the SU a commentary upon the 8,000 according to the terms of chapter 4.

But there is a third work that interposes itself, as it were, between the SU and the 8,000. This third work is called *Abhisamayālaṅkāra* [Ornament of Realization, abbreviated as AA], and is best understood as a "condensed table of contents"[56] for the perfection of wisdom literature as a whole. The AA contains 273 verses in *śloka*-meter. These verses do not directly quote the matter of the 8,000 (or the other specimens of perfection of wisdom literature); instead, they give a very summary presentation of the entire content of that literature, a presentation meant to be used as a guide in studying it but that does not follow the order of the matter in any of the perfection of wisdom works. The AA is therefore not a commentary upon the 8,000 in the terms of chapter 4; it provides, instead, a kind of analytical digest.[57]

The verses (most of them, anyway) of the AA are, however, quoted and expounded in the SU. Indeed, one of Ratnākaraśānti's goals seems to have been to show how the matter of the AA should be coordinated with that of the 8,000. Since, however, the verses of the AA do not follow the order of the 8,000, and Ratnākaraśānti does follow this order in the SU, it follows that he cannot adopt the order of the AA. Instead, he quotes the verses as they seem to him to fit with the matter of the 8,000.

In light of all these facts I'm inclined to follow Ratnākaraśānti's own judgments about the nature of his work, which means to classify it as a commentary upon the 8000, and to think of his use of the AA as of service to his exposition of the 8000 rather than as an additional and separate commentarial act.

Ratnākaraśānti says little of his own purposes in composing the SU: only that (using the rhetoric of modesty) being not very intelligent he will explain the 8,000 in clear and simple words (*vacasā spūṭena laghunā*); that he will provide grammatical analysis (*vibhaj-*) of the matter in the 8,000 and that in the AA; that he will do so in the hope of boundlessly increasing merit and promoting devotion to the perfection of wisdom; and that, as a result, he will encourage the development of internal illumination (203–205).

A better sense of Ratnākaraśānti's method can be had by looking at the way in which he treats one chapter of the 8,000. I've chosen the sixteenth chapter, on actuality (*tathatā*).[58] In the 8,000 this chapter begins with a disquisition by Subhūti on the philosophical meaning of actuality—on the way things really are. In response to this disquisition, the earth shakes as it had when Śākyamuni became a Buddha, and many among the crowd have their understanding advanced. Śākyamuni and Śāriputra then have a discussion in which they comment approvingly upon Subhūti's disquisition and pursue some of its implications. Subhūti and Śāriputra take the matter further, with the latter playing the straight man to the former's learned master. The chapter concludes with a brief statement by Śākyamuni as to the proper method of training (*śikṣā*) for those who want to attain complete awakening.

This chapter is, then, mostly in the form of discussion between identified speakers. It is in prose, and there is a line of argument and a narrative line of sorts that flows through the whole chapter. It's roughly equivalent to 225 verses in length, and Ratnākaraśānti's comments upon this chapter are somewhat shorter, perhaps equivalent to about 175 *ślokas* (102–108). His usual method is to choose a few words from each paragraph and explain them, either lexically or semantically or both. Here's a representative sample (the relevant paragraph of the 8,000 is translated first, followed by that of the SU; I've indicated Ratnākaraśānti's quotations from the 8,000 by putting them in upper case):

> Next, the gods Śakra (who is Indra) and Brahma Sahapati, together with their retinues from the realms of form and desire, spoke to the Blessed One [the Buddha]: "Certainly, Blessed One, this noble hearer and elder Subhūti is an offspring of the Blessed One. Why? Because, Blessed One, whatever doctrine the noble hearer Subhūti teaches, he teaches always with reference to emptiness.[59]
>
> The words beginning NEXT: OFFSPRING: born after, understood transitively [*sakarmaka*]. The action in question is bringing to birth. The agent is the one who is born. Therefore, the word's suffix indicates the agent [*tasmād iha kartari ktaḥ*]. The object is in the genitive case [*karmaṇi ṣaṣṭhi*], and so the proper connection is that SUBHŪTI is the OFFSPRING OF THE BLESSED ONE. The words beginning WHY?: The question is asked of the property of being the offspring that belongs to that one [*tat tasyānujātatvam*]. It is answered by the next words, beginning BECAUSE. The reason is that this son of the Blessed One also, and similarly, gives precedence to emptiness [*śūnyatāv āditvād iti bhavaḥ*]. (103)

It would be tedious to translate more. Most of Ratnākaraśānti's commentary is like this. Most of the words of the 8,000 are not expounded; those that are tend to be treated both syntactically and semantically. So, in the extract translated we learn both what the word "offspring" means, and how it's related to other relevant terms in the sentence. In giving such explanations Ratnākaraśānti is fond of using the technical terminology of Sanskrit grammar, as is evident from the terms given in parentheses in the translation.

Ratnākaraśānti's quotations from the 8,000 are almost always signaled as such (by the use of *iti*, which I indicate by putting the words signaled by it into upper case). But they rarely or never make sense by themselves, and the user of the SU could, on the basis of it alone, gain virtually no idea of what the 8,000 is about. Ratnākaraśānti's focus is unremittingly narrow. He limits himself to the word, the phrase, or the sentence, rarely commenting on the structure of a chapter, much less of the work as a whole.

Rather more than halfway through his exposition of the actuality chapter of the 8,000, Ratnākaraśānti makes some use of the AA, the other work to which the SU is related in a quasi-commentarial fashion. He introduces it as he explains a statement by Śāriputra (in the 8,000) that someone who wants complete and perfect awakening should develop both the perfection of wisdom and skill in proper means (156). The verses that he quotes from the AA treat a topic directly relevant to this: they define the skill in question, and then break it down into its various (and scholastically standard) subdivisions.[60] The details are not of interest here, but Ratnākaraśānti's method of using the AA is. He introduces the quotation by identifying it as one, and saying that it comes from the "Treatise" (*śāstra*)—which is what he always calls the AA. The three verses are quoted in full, though the first is separated from the second by a brief gloss given by Ratnākaraśānti, and the second half of the third is separated from the first half by another, slightly longer gloss, in which he says: "This is just what the Blessed One said in the words beginning WHEN THIS HAD BEEN SAID . . ." (106). The uppercase words are from the 8,000, and they mark the beginning of a six-line speech by the Buddha in whch Śāriputra's comment is approved and expanded using the scholastic divisions also given in the verses from the AA that Ratnākaraśānti quotes. Interestingly, he says nothing more about this six-line speech: he neither quotes nor expounds any of it.

This is an entirely typical case of Ratnākaraśānti's interweaving of the verses of the AA with the prose of the 8,000, and of both with his own exegetical comments and glosses. As I've said, he usually, though not invariably, introduces his quotations from the AA with *ataḥ śāstram* ("hence in the Treatise"); and he usually, though not invariably, introduces those from the 8,000 with *āha* ("he said") or *bhagavān āha* ("the Blessed One said"), or something similar. So the ideal reader is expected to need, or at least to find useful, signals of this kind. But it is equally clear that the ideal reader must have independent access to both the 8,000 and the AA in order to profit from what's in the SU. This is evident in the set of word glosses I translated earlier (which make no sense at all unless the passage from which the words glossed come is independently available), and in Ratnākaraśānti's throwaway mention of the fact that the content of these verses of the AA is substantially the same as that of a speech in the 8,000, when the speech in question is identified only by its first two words.

As with the SS, the SK, and the TBh, the least likely means by which such access would have been had was by poring over a palm-leaf manuscript. Ratnākaraśānti does not make sequential use of the AA; and although he does make such use of the 8000, he often skips large segments of it. If you're treating a work in this way, the difficulties of finding your place in a palm-leaf manuscript such as I've described are very great. But if access to the 8,000 and the AA was not had in this way, the ideal readers of the SU must have had it either memorially (they'd already memorized these works) or through the aural display of the contents of someone else's memory (the teacher expounding the SU—perhaps even Ratnākaraśānti himself—has memorized the 8,000 and the AA, and quotes the relevant passages in full, as necessary). Deciding between these scenarios isn't possible without more knowledge of the context than we have or are likely to get.

Ideal Readers in Buddhist India

These brief studies of four Indian Buddhist works, coupled with what is known about the material culture of books and bookmaking in India during the classical period, strongly support the conclusion that writing was not then of much importance for the composition and display of literary works, and that while many works were stored in writing, this was done for reasons that had little or nothing to do with their redisplay. *Śāstragrahaṇa*, learning a work, was a matter of ears, memory, and mouth. Also, the kind of attention paid to works during this period—evident in the anthologizing of Nāgārjuna and Śāntideva, and in the commenting of Sthiramati and Ratnākaraśānti—is clearly akin to that characteristic of religious reading. The works are read (heard), reread, memorized, pondered upon, excerpted, commented upon, chewed over, smelled, and incorporated. This is what religious readers do; it is not what consumerist readers do.

I haven't, of course, shown that the account of things in the service of which Buddhists in India read and composed was (in the terms of chapter 1) a religious account. To show that, I would have had to enter upon a discussion of what these works say, and that I have for the most part avoided. But as a matter of fact the account of things given in or implied by these works is a religious one: Buddhists in India were religious readers in terms both of their reading practices and of the substance of the account they offered. They also possessed institutional forms and pedagogical methods of the kinds typical of communities of religious readers (sketched in chapter 3): some information about those has been given in the course of this chapter. Buddhists in classical India were religious readers, and we are mostly not; that is among the reasons why we so frequently and deeply misunderstand and misuse their literary works.

6

Commentary and Anthology in Roman Africa

Christian Literature in Roman Africa, AD 193–430

Roman Africa was a narrow strip of coastal land running, at its greatest extent, from the Atlantic coast of Morocco in the west to Libya in the east, taking in goodly parts of Tunisia on the way. The area around what had been old Carthage became Roman territory during the Republican period, but the full extent of Roman power in Africa wasn't reached until the second half of the third century, and Roman influence throughout the area declined rapidly after the beginning of the fifth century. Even at its height, romanization nowhere extended more than three hundred miles inland, and reached, in some areas, far lesser distances. It was most evident and deep-going in the large towns (Carthage, Leptis Magna, Volubilis); outside these centers it was often superficial, and it vanished very rapidly, almost without trace, after the sixth century. The main provinces in Roman Africa were Africa Proconsularis, which comprised the northern half of modern Tunisia (and included Carthage); Africa Bizacena, the southern half of Tunisia; Numidia, which covered roughly the territory of northeastern Algeria and included Hippo, where Augustine became bishop; and Tripoli, which covered most of western Libya.[1]

In the third century the Romans reckoned 600 cities in the African provinces. The vast majority of these had less than 5,000 inhabitants. But Carthage probably had more than 100,000 people at this time, and Leptis Magna possibly 80,000. Carthage may have reached a quarter of a million at its height in the late fourth century. These were major urban centers, and by some measures Carthage was, from the late second through the late fourth century, one of the three or four principal cities of the empire. One measure of the influence of the urban centers of Roman Africa upon the broader empire is the fact that by the 180s more than a quarter of the Roman senate was of African origin.[2] This is a remarkable figure.

There was a significant Christian presence in these urban centers as early as the first half of the second century, and by the late fourth and early fifth that presence had become a dominant one.[3] At least in the larger towns (and most especially in Carthage), Christian institutional and financial presence was probably more significant than that of any body other than the Roman imperium itself, and in some ways more significant even than that. There was a correspondingly lively intellectual life. Christians in North Africa from Tertullian (ca. 160–220) to Augustine (354–430) composed, stored, displayed, and redisplayed an astonishing range and number of works. Composition in Latin was arguably more lively in Roman Africa between the second and the fifth centuries than anywhere else in the Roman world; and most of it was by Christians.

Greek was the language preferred for literary composition by Christians in the western parts of the empire until the end of the second century. Justin, for example, martyred at Rome in 165, composed in Greek even in that center of the Latin world. This Christian preference for Greek had partly to do with the fact that this was the language of the Bible, both Septuagint and New Testament, and partly with the fact that the Church began and went through its early growth in the most solidly Greek-using parts of the empire. But it also had to do with the fact that composition in Latin was in desuetude even in the heart of the western empire (even in Rome) by the first quarter of the second century. By then, Pliny the Younger, Tacitus, and Suetonius were all dead; Hadrian, emperor from 117 to 138, adopted 'Pan-Hellene' as one of his titles, and chose to use Greek for his own compositions; Marcus Aurelius, emperor from 161 to 180, composed his *Meditations* in Greek; and after the accession of Septimius Severus in 193, the renaissance of Greek letters went still further, among both Christians and non-Christians. Clement (ca. 150–215) and Origen (185–254) among Christians, and Plotinus (205–270) and Porphyry (232–304) among non-Christians, dominated theological and philosophical thought in the third century, and they all used Greek.

In the Latin world, by contrast, there was little composition of significance in any of the major genres (poetry, history, the technical literature of learning) after the mid-second century.[4] The literati in Rome in 250 used Greek much as the literati in Moscow used French in 1870. But there was one exception, one place in which Latin letters began to be reborn, almost exclusively at the hands and by the mouths of Christians, and this was Roman Africa toward the end of the second century. Gian Conte puts it this way: "To all effects, Christian literary writing is the principal cultural event in an era that otherwise, at least in the Latin West, does not have many significant writers or important literary movements."[5] Virtually all the significant composition in Latin to have survived from the late second and third centuries is by Christians who were educated in part or in whole in Africa: Tertullian, Minucius Felix (early third century),

Cyprian (ca. 200–258), Arnobius (ca. 250–327), and Lactantius (ca. 260–330). As a result of their work, by the fourth and fifth centuries Latin Christian literature was on a par with Greek, both in volume and subtlety. After Hilary (ca. 315–367) and Ambrose (ca. 339–397) it became a torrent, the strength of whose current enabled it to survive the end of the western empire. Jerome (347–420) and Augustine are its most prominent and prolific practitioners, and the latter, of course, was educated largely in Africa, and composed almost all of his works there.

The predominant genre of African Christian literature was the brief occasional polemical or apologetical treatise ('brief' here means from ten to 100 pages in a modern printed edition), addressed to some specific error of doctrine or practice, engaging some particular opponent, or speaking to some pressing issue of the day on which the Christian communities needed advice. The bulk of Tertullian's output is of this sort: *De pudicitia* [On Chastity], *De cultu feminarum* [On the Appearance of Women], *Ad martyros* [To the Martyrs], and so on. The same is true of Cyprian, who composed works like *Quod idola dii non sint* [That the Idols Are Not Gods], and *De lapsis* [On the Lapsed]. And Augustine's anti-Manichaean, anti-Donatist, anti-Arian, and anti-Pelagian writings are also of this genre. Some of these occasional and polemical works reach a much greater length. The classic example is Augustine's *De civitate dei* [City of God], which is many hundreds of pages long; but Tertullian's anti-Marcionite polemic (*Adversus Marcionem* [Against Marcion]) also reaches a considerable length.

Almost indistinguishable (in terms of genre) from these occasional and polemical essays are works of a more speculative and constructive kind, usually devoted to some topic in philosophical or moral theology. These works differ from those mentioned in the preceding paragraph in that their polemical edge is less sharp, and in that they are somewhat less occasional. Tertullian's *De anima* [On the Soul] and Augustine's *De magistro* [On the Teacher] and *De vera religione* [On True Religion] provide examples. These works, too, are usually relatively brief.

Hagiography is the second major genre of African Christian literature. By this I mean narrative accounts of the lives (and, often, the martyrdoms) of paradigmatic figures. As early as 180 the *Acta martyrum scillitanorum* [Acts of the Martyrs of Scillum], an account of the trial, condemnation, and judicial murder of a small group of Christians, had been composed and had found wide circulation. By the beginning of the third century it had been followed by the *Passio Perpetuae et Felicitatis* [Passion of Perpetua and Felicitas], a harrowing story of the martyrdom of a well-born young African woman together with her slave and catechist. Shortly after the martyrdom of Cyprian his life was composed and the work found wide popularity. It was followed in short order by lives (hagiographies) of other fathers of the Church (Ambrose, Martin of Tours, Augustine), whether martyred or not—and of course after the beginning of the fourth century martyrdom was increasingly rare. The popularity of this genre is suggested by the fact that interest in it seems to have prompted more translations from Latin to Greek and Greek to Latin than anything else. Latin versions of Athanasius' life of Anthony (composed in Greek) were in circulation shortly after 350; and a Greek version of the *Passio Perpetuae* was made early in the third century. Such translational compliments were, by and large, not given to the apologetical and speculative treatises, even though their number was much greater. Apart from these hagiographies and translations of the Bible from Greek into Latin (which had certainly begun to be made in piecemeal fashion in the second century, but were not given final and definitive form until the completion of Jerome's version in 406), there was relatively little translation from Greek into Latin or Latin into Greek done by African Christians in the period under investigation here.

Biblical commentary, a third genre, is hardly evident in Latin before the third century. The first surviving self-contained commentaries on biblical books to have been composed in Latin were by Victorinus of Petrovium (d. 304), who was active in what is today Slovenia (although he too was probably partly educated in Africa). Among his works, only a commentary on Revelation survives. A little earlier in Roman Africa, portions of various polemical works by Tertullian were composed in commentarial form (for example, the fourth book of the *Adversus Marcionem*, on Luke, which I shall treat later in this chapter), even though Tertullian composed no works whose sole purpose is commentary on a particular biblical book. Probably the first African Christian to have composed commentaries on particular biblical books was Gaius Marius Victorinus (ca. 275–350, born in Africa but active in Rome), who composed commentaries on the Pauline letters; Augustine seems to have known these and been influenced by them.[6] Victorinus' commentaries follow the word-by-word and paraphrastic methods of the commentaries on the classics produced in the non-Christian schools; it's probable, as this suggests, that Christians learned their commentarial methods from non-Christian Latin commentators. But biblical commentary only really begins to flourish with Ambrose, Augustine, and Jerome, all of whom composed many—or, perhaps more accurately, all of whom devoted many sermon series to the exposition (line-by-line and often word-by-word) of biblical books, some of which were then recorded and handed on in written form.

Anthology, a fourth genre, is also quite scarce in Roman Africa. The only two clear cases I've been able to find are the works by Cyprian and Augustine, both of which will be treated in detail later in this chapter. The most obvious reason for the relative scarcity of anthologies is that Latin Christian literature was at its beginning in this period: there wasn't yet much to anthologize. After the death of Augustine, anthologies became much more important in the Latin West, in part because by then there was much more to anthologize, and the tradition had a more developed sense of what is worth anthologizing. In Cyprian's time, and even perhaps in Augustine's, the only thing clearly worth anthologizing was the Bible, and both their anthologies are biblical.

Poetry and hymnody, a fifth genre, is also relatively scarce. It's first evident in the work of Commodion, whose dates are unknown, but who probably lived in the second half of the third century and was possibly active in Africa a little after the martyrdom of Cyprian. He wrote two lengthy didactic poems: the *Instructiones* [Teachings], criticizing pagans and Jews and exhorting Christians to be better Christians; and the *Carmen apologeticum* [Apological Poem] on the history of the world. Not long after, Lactantius may have composed *De ave phoenice* [On the Phoenix], an elegy on the phoenix as a symbol of Christ. There are other examples; and hymnody, like anthology, becomes an increasingly important genre of Christian writing after the death of Augustine.

Teaching and Learning Literary Works in Roman Africa

William Harris's study of the extent and nature of literacy in the ancient world shows quite clearly that, even in the major urban centers of the Roman world in the first century (Rome, Alexandria, Athens), literacy never exceeded 20 percent, and in most areas of the empire was much lower.[7] It's true that Harris uses a restrictive definition of literacy: the ability to read and write with ease in some language. But even if the definition is relaxed to include those who can read literary works, but who have little or no competence in writing, or those who have sufficient skill in letters for business purposes but not for literary purposes, and who would never choose to read for pleasure, it's unlikely that the percentage would increase dramatically. And if we focus upon literacy in Greek and Latin, the two languages in which most composition of literary works in the early empire was done (there were, of course, many other languages, both spoken and written, in the early empire, and many inhabitants of it, including some citizens, who knew not a word of either Latin or Greek), any increase would be balanced, for some people were literate in languages other than Greek or Latin. So it's probably safe to assume that literacy in Greek or Latin in Rome at the time of Jesus' death, even in a more relaxed sense than that used by Harris, did not exceed 20 percent. This should not be surprising. Even in the United States at the end of the twentieth century, a country with universal adult literacy as an aspiration (not one that would have seemed reasonable to anyone in Rome at the time of Claudius, or indeed anywhere until the nineteenth century), probably no more than 50–60 percent of the population has Harris's kind of restrictive literacy in English; and a very much smaller proportion is sufficiently literate to derive pleasure and profit from reading literary works.

The system of formal education, such as it was in the early empire, began with the skills of reading and writing.[8] From this it follows, given the extent of literacy, that only a small proportion of the populace enjoyed (or suffered) such an education. For those who did, it began with letters and numbers. Letters were learned both for recognition and reproduction: you had both to read them and write them. The standard tool for doing the latter was the wax tablet (*tabella*), inscribed with a stylus and then smoothed over to be reused. Examples of unerased school exercises of this sort from the Mediterranean world have survived: some are abecedaria, and some are multiple copyings of lines from the poets. It's clear from the accounts of such education left by those who experienced it (the most detailed is by Quintilian, who was born in Spain in AD 35, but there are interesting comments dropped along the way by many others) that its main goal was to produce rapid and accurate recognition of written letters, the ability to read aloud with good pronunciation, to write in a good hand, and to be able to perform simple arithmetic.

At this level of education, as also at the subsequent ones, memory, ear, and tongue were the principal instruments. Augustine recalls chanting the multiplication tables as a boy,[9] and Quintilian offers advice to the teacher of boys on how important it is to assess their capacity to memorize.[10] Writing instruments and written objects were of course used; but they were principally adjuncts to memory and speech.

At the higher levels of education, grammar and rhetoric were studied. Grammar meant analysis of the parts of speech, of syntax and metrics, and of pronunciation and articulation. Students were meant to develop the ability to do these things themselves, and so they were also expected to know what was necessary in order to do so. A fairly standard pattern of instruction was followed in order to develop all these skills. At the end of the day, a passage from one of the poets or historians would be set for memorization; students would begin their work in class the next day by reciting the passage from memory (it would have been learned between the end of school one day and its beginning the next morning); the teacher would then offer comments on the formal features of the passage; and students would be asked to identify the parts of speech in each sentence, as well as syntactical features of the passage as a whole. Comments would be offered by the teacher on student pronunciation and articulation.[11]

The skills produced by a grammatical education were meant partly to permit the appreciation of works of literature, history, and philosophy; but were more importantly intended to equip students for the composition and oral delivery of set pieces on questions of legal, historical, or literary interest. These set pieces typically drew their themes from literature (What did Helen feel when she first saw Paris?), or history (Why did Hannibal decide to invade Italy by land?), or law (How does the principle of primogeniture work in the case of male twins removed simultaneously from their mother's womb?); and the speeches produced on them would be designed both to persuade and to delight by demonstrating the skills mentioned.

Rhetoric was supposed to follow grammar, and to be the culmination of a formal education; so all the classical models suggest. But the pedagogical method used in the rhetorical schools was hardly distinct from that used in the grammar schools, and the distinctions between the two seem never to have been as clear as some Roman theorists (Quintilian, for instance) and western scholars suggest. A rhetorical study of a passage involved, first, reading it aloud (this was the initial *lectio*); students might copy it in writing as it was read, or they might learn it by heart by repeating it to themselves after the teacher's reading (the teacher might read or recite the passage a number of times to make this possible). The *lectio* was followed by exposition (*enarratio*), which might take the form of a word-by-word exposition of the work expounded, or of a more wide-ranging lecture. Discussion might follow, but the goal seems always to have been the fixing in the mind of the student of a fairly extensive body of strictly grammatical knowledge; of a resonant manifold of memorized works; and of a thoroughly learned set of *topoi* or *loci* (recall the discussion of mnemotechnique in chapter 4), together with a standard set of rhetorical forms—the *loci* would work together with the rhetorical forms to permit the rapid extemporaneous composition of fluent and (sometimes) elegant expository or argumentative prose. Stanley Bonner says: "We must accept that for the Romans of our period [he speaks of the second century] effective public speaking was the prime objective of the standard school curriculum."[12] He seems, oddly, to regret this, and to think he has to apologize for it; perhaps he thinks that the goals of our educational practices are more noble?

The early empire had virtually no translocal educational institutions—certainly nothing of the size and international significance of Nālandā or Vikramaśilā. The teaching of letters, numbers, and grammar was local and small-scale: it was typically not sponsored by the state at all (though at some periods in some places tax benefits were given to teachers of letters and grammar),[13] and it was exceedingly rare for a local grammar school to have more than a few dozen students, or to possess a permanent building for its use. Much teaching at this level was done outdoors, or in the covered porticoes of the public squares in larger towns. The state did sometimes take a part in financing 'higher' education, meaning the teaching of rhetoric. Suetonius says that Vespasian (emperor from 69 to 79), for example, paid the salaries of holders of (what we would call) chairs of rhetoric at Rome;[14] Quintilian held one of these positions, and was handsomely rewarded by the state for it. Later emperors, in the second and third centuries, did the same for other cities. But these seem to have been sinecures without institutional support or many other duties, rather like the position of poet laureate in England. Those who held such positions typically also had students who paid fees for being taught, just as did non-state-sponsored teachers of grammar; so the fact of state sponsorship made little difference to institutional presence.

Insofar, then, as there were educational institutions that attracted students from a wide geographical area, they were a result of the presence of a teacher with an especially attractive reputation: Quintilian at Rome in the first century, Clement and Origen at Alexandria in the second, Ambrose at Milan in the fourth. There were no permanently endowed translocal institutions in the early empire or anywhere in Roman Africa in the period under discussion here. Neither were there, in all probability, any schools at any level with more than a few hundred students at any one time. The elder Seneca attended a school in Spain that had more than 200 students,[15] but this was clearly thought unusual and worthy of special note. A typical school for the teaching of grammar or rhetoric would have drawn its students only from the immediate neighborhood.

Literacy may have been a necessary condition for grammatical and rhetorical training, but it was not a sufficient one. Much of the reading and writing in the empire between the first and the fourth century was done by professional scribes: men (usually) who read and wrote letters, contracts, and accounts for their employers, who either could not or did not want to do these things for themselves. Many of these professionals were also employed to teach (usually at home) their employers' children their letters and their numbers. Such professional scribes were also often slaves; and it seems to have been atypical for them to have had an education in rhetoric, or an interest in reading or composing literary works. They were professional readers and writers without high status, people who met certain practical and administrative needs, but who were not much concerned with the teaching and learning of literary works. Their existence shows that the ability to read and write with ease and fluency was not closely tied to literary interests.

Also, the teaching and learning of literary works was not limited to those with an education in rhetoric. It's likely, though hard information is naturally difficult to come by, that many who lacked even basic skills in reading and writing (and there were many such even in the wealthier strata of Roman society) would have known (memorized) Plautus or (later) Virgil, just as many illiterate Buddhists in India might have known (memorized) Aśvaghoṣa or Candragomin. In general, it seems right to say that while in the early empire the teaching and learning of literary works in a formal setting was deeply implicated with the possession of literacy, the skills of reading and writing were somewhat peripheral to its practice. You were taught to read and write, but once taught, you did the vast majority of your work as a student of grammar and rhetoric with ear, memory, and tongue. The whole of Homer or Virgil could be taught and learned in this way, as could Cicero or Plotinus; and complex and powerful set pieces could be composed and delivered using only these tools.

So much, in general, for the institutions and practices of Roman education in the early empire. None of this changed significantly between the accession of Septimius Severus in 193 and the death of Augustine in 430; and what was true of the western empire as a whole was true also of Roman Africa. What then of the material culture of books? How were books produced and used, and what were they like?

Tools for Writing in Roman Africa

During the second, third, and fourth centuries, literate Romans used two kinds of object for the permanent storage of lengthy written works.[16] One was the roll, the *volumen*; the other was the codex, a word that serves in contemporary English as well as classical Latin. Many other surfaces were written on, of course: walls for graffiti (hundreds of examples have been uncovered at Pompeii and Herculaneum), erasable wax tablets for school exercises and accounts, stone tablets for inscriptions, clay pots for makers' marks, wooden boards for shop signs—and so forth. But aside from the roll and the codex, all these other surfaces were used only for short pieces of writing (*arma virumque cano*, the opening of the *Aeneid*, was a common graffito throughout the empire—a memory from school days, no doubt), or for occasional writing that did not need long-term storage. But if you wanted permanently to store a long work in writing in these centuries, the roll and the codex were your only options (though this is not to say that the roll and the codex were never used for other kinds of storage; early codices, for example, appear often to have been used for the keeping of accounts).

Rolls were almost always made from prepared papyrus leaves. Papyrus is a reed (*cyperus papyrus*) that then grew most abundantly in Egypt, in the Nile valley. The most detailed description of the methods used to turn papyrus leaves into sheets ready for writing to have come down to us from the empire is that given by Pliny the Elder in his *Naturalis Historia*, probably completed in AD 77.[17] The process was complex and expensive, and by his time a trade with several centuries of practice behind it was well established. A prepared sheet of papyrus was typically ten to twelve inches high and seven to eight inches wide; sheets were pasted together to make a continuous writing surface that could be as long as thirty feet, but was more typically about twenty. It was written on in columns (*pagina*) of matter, usually no more than four inches wide, each column separated from the next by plenty of white (actually brownish yellow) space. The columns began at the left and marched to the right; readers would hold the roll in both hands, rolling up what had been read and unrolling what remained (Roman art is replete with images of such readers). Papyrus, when properly prepared and treated, is a very durable material: many hundreds of examples of Latin works written on papyrus rolls survive from the third and fourth centuries.

A codex was made by taking a number of sheets of writing material, folding each sheet in half, and then sewing the sheets together down one edge. Each sheet would thus yield two double-sided leaves, both sides of which would typically be written on, just as with our printed books. The sheets before folding were usually of the same dimensions as those used in the preparation of a manuscript roll, a *volumen*; after folding and binding, then, a typical codex leaf would be eight inches high and about six wide—though there are a number of examples where each leaf is smaller and closer to square (about six by six inches), and several with much larger dimensions (up to eighteen by twelve inches for a leaf). These last would have been made from especially large and expensive sheets. Most often, each leaf was written upon in two narrow columns. A typical example is the second-century codex of Demosthenes' *De Falsa Legatione*, whose double-columned leaves are 7½ inches by 6½ inches, with each column of matter being just a hair more than two inches across.[18]

The sheets from which codices were assembled were often made of papyrus; but increasingly often after the second century they were made of parchment (*membrana*). This word refers to untanned animal skin (most often that of sheep or goats; Matthew 25:31–46 does not seem to have led Christian parchment makers to abandon the latter as a source), prepared for writing by being soaked in lime, scraped, stretched, and smoothed. Like papyrus, parchment is a durable medium for the long-term storage of literary works. But unlike papyrus, it cannot easily be pasted, and this means that it is effectively unusable for making rolls, since the joins between the sheets would have to be sewn rather than pasted, and this would make for an impossibly bulky roll that would not have a continuous, smooth writing surface. So parchment was used only for codices, while papyrus was used for both those and rolls.

The codex (whether parchment or papyrus) and the roll (always papyrus) were written upon in identical fashion, which is to say with pen and ink, in majuscule *scriptio continua*, and in narrow columns. Pens were of various sorts (split reed, metal, horn), as also were inks (from the cheapest gum-plus-lampblack to the most expensive silver and gold), but variations in these materials have no effect upon the questions that concern me here. The question of scripts and punctuation is, however, directly relevant, since information about these is suggestive for conclusions about how the written manuscript was used.[19] Virtually all Latin manuscripts from our period are written in majuscule scripts, which is to say those in which all letters are of the same height, and are without ascenders and descenders. Not all majuscule scripts used in this period are identical: there are uncial scripts, scripts using so-called rustic capitals, and so on, but these variations don't affect the fact that all majuscules present the same basic appearance of a continuous string of matter of invariant height. *Scriptio continua* (continuous writing) means script without word breaks, paragraph divisions, or any other marks of punctuation. This, too, is characteristic of almost all Latin manuscripts from the period.

On the question of punctuation: Latin inscriptions from the centuries immediately before Christ typically use a point to indicate the boundary between one word and another. But Latin manuscripts from the first century after Christ onward typically show no such divisions. The only exception to this generalization is Latin manuscripts of the Bible, which always indicate chapter divisions (though these breaks were put in different places in different manuscripts), and often also phrase divisions, breaks marked to help in reading the work aloud. The beginning of a phrase was often indicated by a space, or by an initial letter of a larger size than the rest; and a phrase typically contained about as much matter as could be read aloud in a breath (with due attention to sense, of course). The divisions that Jerome made in his Latin version of the Bible at the end of the fourth century were on this principle (*per cola et commata*, as the tag has it). But virtually all manuscripts other than biblical ones written in Roman Africa between 193 and 430 were without punctuation.

What were the costs of the materials used for writing? Assuming that the cost of pens and ink was minimal, the main costs would have been for the purchase of prepared sheets of papyrus or parchment, and on this there is some information. In Egypt in the first century after Christ a prepared (but unwritten) roll of papyrus cost approximately eight times as much as what was then the daily wage for an unskilled laborer. At 1997 dollar rates in the United States, this means that a prepared papyrus roll might go for about $250—and this before the costs of having it written upon were paid. The cost of prepared parchment sheets is unlikely to have been much less, so that a quire of fifty sheets of parchment (a fairly typical size for a third-century codex), would have cost roughly the same as a thirty-sheet roll.[20] Some contrasts are useful: a printed mass-market paperback in the United States in 1997 sells for not much more than the hourly (not daily) minimum wage, while even an expensive academic hardcover typically doesn't cost more than twice the daily minimum wage. While the cost of employing a scribe to write on a fifty-sheet codex or a thirty-foot roll is difficult to assess, it must have been at least as much as the cost of materials. The upshot is that the cost of a written roll or codex would have been at least fifteen times the daily wage of an unskilled laborer. This is not far from what a printed and bound book cost in eighteenth-century England: in both Roman Africa and eighteenth-century Europe books were, because of expense, rare and precious items. Hardly anyone could afford to own them, and only the very rich could have a large library.

Between the second and the sixth century the papyrus roll passed from being the object of choice for the storage of literary works to being scarcely used at all for that or any other purpose. It was replaced by the codex. The reasons for this change remain unclear despite the extensive scholarly debate given to the matter.[21] The advantages of the codex in cost, ease of production, and portability are relatively minor; perhaps the fact that the codex is somewhat easier than the roll to use for reference had something to do with it: you can mark a page and quickly find a place in a codex, much as you can in a modern bound book. But whatever the reasons, it's clear from the surviving manuscripts of all types that Christians had an almost exclusive preference for the codex over the roll from the very beginning, and that this preference was only gradually imitated by the rest of the Roman world. Harry Gamble puts it this way:

> The relevant evidence indicates that early Christianity had an almost exclusive preference for the codex as the medium of its own writings and thus departed early and widely from the established bibliographic conventions of its environment.[22]

Christian attitudes to the material culture of bookmaking in the early centuries (certainly until the death of Tertullian) were heavily influenced in various ways by the fact that Christianity was an outgrowth of Judaism. Judaism, both before and after the destruction of the Second Temple in AD 70, placed a higher valuation upon the scrolls upon which the Tanakh was written than it did upon almost any other material objects; and this led to (or was strongly implicated with) a higher valuation of books in general, and the ability to read them, than was common in late antiquity. Jewish literacy rates were much higher than those in the rest of the Mediterranean world at the time of Jesus and immediately afterward. And Christians shared, to some extent, in those attitudes. Apart from Jews, they were the only large-scale religious movement in the empire to produce a significant literature in the first three centuries. That Christian literary production from the first century onward was stored almost exclusively in codices rather than rolls may have been part of the early Christian movement's attempt to differentiate itself from Judaism. But this is speculation; it is relatively certain that insofar as works by Christians in Roman Africa were stored in written form, they were stored on papyrus or parchment sheets bound into codices and written upon in majuscule *scriptio continua*. This is how Tertullian's, Cyprian's, and Augustine's works were stored.

Christian Educational Practices

By the end of the second century, Roman Africa was the home of a minor renaissance in Latin letters and of Latin rhetorical education. Carthage had become one of the empire's main urban centers and was beginning to attract some of the best teachers of rhetoric from outside Africa. Roman Africa was also, by the time of the accession of Septimius Severus, a place with a very substantial Christian presence. Against the general background of Roman teaching and learning of literary works and the material culture of books, it is now important to ask how Christians taught and learned the works they judged significant.

Christians in the Roman world from the second to the fourth century showed neither special interest in nor special animus against the ordinary educational practices of their place and time. They seem not to have been significantly different from their non-Christian peers in either possession of or attitude toward literacy or grammatical and rhetorical education: wealthy Christians typically were literate and possessed such an education, just as did wealthy non-Christians; poor Christians and non-Christians both lacked them. What counted was social class, not religious affiliation. The great Christian literary figures of Roman Africa (Tertullian, Cyprian, Augustine) were all of the middle or upper classes, and had all received the rhetorical education that was a perquisite of their class. Their hearers, when they preached in church or gave catechetical instruction, would mostly have been illiterate (incapable of reading or writing Latin), just because they were from the social classes in which this was the normal state of things.

It is true that some Christians in Roman Africa fulminate against traditional Roman education, and against the usefulness of the works studied in the grammatical and rhetorical parts of that education. Tertullian, with a characteristically aggressive tone, has strong words to say in his *De Idololatria* [On Idolatry] (composed perhaps at the end of the second century) against schoolmasters (*ludimagister*), by which he means teachers of literature in general.[23] He takes this to be an improper profession for Christians because it is almost inevitably idolatrous, and he gives two reasons for thinking so. First, schools are unavoidably implicated with observance of feasts and rituals belonging to pagan gods: it's usual, he says, for the feasts of Minerva and Saturn, and for the calendrical festivals of the new year and of midwinter to be kept in schools, and these are all instances of idolatry, deeply inappropriate for Christians. Second, and more damaging, the works taught in these schools assume the reality of the pagan gods, and in teaching them the schoolmaster will almost inevitably give at least the appearance of doing the same: "Consider whether the one who catechizes about idols isn't guilty of idolatry!" (*quaere an idololatrium committat qui de idolis catechizat*).[24] Tertullian does not wish to place a ban upon the study of non-Christian literature by Christians. He acknowledges that such study is a necessary condition for properly Christian learning. But Christians should treat it as they would treat a poisoned drink: it may have benefits and attractions (of color and smell), and these may properly be relished and used. But if you drink it, it will kill you. And, says Tertullian, this kind of limited use is not possible for professors of literature because they are swilling it around their mouths every day. Even for students it is difficult not to swallow the deadly brew.

Augustine, in somewhat different vein, is harsh in his criticisms of the rhetorical education that was standard in Africa and Italy during the fourth century. In his work *De catechizandis rudibus* [On Catechizing the Uninstructed], composed in about 405, he categorizes those "coming from the ordinary schools of grammar and rhetoric" (*de scholis usitatissimus grammaticorum oratorumque venientes*) as not to be numbered among the foolish (*idiotae*), but also as not to be called very learned (*doctissimi*) as are those who have studied philosophy.[25] The *rhetor*, he says, is likely to be both arrogant and unable to perceive what the really important questions are, and will therefore need careful handling, pedagogically speaking. And when Augustine comes to reflect upon his own education in grammar and rhetoric, he has little good to say about either the methods used or the virtues of what was read.[26] And, famously, Jerome was extremely ambivalent about the pleasure he took in reading Virgil and Horace, and tried to stop reading them in favor of the Bible and other explicitly Christian works—though with only partial success.[27]

But Tertullian's and Augustine's and Jerome's criticisms of traditional Roman education are not directed at the skill of literacy, nor even at the reading of Virgil as such. They are directed instead at the place that such learning should have in the life and reading of a Christian, and about the ill effects that may follow if it is given the wrong place. If Virgil and Ovid are loved for themselves rather than for the usefully decorative place they might have in ornamenting and complementing a Christian account of things, the result will be idolatry, and (usually) an improper inflaming of the passions and desires. Recall that Tertullian states his strongest reservations about rhetorical study as part of his treatment of idolatry. Concerns of this sort are entirely typical of religious readers. Such readers offer a comprehensive, unsurpassable, and central account of things; they do not want to read anything that cannot be inscribed into the margins of this account, and if something begins to be treated as if it had worth or significance independent of the religious account offered by its readers, then Jerome's or Tertullian's response is the natural and appropriate one. Religious readers are more alive to the dangers of reading than their nonreligious counterparts, precisely because of the fact that they read religiously rather than as consumerists.

Christians, then, were literate and educated to the same extent and in the same way as their non-Christian counterparts in our period. They had no in-principle objections to Roman schooling, properly contextualized:

> Whatever misgivings they may have had about them in the past, by the middle of the fourth century few Christians had any reservations about sending their children to school, where they would receive the standard form of traditional education, with its strongly literary and grammatical bias.[28]

But Christians did, of course, have a special interest in teaching and learning a set of works that were not taught in the schools of the empire. These were the four quasi biographies, the historical narrative, the twenty-one letters, and the apocalyptic treatise (all composed in Greek) that were eventually collected under the title "New Testament"—together with their extended prolegomenon, variously limited and enumerated, but amounting to between thirty-nine and forty-six books, composed in Hebrew, Aramaic, and Greek, and collectively eventually called "Old Testament." Most (perhaps all) of these books were available in Latin versions in Roman Africa by the time of Tertullian, though some of them appear to have circulated in a number of different versions, and there was no standard Latin version for use in public worship or private study until the general acceptance of Jerome's version in the fifth century. Nonetheless, this collection of works provided the framework, the grammar of the religious account offered by Christians at this time (as also now). It had to be taught and learned by those who did not know it, most of whom would not have been able to read it for themselves. Its meaning for Christian life had also to be taught, as did the proper ways of understanding and using it. All these were educational demands placed upon Christians in Roman Africa, demands that, if properly met, would produce people who could offer a Christian account of things, who could read the world in Christ with the Bible as their main tool. Fortunately, something is known about how these needs were met—about, that is to say, the development of the catechumenate.[29]

From the second century on, the Christian church was a rapidly expanding institution. Decisions had to be made about what those who wanted to join it should know and be able to do before membership was granted, and once those decisions had been made (or, more precisely, were continually made and remade), further decisions were necessary as to how the required knowledge and skill was to be imparted. The most general rubric used by Christians in our period for the various processes by which these things were done was the verb 'to catechize', either in its Greek form (*katechizein*), or in its Latin form (*catechizare*). Etymologically, this verb carries with it connotations of sounding, resounding, and sounding through; it came to refer, on the lips of Christians, specifically to the sounds produced by giving oral instruction and hearing a response to that instruction. It is not very archaic English to say that I had some information dinned into me at school; and this image preserves an important part of the meaning of the verb 'to catechize'. Of course, catechizing did not mean, for Hippolytus at Rome in the early third century, for Cyprian in Carthage a few decades later, for Cyril in Jerusalem or Ambrose in Milan in the middle of the fourth century, for Egeria on pilgrimage to the Holy Land at the end of the fourth century, or for Augustine in Hippo at the beginning of the fifth (these are some of our principal witnesses to the development of catechetical practice), just any oral teaching. It meant specifically teaching aimed at permitting its recipients reception into the Church: teaching aimed at the formation of religious readers.

Approaches to catechizing varied considerably from place to place and time to time, even within our period; the sketch to follow probably does not reflect exactly what was done anywhere in Roman Africa, but some of its elements would have been present everywhere after the early second century, and virtually all of them are presupposed by Augustine in the early fifth. Also, what follows will have to do only with the teaching and learning of verbal works, preeminently the Bible and the Apostles' Creed; there is, of course, much to say about the strictly liturgical elements of the catechetical process (and there is an enormous literature on it); but these matters fall outside my scope.

The catechetical process was usually divided into four stages among Latin-using Christians in Roman Africa. At the first stage you were an *accedens*, a petitioner or inquirer who had expressed interest in becoming a Christian. You were interviewed by a catechist who questioned you about motive, style of life, and knowledge of Christianity. Some motives (desire for professional advancement, to please a spouse, or to have a better social life) were judged inappropriate, as were some ways of earning a living (anything that could be construed as supporting the worship of pagan gods; prostitution; and—by some—military service). If improper motives or livelihood were apparent, the process could cease at that point; although some (certainly Augustine) seem to have thought that dubious motives might be transformed by good catechesis into proper and even praiseworthy ones.[30] Questioning about the extent to which Christianity is already known was meant to show the catechist what sort of instruction will be appropriate at a later stage of the process, and what sort of preliminary statement of Christan teaching ought to be given at the initial interview. After this questioning the petitioner was given a brief version of the Christian story, usually beginning at the creation of the world and ending at the present, and was exhorted to take this story to heart and to try and live by the recommendations for human life implied by it, as well as to come to see these implications more fully. If all went well, the *accedens* was then transformed by an appropriate ritual act (usually, a signing with salt) into a *catechumenus*, one who has been admitted to formal catechetical instruction, but who has not yet asked for (or been promised) baptism.

The *catechumenus* then entered an open-ended period of largely oral instruction, most of which took place during communal worship and took the form of exegetical commentary upon scriptural texts. Attendance at such worship was certainly weekly, and may in some places and at some times have been daily. Hearers of these sermon series (an instance of which will be treated in my discussion of Augustine's commentary on the Johannine letters) typically heard them without book (as they were also usually delivered); and since a goodly proportion of catechumens were not capable of reading the Bible themselves, this form of oral instruction would have been the only way in which they could have learned it. There is no evidence at all that catechumens who could not read were encouraged (much less required) to learn to do so. Literacy seems to have held little interest, one way or another, for catechists: William Harris suggests that Cyril of Jerusalem thought of illiteracy among catechumens as the normal state of affairs,[31] and there is some evidence that it was not uncommon for those who held official positions of some significance in the Church to be illiterate.[32]

The catechumenal stage was open-ended, but it seems not uncommonly to have lasted for three years.[33] The oral instruction was intended to provide a resonant manifold of memorized words, to textualize the catechumens, and by so doing transform them into people who, as a result of becoming textualized—having the blood in their veins replaced, corpuscle by corpuscle, with the words of Scripture—will act in accord with what these words prescribe. Oral instruction was linked throughout with nonverbal instruction, with the postures and actions and spaces of the liturgy; but a repetitive hearing of the words of Scripture coupled with teaching about their meaning was the heart of being a catechumen.

When the catechumenal stage came to an end, if it seemed good both to the catechumen and to the Church baptism was requested and promised. This usually happened at the end of the season of Epiphany, just before the beginning of Lent: at this point the catechumen became one of the elect, someone who has been judged competent to receive baptism. Such people were called *competentes, electi,* or *illuminandi*. Since this third stage was entered upon only at the beginning of Lent, and those in it were baptized at the dawn of Easter Sunday, it lasted only forty days. It was a period of still more intensive oral instruction in the Bible. Egeria, in describing the catechesis of this third stage in Jerusalem at the end of the fourth century, says that it took three hours a day seven days a week, and that the catechist "goes through the whole Bible, beginning with Genesis . . . first relating the literal meaning of each passage, then interpreting its spiritual meaning."[34] According to Egeria, instruction was entirely oral: the elect gathered in a circle around the catechist to hear his teaching (he was often the bishop of the diocese), and there is no mention of question and answer, or of oral response of any kind from those being instructed.

Biblical instruction was not the only kind given during this third stage. Lent was also the period when, typically, the *illuminandi* were taught and asked to memorize both the Apostles' Creed (the teaching of this was called *traditio symboli*) and the Lord's Prayer (whose teaching was called *traditio orationis*). Both the creed and prayer were usually also made the topic of explicit exegesis and teaching, and a number of examples of catechetical instruction on them survive, most notably those by Augustine, Ambrose, and Cyril of Jerusalem.[35] Memorization of these short works was essential; Augustine, in speaking to catechumens of the importance of memorizing the creed, says:

> Receive the rule of faith which is called the Creed [*symbolum*]. And when you have received it, write it on your heart and say it to yourselves every day [*et cum acceperitis, in corde scribite, et cotidie dicite apud vos*]. Before you sleep and before you go out arm yourselves with your Creed. No one writes the Creed so that it may be read [*symbolum nemo scribit ut legi possit*], but rather for rehearsal of it; so that forgetfulness might not erase what diligence has delivered. Let your memory be your codex [*sit vobis codex vestra memoria*].[36]

The maxim that your memory should be your codex should be taken to apply much more broadly than to memorizing the creed before baptism. For most *electi* in Roman Africa the papyrus or parchment pages of a book were either not available (because of expense) or not usable (because of illiteracy). But for the catechists of the period, the pages of the memory (*memoriae paginae*, a phrase often used) were always preferred to the pages of a codex (*codicum paginae*) anyway.

The fourth and final stage of the catechumenal process took up the week immediately following baptism at Easter. The newly baptized at this stage were called *neophyti*, and in this week they had explained to them the ritual mysteries (especially that of the Eucharist) from which until then they had been barred. With the completion of the Octave of Easter (which ends with the Sunday after Easter), the catechumenal process came to an end.

The teaching and learning of verbal works in the catechumenate in Roman Africa was clearly a local affair. You were catechized where you happened to live, and while there were certainly famous and influential catechists (Augustine himself was one), it doesn't seem that any of them developed (or would have wanted to develop) translocal catechetical schools. The learning that went on in these local settings was not aimed at fostering or encouraging the technical skills favored by consumerist readers (or those possessed by *rhetors*); it was meant to provide, instead, a knowledge of the biblical narrative of a kind that could embrace every aspect of its possessors' cognitive and affective lives; and it was meant to encourage sufficient memorization of key works that the resonant manifold of catechumens' memories would resound principally to the vocabulary and rhythms of creed, prayer, and hymn. As Victor Saxer puts it, "le catéchuménat est donc essentiellement un temps de formation morale et religieuse";[37] or, as I would prefer to put it, the completion of catechesis laid the foundation for the cultivation of religious reading. It's remarkable, too, that Christians in Roman Africa saw no other kind of education (not even that leading to literacy) as essential to the formation of Christians.

With these remarks on specifically Christian educational practices in mind I now turn to some examples of works composed in Roman Africa. As in chapter 5, I'll treat four works (two commentaries and two anthologies). The criteria for choice are similar: the works treated were all composed in Latin, and there is at least one printed edition of each. The same formal questions will be asked of these works as of the Sanskrit works discussed in chapter 5, and with the same goals: to ascertain what can be ascertained about their ideal readers, and to see how closely their reading habits conform to those of religious readers as I've analyzed these. As with the works chosen in chapter 5, my goal here is only to take soundings, not to provide a complete view of what can be learned from the formal features of Christian works composed in Roman Africa.

The four works to be treated are Cyprian's *Testimoniorum libri tres ad Quirinum* [Three Books of Testimonies for Quirinus]; Augustine's *Speculum de scriptura sacra* [A Mirror of Sacred Scripture]; the fourth book of Tertullian's *Adversus Marcionem* [Against Marcion]; and Augustine's *In Ioannis epistulam ad Parthos tractatus X* [Ten Books on the Letter of John to the Parthians].

Testimoniorum libri tres ad Quirinum [Three Books of Testimonies for Quirinus]

Cyprian of Carthage, the compiler of *Testimoniorum libri tres ad Quirinum* [Three Books of Testimonies for Quirinus],[38] was born around 200, probably in Carthage. His family was pagan, and at least middle class; he was given a traditional grammatical and rhetorical education, and himself became a teacher of rhetoric. This might suggest that Cyprian was literate in both Latin and Greek; however, it's unlikely that he knew Greek. He never quotes works in that language, or uses it himself, and he never even mentions that the New Testament was composed in Greek.[39] In the mid-240s (probably in 246) he was baptized, for reasons and with motives that remain obscure. Within two years of his baptism he was a presbyter, and very soon after that was made bishop of Carthage (in 248–249).

Cyprian went into exile in 250–251, during the Decian persecution (so-called; more accurately an attempt by the Emperor Decius to produce a certain kind of political stability by requiring public performance of acts taken to signify loyalty to the empire; it was not aimed at Christians, though they certainly suffered from it). Upon his return he was faced with a profound and troublesome theological controversy about what to do with those Christians who had sacrificed to the Roman gods under pressure from the state. One of his treatises, *De Lapsis* [On the Lapsed], and many of his letters reflect the events of 250–251 and their aftermath. In 253 Valerian became emperor, and pressure was again brought to bear upon those who did not practice the Roman religion (*eos qui romanam religionem non colunt*) to acknowledge the validity of Roman rites (*debere romanas caeremonias recognoscere*).[40] Cyprian was a target because of the prominence and power of his position; he refused to do what the proconsul of his province required, and as a result was first exiled and then (in late 258) beheaded by the state.

The unpleasantnesses of the decade from 249 to 259 were the last major difficulties that Christians in Africa had with the Roman state. They produced the last important crop of martyrs, too, among whom Cyprian was the most influential. But Cyprian's episcopate was important not only for the fact that as the story of his life and death was told and retold he became a prototypical episcopal martyr; it was important also because it represented the increasing importance of a certain kind of voice in the public life of the Church: the voice of the Roman intellectual. After Cyprian, to a greater and greater extent, it was natural for such men to become (or already to be, by birth) Christians. Before him it had been, in Roman Africa, anomalous (Tertullian was anomalous in this respect, as in most others). Just as the renaissance of Latin letters after the accession of Septimius Severus was largely at the hands of Christians, so also was the intellectual life of Roman Africa mostly a Christian affair after Cyprian.

Cyprian was faced with a rapidly expanding Church, and with precisely the sorts of pedagogical questions I've outlined. Most of his works (his letters and his treatises) were addressed to particular issues of concern to the third-century Church. But at least one, the three books of testimonies addressed to Quirinus (usually known as the *Ad Quirinum*), is an anthology of biblical excerpts specifically designed to meet some of the educational needs of a Church attracting large numbers of converts who typically knew nothing of the Bible, and who may have been illiterate. This work probably belongs to an early period of Cyprian's life as a Christian, before the difficulties of 251, and perhaps even before he had been made bishop; 248 would be a good rough guess as to the date of its composition.[41]

The *Ad Quirinum* is about 33,000 words long. At a moderately fast reading speed of 160 words per minute (roughly the same as the nine-verse-per-minute speed used to assess the time it would take to chant the Buddhist works discussed in chapter 5) it would take about three and a half hours to read aloud. It contains rather more than 700 excerpts, many very short (less than ten words), but many also quite long. The longest is an excerpt of about 300 words from Matthew 25 (71–72). The majority contain between ten and fifty words. The beginning of each excerpt is signaled clearly with words indicating its source (though the source is identified with varying degrees of precision, a matter to which I'll return), and its end is marked either by words introducing the next excerpt or by a heading that begins the next chapter (if the excerpt is the last in a chapter). The user of Cyprian's work can therefore never be in doubt as to whose words are being heard or read: either the compiler's (Cyprian's), or those of the biblical book from which the excerpt is taken. This clarity was obviously important to Cyprian.

Cyprian provides three levels of structural help for his readers. First, the entire work is divided into three books (*liber*) of unequal length, the third being longer than the first two combined. It's possible that the third was composed or compiled after the first two and intended as an independent work; this is suggested by the fact that there are prefaces addressed to Quirinus at the beginning of the first and third book, but not at the beginning of the second. The prefatory remarks at the beginning of the first book say that the work to follow comprises two books (*conplexus sum vero libellus duos pari qualitate moderatos* [3]); it makes no mention of a third, and the preface at the beginning of the third book makes no mention of the first two. But whatever may be the correct historical story to tell about the composition of the *Ad Quirinum*, the first-level division of the work as it now stands is into three books, and the second-level division is by subject heads (*capitulum*). There are altogether 174 of these (twenty-four in the first book, thirty in the second, and 120 in the third). Cyprian gives a list of those found in each book at the beginning of each book—a kind of table of contents. Each head is also given at its proper place in the book. The third-level division is by individual excerpt under a head (I'll explain in a moment how each excerpt is marked). The excerpts gathered under a particular head appear to follow no readily predictable order. For instance, the nineteenth *capitulum* of the second book is "that Christ and the Church are spouses" (*quod ipse sit sponsus ecclesiam habens* [55]). Under this head are given ten excerpts, in the following order: Joel, Jeremiah, Psalm 119 (following the enumeration in the Hebrew Bible and in most Protestant Old Testaments), Revelation, John, Joshua, Exodus, John again, Luke, and Revelation again.

Cyprian takes his extracts solely from the Bible. Of the seventy-three books contained in the so-called Alexandrian Canon reflected in the Septuagint (Cyprian of course knew an Old Latin version of the Septuagint; that version or versions no longer survive), Cyprian takes excerpts from fifty-seven. His favorites are the Gospels (especially Matthew and John), Psalms, Isaiah, Jeremiah, Romans, and I Corinthians, each of which provides more than twenty-five excerpts. Least often excerpted (save for those not excerpted at all) are II Chronicles, I and II Esdras, Nahum, Haggai, I Thessalonians, and I Peter, each of which provides Cyprian with only one excerpt. Usually, Cyprian identifies the source of an excerpt simply by giving the name of the book from which it came (*in epistula Pauli ad Galatas, apud Esaiam*, and so on). But there are exceptions. Excerpts from the Psalms are consistently identified by the number of the psalm from which they are taken (*in psalmo XXII . . .*). And when a string of citations from the same biblical book is given, the name of the book is usually not repeated, but connectors like *item ibi* and *item illic* are used. This is never done, though, when uncertainty about an excerpt's origin might result. Cyprian permits such doubt only when he uses the phrase *item in euangelio* (likewise in the Gospel) without specifying which Gospel. These instances are few; they may indicate that Cyprian sometimes judged it less important to identify from which of the four gospels an excerpt was taken than to say simply that it was a Gospel passage. But they may also be the result of the loss of an immediately following phrase (*cata Iohannem* or *cata Mattheum* or the like) due to scribal error (though there is no textual evidence for this). It is not now possible to decide which is the correct explanation; but it is clear that, by and large, Cyprian's ideal readers are intended to know just where each excerpt begins and ends, and which biblical book it comes from.

The vast majority (more than 90 percent) of the words in the *Ad Quirinum* belong to the excerpts, and so are not Cyprian's own. Apart from the formulaic introduction of each excerpt (*et in apocalypsi*, and so on), some prefatory remarks at the beginning of the first and third books, and the subject headings provided to organize the excerpts, Cyprian offers almost no comment upon or explanation of the excerpts he provides. Sometimes, as well as providing a string of excerpts upon a particular topic, he gives in his own words a summary or list of other places in the Bible where a topic is treated, without providing excerpts from these places. For instance, at the end of a collection of excerpts on the topic of Jesus Christ as precious stone (*lapis*), Cyprian concludes by saying:

> This is the precious stone in Genesis, which Jacob put at his head . . . this is the precious stone in Exodus, upon which Moses sat on the hilltop when Joshua, son of Nun, was fighting against Amalek . . . this is the great precious stone in First Kings on which the Ark of the Covenant was placed. (52–53)

Another example is Cyprian's collection of excerpts treating the impropriety of Christians marrying non-Christians (*matrimonium cum gentilibus non iungendum*). In addition to the excerpts on this topic, he also makes brief mention of other places in the Bible where there is relevant matter ("also in Genesis Abraham sends his servant to get Rebecca, his kinswoman for his son Isaac" [153]). Such cases are very much the exception; but even when they occur, Cyprian always provides sufficient information that his summary (in the instance just mentioned it is of an episode in Genesis 24) makes sense as it stands and does not require (though it would benefit from) independent reference to the biblical work cited.

In addition to helping the user of his anthology by organizing its excerpts by books and subject heads, Cyprian also makes some comments in his prefaces about the proper uses of his work. In the first preface he says (addressing Quirinus):

> And in accord with what you asked, I have composed a discourse [*sermo*], a treatise [*libellus*] arranged systematically into a brief compendium so that I might not spread out too much what has been written, but to the extent that my mediocre memory makes possible [*mediocris memoria suggerebat*] I might collect what is necessary in connected excerpts placed under subject heads [*excerptis capitulis*

> *et adnexis necessaria quaeque colligerem*] . . . Further, brevity of this sort is very useful for readers [*sed et legentibus brevitas eiusmodi plurimum prodest*], for a longer work would dissipate the reader's understanding and comprehension, while a tenacious memory holds on to what has been read in a cleverly ordered compendium [*sed subtiliore conpendio id quod legitur tenax memoria custodit*]. (3)

In the second preface he says:

> You asked that I would excerpt for your instruction from the Holy Scriptures some subject heads pertinent to the religious discipline of our sect [*excerperem de scripturis sanctis quaedam capitula ad religiosam sectae nostrae disciplinam pertinentia*]. For you are seeking a succinct method of sacred reading, so that your mind [*animus*], which has been given to God, might not be fatigued by long or numerous books [*non longis aut multis librorum voluminibus fatigetur*], but, instructed by a brief summary of heavenly precepts [*sed eruditus breuiario praeceptorum caelestium*], might have a wholesome and exhaustive compendium that will serve the needs of your memory [*ad fouendam memoriam*]. (73)

Cyprian's goal is to provide a compendium whose brevity and systematic order make it easy to read and to remember (to memorize). Excessive length and lack of order do not, in his mind, serve the memory's needs; hence the subject heads, the tables of contents, and the clearly marked excerpts.

What then of the *Ad Quirinum*'s ideal readers? First, they were expected to read, or to hear, the work with a view to inscribing it upon the pages of their memories. The use of *legere* ('to read') in the passages just translated does not necessarily mean that Cyprian imagined that all users of his work would have a codex in their hands and be running their eyes over pages of majuscule *scriptio continua*. The verb can also suggest the following of a trail or trace (*vestigium legere*), and this can be done as well by ear as by eye. The goal, in any case, as is typical of religious readers, is memorization, whether achieved by ear or by eye. Cyprian also suggests that his own memory has been an important tool of storage and composition ("to the extent that my mediocre memory makes possible").

Further, the *Ad Quirinum*'s ideal readers aren't expected to have the complete Bible available to them independently of Cyprian's work. Cyprian is very careful to make his excerpts comprehensible as they stand, and it is easy to see how a work of this sort could have been used as part of the instruction of catechumens: to be supplemented, of course, by the biblical instruction given in sermons, and ideally to be expanded by independent study—but perfectly usable as it stands. Finally, the *Ad Quirinum*'s ideal readers were expected to need and to benefit from a systematic and clear ordering of (what Cyprian took to be) the central topics of Scripture. The provision of *capitula* achieves this, and again it is easy to imagine both the pedagogical and polemical benefits of this approach. Catechumens needed (and need) to know what the Bible teaches about Christ, or marriage, or the Jews, because these things are essential parts of the comprehensive, unsurpassable, and central account of things they are forming and developing within the catechumenal process. They also need to be able to instruct others on these matters, and to meet objections when they are made. The

Ad Quirinum, then, is a work whose formal properties strongly suggest that it was intended for use by religious readers; and this impression is confirmed by what is known on other grounds of the educational practices of the time.

Speculum de scriptura sacra [A Mirror of Sacred Scripture]

Speculum de scriptura sacra [A Mirror of Sacred Scripture] is attributed to Augustine of Hippo, though there remains some doubt as to whether he was its compiler.[42] I shall assume that he was, though even if he was not it must date from roughly his time, since it is attributed to him by his first biographer, Possidius, writing not long after his death. The work may, at any rate, reasonably be taken as a witness to one kind of literary composition being done by Christians in Roman Africa at the beginning of the fifth century, some 250 years after Cyprian. Augustine's life is well known and much written about, so I won't recapitulate it here, except to say that if the work was compiled by him, this was almost certainly done after the beginning of the fifth century, when he was in Hippo as bishop.

The *Speculum* is roughly 60,000 words long. Following the measure already used for Cyprian's work, it would take something over six hours to read aloud at a speed of 160 words per minute. It contains a little over 800 excerpts, of very varied lengths. The longest is seven pages (xxv), containing almost all of Matthew 5–7; there are a number of very short excerpts (for example, a few words from Amos 2:8, *damnatorum bibebant in domo dei sui* [xiii]); and there is everything in between. The mean length of an excerpt is about seventy words, but there are few of just that length. Augustine, much more than Cyprian, is happy to give lengthy excerpts interspersed with very brief ones. There is no standard length for an excerpt.

Augustine almost always signals the beginning and end of his excerpts with clarity, though his conventions for doing so are rather different from Cyprian's. The *Speculum* is divided into chapters, each of which contains excerpts from only one book of the Bible. The name of the book is given at the head of the chapter and is usually not mentioned again in the body of the chapter. The user of the work then assumes that every excerpt in the chapter is from the work mentioned at the head. When (rarely) Augustine gives an excerpt from a book other than that given in the chapter head (as when he provides an excerpt from I John in his chapter of excerpts from the Song of Songs in chapter ix), he always explicitly signals the book from which this alien excerpt comes (*ait Iohannes in epistula sua . . .*). Augustine is also concerned to give the user of his work some idea of how much matter intervenes between one excerpt and another. For instance, in his chapter of excerpts from Tobit (xxiv), the first excerpt is Tobit 4:3–4, and the next excerpt begins at the end of 4:5 and extends to 4:16. Augustine notes that the second excerpt begins "after two lines" (*post II versus*), so telling the reader that not much matter has been omitted. But the amount of matter skipped between his fourth excerpt (which ends at the end of chapter 4) and his fifth (which begins at 12:6) is much greater, and Augustine notes this by saying "and after many [lines]" (*et post multa*).

The user of Augustine's work is therefore never in doubt either as to from which biblical book the words of some excerpt are taken, nor as to whether, in the book from which they are taken, they are close to or far from those in the excerpt that precedes them. The second kind of information, entirely absent from Cyprian's anthology and from the two Buddhist anthologies studied in chapter 5, may indicate that Augustine was concerned to make it easy for users of the *Speculum* to find his excerpts in their original context, a concern that is more typical of consumerist readers than of religious ones.

Augustine is in fact explicit about his desire to make it possible for the users of his work to retrace the excerpts he provides to their original locations. At the end of his chapter of excerpts from the Psalms (vi), he says that his own interpositions (meaning phrases like *et post III versus*) are meant to indicate to the reader (*lectorem*) that the excerpts he's woven together so that they might be read as if they were a single psalm (*tamquam unum psalmum contextim legat*) are in fact only parts of a psalm; and that his interpolations are there to enable location of the excerpt in the original (*ut si voluerit inspiciat ubi sit scriptum quod posui id est quoto vel in quo loco eiusdem psalmi*). But, he hastens to add, if you want to read the words of the psalms that he provides without paying attention to his indications of location (his source notes, we might say) this is fine: such a reader might derive greater benefit (*his enim praetermissis qui lectione continuata inspexerit sola verba psalmorum multo iocundius et ob hoc utilius ex divinis afficietur eloquiis*). Retracing is therefore not necessary for learning what you need to know, morally speaking; the words of the psalms can have their transformative effects, can provide juicy gobbets to chew upon, even if you choose to ignore Augustine's indications as to the locations of these gobbets.

As to Augustine's sources and the accuracy with which he quotes them. All the excerpts in the *Speculum* are biblical. All twenty-seven books of the New Testament are excerpted, as are twenty-four of the twenty-six Old Testament books. Augustine's favorites are the wisdom books: Psalms, Proverbs, and Ecclesiasticus together account for more than 300 of the 800 or so excerpts in the whole work (there are reasons for this emphasis that I'll come to in a moment). Next come the Gospels (especially Matthew and Luke) and the prophetic books (especially Isaiah, Jeremiah, and Ezekiel). The historical books of the Old Testament are not excerpted at all, and the Acts of the Apostles warrants only five excerpts. It's not possible to say anything very useful about accuracy of quotation; the work as we have it bears some traces of the Old Latin versions that must have been its original source; but it also seems to have been largely assimilated by copyists to the Vulgate version. However, there is no reason to doubt that Augustine intended to quote his sources verbatim.

The main structural help provided by Augustine has already been mentioned: the division of the excerpts into fifty-one chapters, and the provision of chapter heads indicating the biblical book in question. In addition to this, the excerpts within each chapter are arranged sequentially: they follow the order of the book from which they are taken, so that an excerpt from Romans 2 comes before one from Romans 3, and so on. Users of the *Speculum* thus know that if they study the excerpts in a particular chapter in order they are also following the order of the book from which they were taken. Further, as already indicated, Augustine is concerned to give users some idea of how much of a book has been omitted between excerpts. If the sentences (lines, *versi*) in which the entire biblical text consists are like beads on a string, Augustine chooses perhaps one-fiftieth of the beads, removes them from the string, restrings them in the same order they had on the original string, and lets the user know roughly how many beads would have been found between one bead and the next in the original necklace. The beads on the string of the new necklace (the anthology) are comprehensible as they stand, both severally and together; but Augustine does not want those who use his work to forget where the beads come from and that there are many more and more precious stones to be found in the original necklace.

Augustine also explains to his readers why he has chosen to compile a work like the *Speculum*. The work is, he says, addressed to those ignorant of the content of Scripture, in order that they might understand and have faith in what's said there (*ut tantum scirentur et crederentur*), and more specifically so that they might come to know what they ought do and not do: what is required of Christians, what forbidden them, and what permitted them. Augustine's goal is to have collected all the parts of Scripture of this kind (*omnia talia de canonicis libris colligam*), so that people may easily inspect them as if they were visible in a mirror (*ut facile inspice possint, in unum tamquam speculum congeram*). He does not want to engage in apologetics, to deal with difficult or disputed texts that must be given figurative or allegorical readings, but only to address those who already have faith and want to know how to do what God wants (*sed eum qui iam credens oboedire deo voluerit*). This explains, in large part, why such a large proportion of the work is devoted to the Old Testament's moral precepts as found in the wisdom literature (Augustine thinks of these as binding upon Christians), and why so much of what is excerpted from the New has to do with Christian life (the whole of the Sermon on the Mount, for instance). If Augustine had excerpted the historical books of the Old Testament, for example, his stated purpose would not have been served.

The vast majority of the words in the *Speculum* are excerpted from the Bible—about 97 percent. The rest are mostly the kinds of brief connecting phrases I've noted, together with occasional longer comments, including the introductory remarks summarized above, and the remarks on how to read the Psalms. In addition to these, Augustine offers occasional explanatory statements about such matters as the meaning of the Song of Songs (ix); the relations between the books of Wisdom and Ecclesiasticus (at the end of xxi); which books of the New Testament he will excerpt, and why (at the end of xxiv); and why the Acts of the Apostles doesn't contain much material suitable for excerpting in the kind of work Augustine wants to compile (xxix). But for the most part the words are biblical.

What then of Augustine's ideal readers? They are not learned: they do not yet know what the Bible teaches about the Christian life, and they need to know. A work like the *Speculum* might have had uses in the second stage of the catechumenal process, in which the catechumen is being instructed, but has not yet received baptism. But the primary purpose of the anthology does not appear to be the communication of information (if this were its central purpose there would be every reason to classify it as a work produced by and for consumerist readers). Instead, a proper reading of the *Speculum* is supposed to move the hearts of readers in such a way that not only do they give assent to the claim that Christians are supposed (for example) to love their enemies, but also that they are able (or that they begin to be able) to act as if they did. That this is Augustine's purpose is evident both in his introductory comments and in his analysis of how to read the excerpts he provides from the Psalms. But, as we've seen, Augustine also has in mind the reader who might benefit from using the *Speculum* as a guidepost to the Scriptures themselves, and it's for readers like this that he provides the source notes I've indicated. And, interestingly, Augustine is himself clearly aware of the difference between reading the *Speculum* in the latter way and reading it in the former, and feels the need to offer an apology for the source notes: he doesn't want to be construed as offering a work for consumerist use. It seems, too, that Augustine thinks that the transformative effects that might be wrought upon religious readers by reading the *Speculum* are not essentially different from those that might be produced by reading the scriptural books themselves. The content of the parts is more important than the order of the whole, and that this is so is what makes the anthology such an attractive genre for him and for his readers.

There are no clear indications in the *Speculum* as to whether its ideal user read it in a majuscule parchment codex or heard it spoken by a teacher. Neither are there clear indications as to whether the ideal reader stored it in memory or kept it on the shelf to consult later. The controlling metaphor of the work as a whole and of Augustine's introductory comment is visual: the work is like a mirror in which all the relevant parts of Scripture can be seen with ease and at once. There is no use of the mnemotechnical terminology evident in Cyprian's work. But this may not mean much one way or the other; the visual image of the mirror is neutral as to whether the work to which it is applied is meant to be memorized. To say that a work is like a mirror is not to say that it is meant to be read from the page, but to say that it has everything necessary to the topic at hand laid out in such a way that it can be apprehended quickly and easily. More suggestive, perhaps, is the much greater variation in length of excerpts evident in Augustine's anthology than in Cyprian's. This may suggest (though not very strongly) that the *Speculum* was designed to be read from the codex rather than heard. But whether or not this is the case, the central point that it is a work for religious readers remains. That this is so goes a good way toward explaining why it has been ignored by contemporary consumerist scholarship.

Adversus Marcionem, liber IV [Against Marcion, book 4]

The *Adversus Marcionem* is Tertullian's longest surviving work.[43] It is divided into five books, and into chapters within each book, and contains altogether about 130,000 words. At a moderate reading speed of 160 words per minute, the entire work would take between thirteen and fourteen hours to read aloud. It is thus about four times as long as Cyprian's *Ad Quirinum* and twice as long as Augustine's *Speculum*. It had reached the form in which we now have it by about the year 212, when Tertullian was in his forties, perhaps twelve years after he had become a Christian; and it was by far the longest Christian work to have been composed in Latin by the first decade of the third century.

A complex history of composition underlies the work. Tertullian explains a good part of it himself, at the beginning of the first book (i.1). The details are outside my scope, but it is worth noting that the matter of the first three books is a reworking of material in earlier works by Tertullian, and that the fourth and fifth books were probably added later, perhaps several years later. The entire work takes the form of an argument against the teachings of Marcion, a heretic who had died probably about the time Tertullian was born (ca. 160), which had a good deal of influence in Roman Africa, especially at Carthage, at the end of the second century. Books one through three deal with strictly doctrinal matters, and books four and five with Marcion's interpretation of the Bible (book four with the Gospel of Luke, and book five with the Pauline letters). Tertullian has no high opinion of Marcion, and with characteristically excessive rhetoric he begins his work with a dithyramb on the horrors of life at Pontus on the Black Sea, which is where Marcion is said to have been born, sometime early in the second century. People there are uncivilized, the climate is bad, the women go half-naked, and the people eat the dead bodies of their parents along with those of their livestock (*parentum cadauera cum pecudibus caesa conuiuio conuorant,* [i.1]—it's not clear whether the fact that parental flesh is mixed with that of domestic livestock makes matters worse than they would have been had it been eaten alone). Pontus, anyway, is a very bad place, but the worst thing about it is that Marcion was born there (*sed nihil tam barbarum ac triste apud Pontum quam quod illic Marcion natus est* [i.1]). Marcion's thought, terrible and disgusting as it is in Tertullian's mind, warrants lengthy and careful refutation, and this is what he gives it in the *Adversus Marcionem*.

Tertullian was a native of Carthage, and, like Cyprian, received a fairly typical upper-middle-class education in grammar and rhetoric. Some of his works suggest that he was also trained in law, and he may have practiced that profession before his conversion to Christianity, either in Carthage or at Rome. He was literate in both Latin and Greek, but all his significant composition was in Latin. He became a Christian sometime in the mid-190s; it is not clear whether he ever became a priest, but the rest of his life was given to the composition of increasingly passionate and extreme defenses of Christianity against both its pagan detractors and its (in Tertullian's eyes) excessively lax defenders. Tertullian has a rigorist view of Christianity: Christians, he thinks, should be easily identifiable by their style of life—especially by their attitude to the power of the state, their sexual behavior, and their use of money; they should not be subject to the mores of the non-Christian context within which they happened to find themselves, and insofar as they are, heresy and schism are a continual threat. Tertullian himself ended his life (it is not known when, where, or how) as a Montanist, a follower of the ultrarigorist Montanus, whose movement was later judged heretical and schismatic by the Church. Tertullian's thought has ever since been an object of ambivalent admiration by Catholic Christians: he is admired for the fervor of his faith and his defense of Christianity as something distinctive and demanding, and rejected for the extremes into which these views led him. He appears to have had no official teaching or administrative position in the Church during his life.

A central theme in Marcion's thought was the distinction between Law and Gospel. The former he identified with the wrathful and vengeful God of the Old Testament, and the latter with Jesus and the merciful and forgiving God of the New. But for Marcion, Law and Gospel were not just distinct; they were irreconcilably opposed in both theory and practice, and this led him to advocate that Christians should abandon the Old Testament as sacred Scripture, and that they should be deeply selective even about which works of the New Testament they treated as such. Among the four Gospels, Marcion approved of Luke, though he recommended that Christians should read a bowdlerized (as Tertullian has it, *adulteratus* [iv.2.1]) version even of that, so that they should not be led astray by apparent continuities between what the Old Testament says and what Jesus and the New Testament say. Tertullian devotes the fourth book of his work to showing that even Marcion's adulterated or mutilated version of Luke cannot reasonably be read in such a way as to support or give credence to Marcion's own theological positions. Marcion, says Tertullian, has deleted from Luke everything that appears to contradict his own position (*certe propterea contraria quaeque sententiae suae erasit* [iv.6.2]); if, then, it can be shown even from what remains that his position is untenable, Marcion's true blindess and depravity will have been demonstrated (*haec* [what remains in Marcion's version of Luke] *conveniemus, haec amplectemur: si nobiscum magis fuerint, si Marcionis praesumptionem percusserint, tunc et illa constabit eodem vitio haereticae caecitatis erasa quo et haec reservata* [iv.6.2]), and a very strong case will have been made.

To achieve these ends, Tertullian follows the order of Luke as Marcion gives it, commenting upon the Marcionite Gospel section by section. The exact extent of Marcion's Gospel has been a matter for considerable debate, and some points of detail remain unclear; but the consensus, from the evidence provided principally by Irenaeus and Tertullian himself, is that it began at Luke 3:1 (omitting the birth and genealogy), skipped to 4:31 (omitting John the Baptist, Jesus' baptism, and the temptations), and then included all the rest of the Gospel with only minor omissions and changes. Tertullian's comments on this truncated Gospel are then an especially interesting artifact: a work that is mostly commentarial in form, by the criteria given in chapter 4, but that has as its object a work created by an opponent, and as its goal the refutation of the view that this work should be read as its creator intended it to be read. The bulk of the fourth book of the *Adversus Marcionem* is therefore a polemical commentary, designed principally to show that someone else's reading of the work commented upon is indefensible. It is motivated, that is to say, by the desire to refute; but not the desire to refute the work commented upon so much as a particular reading of that work. It is also, of course, not designed to affirm in any way the view that

Marcion's Gospel should be read by Christians as an authoritative presentation of the Christian message; it affirms only the conditional that if it were so read Christians would still conclude that the God of Jesus of Nazareth was also the God of Isaiah and Jeremiah and Moses; and that Jesus was the Messiah promised by the prophets.

Tertullian's treatment of Marcion's Gospel begins at iv.7 and extends to the end of the book. It concludes with these words: "You have my pity, Marcion, for you have labored without result: the Christ in your Gospel is mine" (*Misereor tui Marcion: frustra laborasti. Christus enim in evangelio tuo meus est*). While all of it is broadly commentarial in form (it is a metawork whose structure and order are largely given it by those of the work to which it is a metawork), much of it does not appear, at first glance, to meet the criterion that the signs of the presence of another work in it should outweigh, either quantitatively or qualitatively, other elements in it. This is because Tertullian very often quotes or mentions a verse or two from Marcion's Gospel and then spends several hundred words not directly discussing any of the elements in the matter quoted, but instead quoting relevant or illustrative material from the Old Testament, or giving theological reasons why the matter quoted comports better with orthodox Christianity than with the Marcionite version. This means that no more than 2 or 3 percent of the words in this book of Tertullian's work are quoted directly from Marcion's Gospel; a much higher percentage (perhaps as much as 20 percent) are quoted from elsewhere in the Bible, Old Testament and New; and the rest are Tertullian's own words. The book as a whole is still a commentary, though, even if very few words from the work commented upon are quoted; this is principally because Tertullian's quotations from elsewhere, as well as his own theological discussions, are always turned back to the service of his anti-Marcionite argument as to the proper way of reading whichever part of the Gospel is under discussion. They never take on significance independent of this goal.

Some examples of Tertullian's method will be helpful at this point. In iv.19 he explains passages from Luke 8, beginning by quoting part of 8:3: "which ministered unto him of their substance" (*de facultatibus suis ministrabant ei* [iv.19.1]). The reference is to those women like Joanna and Susanna (named in 8:3) who took care of Jesus' needs, but Tertullian does not explain this, nor signal in any way that he is quoting the Gospel. Instead, he weaves the quotation into a longer sentence ("the fact that some rich women followed Christ which ministered unto him of their substance . . ."), and then immediately explains this with a quotation from Isaiah 32. Users of Tertullian's work who did not already know the Gospel story alluded to (and its precise words) would be able to make no sense of what he says, and would certainly not recognize the quotation as such.

After mentioning and explaining the rich women, Tertullian makes an abrupt and unexplained transition to the topic of parables, explaining what they are and why Jesus used them, and then quoting parts of Luke 8:8 and 8:18, both signaled explicitly as something Jesus said, but without their relation and connection in the Gospel being explained at all—and, indeed, without mention of the fact that these sayings about parables follow hard upon the mention of Joanna and Susanna in Luke. Again, if users of Tertullian's work did not know what was in Luke 8, and in what order the matter therein is set forth, they would not have known why Tertullian turns to this topic immediately after treating the saying about the women. Tertullian follows his discussion of the first part of 8:18 with a quotation of the second half of that same verse, this time signaling that the matter quoted follows immediately upon that quoted before (*subiacens sensus* [iv.19.4]).

Another abrupt transition is then made ("We now come . . ." / *venimus enim ad* . . . [iv.19.6]) to the question of whether those called Jesus' mother and brothers (Luke 8:19) were indeed such. Marcion thinks not; Tertullian thinks so. The reasons need not detain us, but once again it's important to note that although the question "Who is my mother and who are my brethren?" (these words are actually from the Matthaean parallel [12:48] to the Lucan story; it's no longer possible to tell whether they were included in Marcion's Gospel or whether Tertullian introduced them at this point) is explicitly signaled as something Jesus said, its relation to the discussion immediately preceding it is not explained at all. Reading this section of the *Adversus Marcionem* without a copy of Luke's Gospel open before you (or without it resounding in your memory) would be a deeply puzzling experience.

In iv.19, then, several verses from Luke 8 are quoted in due order. They are expounded, sometimes at length; but their relationship one to another within the Gospel is not explained at all, and they are not always signaled as quotations. Tertullian offers no analysis of syntactic or grammatical features; he is interested only in how the matter from the Gospel that he quotes ought to be taken to be supported by matter from the Old Testament, and so also to provide support for his overarching thesis, which is that the God of the Old Testament and that of the New are not different.

Another brief example: *Adversus Marcionem* iv.10 treats Luke 5:16–26. In this story Jesus forgives the sins of the paralyzed man, and meets with controversy from the scribes and Pharisees for doing so. Tertullian mentions the story at the beginning of his chapter (iv.10.1) but neither retells it nor quotes any part of it directly. Knowledge of the story is assumed, and Tertullian devotes most of his space to showing, by quotation from the Old Testament, that the Jesus who forgives sins in this story is continuous with the Messiah of whom just this is prophesied in the Old Testament. But no detailed exegesis of the relevant section of Luke is given: Tertullian assumes that the user of his work knows the story, that its plain sense is indeed plain and that his understanding of it is the same as Marcion's; he then has to show only that what the story suggests about Jesus (and about God) is not discontinuous with what the prophets said or with what the Old Testament as a whole implies. This chapter is perhaps chiefly remarkable for the fact that no quotations from Luke 5 occur anywhere in it, even though it is, formally, a commentary upon some verses from that chapter.

What, then, were Tertullian's ideal readers like? First, they had independent access at least to the Gospel of Luke, and perhaps also to Marcion's Gospel. It is possible that they read the *Adversus Marcionem* as I do, with a copy of Luke (in their case in an Old Latin codex) open before them. It is possible also that they had in the resonant manifold of their memories the entire Gospel, either in its gist, or verbatim. The latter scenario is perhaps more likely. If, as is frequently the case in Tertullian's work, a quotation or a reference is made without its being signaled as such, it's much more difficult to pick it out as a quotation or an allusion if you have to scan the *scriptio continua* of a second-century codex (even one of the Bible, which would have some breaks or markers in it, and so would not be written strictly *scriptio continua*) to find it than it is if it resonates with something in your memory. But either scenario is possible. Tertullian's ideal readers also knew, or had easy access to, at least the outlines of the Old Testament. They knew what it meant to cite Isaiah or Jeremiah or the Psalms, and could make sense of, and often supply the context of, brief quotations from these and other Old Testament works without having that context supplied for them by Tertullian.

Tertullian's ideal readers would also understand and appreciate rhetorical ornament: a good example is the already-mentioned dithyramb of i.1, setting out the barbarities of Pontus in extreme terms and then overmatching them with the barbarities and enormities of Marcion's teachings, but there are many other instances (i.13, a hymn to the varieties of creation theory offered by non-Christian philosophers, is one). Similarly, they would understand the forms of legal and logical argument: the work is replete with phrases like *ex abundanti causas* (iv.19.8 and passim), a technical legal/logical term meaning "by superfluous reasons" and used to introduce an argument *ex hypothesi*, against a position or a reading that one does not allow, but that can be refuted in its own terms even if one did. The whole of the *Adversus Marcionem* can be construed as an extended example of this sort of argument: if one allows (which Tertullian did not) Marcion his way with the Gospel, even then it cannot be read as he reads it.

Tertullian was, then, composing for highly educated Christians: in the first instance, it seems fair to assume, for the elites of Carthage at the beginning of the third century, toying, as many of them were, with, among other options, Marcion's version of Christianity, with Catholic Christianity, and with Montanism. He was not composing for the uneducated; his rhetorical flights would have been lost on them. And this, in turn, increases the probability that Tertullian expected his work to be read rather than heard, since most of those who would have had the education to appreciate his style would also have been able to read and write.

In Ioannis epistulam ad Parthos tractatus X [Ten Tractates on John's Letter to the Parthians]

In Ioannis epistulam ad Parthos tractatus X [Ten Tractates on John's Letter to the Parthians] is another work of Augustine's, and this time there is no serious doubt as to authorship.[44] All the early witnesses attribute it to him. It was composed and delivered as a series of ten sermons or homilies during the period immediately after Easter. The first six were probably delivered on successive days during the Octave of Easter (the second, fourth, fifth, and sixth refer to what was said yesterday, *heri*), and the last four must have followed at no great distance in time, perhaps at the Feast of the Ascension that same year. The year is not certain, but may have been 415.[45] It's likely that the sermons were preached at Hippo, at a time when Augustine was an experienced bishop and catechist, and at a time when he was composing his greatest systematic works (*De civitate dei* [On the City of God] and the *De trinitate* [On the Trinity]), and some of his most extensive and subtle commentaries on Scripture (*Enarrationes in Psalmos, Tractatus in Evangelium Ioannis*).

The work's title is both illuminating and puzzling. It's not at all clear why Augustine thinks that I John was addressed *ad Parthos*, "to the Parthians." The letter does not say so itself, and Augustine does not take the matter up. There has been endless scholarly speculation about this, but not to any good effect so far as I can tell.[46] More helpful is the fact that Augustine calls the work a tractate (rather than an *expositio* or an *enarratio*). The term has a general sense for him: it means an oral exposition of some work, usually some passage or book of Scripture, delivered from the pulpit as a sermon.[47] It therefore indicates a work composed and displayed without the use of writing, a work heard rather than read, and a work that came to be stored in writing only when scribes recorded it from Augustine's spoken words.

The work as a whole contains about 43,000 words, unequally distributed across the ten tractates. The two longest (the first and the sixth) have a little over 5,000 words each. The shortest (the seventh) has about 3,000. The rest are scattered between these extremes, yielding a mean of about 4,300 words per tractate. Using my standard measure of about 160 words per minute, Augustine's audience would have listened to him for between twenty minutes and half an hour on the occasion of his preaching each tractate.

The First Letter of John, which Augustine expounds in these tractates, is itself quite short, perhaps one-tenth the length of his sermon sequence. He does not treat an equal amount of the letter in each tractate. The first treats 1:1–2:11 (twenty-one verses); the second, 2:12–17 (six verses); the third, 2:18–27a (ten verses); the fourth, 2:27b–3:8 (eleven verses); the fifth, 3:9–17 (nine verses); the sixth, 3:18–4:3 (ten verses); the seventh, 4:4–12 (nine verses); the eighth, 4:12–16 (five verses); the ninth, 4:17–21 (five verses); and the tenth, 5:1–3 (four verses). There is no commentary upon the remainder of the fifth chapter of the letter (5:4–21) in any manuscript of the work. It remains unclear whether Augustine ever delivered a sermon on these verses; while the tenth tractate ends suddenly, and gives the impression of being incomplete, it is almost as long as the longest tractate as it stands, and it seems unlikely that the remaining eighteen verses could have been commented upon by Augustine in the small space that remained to him in the tenth tractate. So it is possible that he never completed the sermon series. Paul Agaësse has noted, perceptively, that the number of verses commented upon by Augustine in each tractate decreases as he advances through the letter, and has suggested that this is because, as Augustine warms to his theme and develops his thought, he gives freer and freer rein to his own words, and as a result feels himself less and less tied to the work he's supposed to be expounding (the small number of verses treated in the second tractate is an anomaly caused by a long excursus on the story of the disciples on the road to Emmaus).[48] This is a reasonable, indeed an illuminating, hypothesis.

There's no doubt that, formally speaking, the work as a whole is a commentary. Its order and structure are given it by John's letter; without this letter it is, as a whole, incomprehensible; and the signs of the presence of John's letter in it certainly dominate it qualitatively, if not quantitatively. In the first tractate, twenty-one verses are quoted complete, verbatim, and in the proper order. Sometimes the quotations from John's letter are marked as such, and sometimes they are simply woven into the fabric of the exposition. Here is a typical example:

> Perhaps we say this [i.e., what Augustine has just said] too quickly? But he himself [i.e., John] is about to make it clear in what follows [*ipse hoc manifestet in consequentibus*]. Recall that at the beginning of our discourse it was said that the Letter commends charity. "God is light," he says, "and in him there is no darkness at all" [1:5b]. And what had he said earlier [*et quid superius dixit*]? "That you might have fellowship with us, and that our fellowship might be with God the Father and with his Son, Jesus Christ" [1:3b]. But perhaps if God is light and there is no darkness at all in Him, and we must have fellowship with Him, then it follows that darkness must be driven away from us and light brought into being in us. This is because it is impossible for light to have fellowship with darkness. Furthermore, pay attention to what follows [*ideo vide quid sequatur*]: "That if we say we have fellowship with him, and we walk in darkness, we lie" [1:6]. Also you have the Apostle Paul saying: "And what fellowship is there between light and darkness?" [II Cor. 6:14]. You say that you have fellowship with God, and you walk in darkness; and "God is light and there is no darkness at all in him" [1:5b]. How then is there fellowship between light and darkness? (i.5)

The parenthetical references to chapter and verse are, of course, supplied by me. This extract illustrates a number of Augustine's methods. First, earlier and later sections of the letter are referred to ("in what follows," "in what he had said earlier"); ideal readers are intended to have more in mind than the verse being analyzed at the moment. Augustine also refers back to what he has said earlier ("at the beginning of our discourse"). The quotations are signaled as such, for the most part ("he says," "pay attention to what follows"). But Augustine also quotes again a passage he has already quoted, gives no indication of whether "what follows" (in this case, 1:6) follows directly upon 1:5, or whether it is separated from it by other matter, and quotes from the Second Letter to the Corinthians without saying anything other than that these are the Apostle Paul's words.

Consider this example from the beginning of the tenth tractate:

> I believe that those of you who were here yesterday will have remembered the place to which, in the Letter's course, our treatment had arrived [*quem locum in progressu huius Epistolae pervenerit nostra tractatio*]. It was: "How is it possible for the one who does not love his brother, whom he sees, to love God, whom he does not see? And we have this commandment from him, that whoever loves God should also love his brother" [4:20b–21]. Our argument went to this point [*huc usque disputatum erat*]. Therefore we should now see what follows next in due order [*quae sequuntur ergo ex ordine videamus*]. "Everyone who believes that Jesus is the Christ has been born from God" [5:1a]. (x.1)

Augustine is concerned, at the beginning of a new sermon, to refocus his hearers' minds upon the point where the previous day's sermon had ended. To do this, he quotes, with an explicit signal, the words of the letter last discussed. He then moves to the next section to be expounded, quotes it, and begins a long dicussion (in the course of which he quotes, sometimes with a signal and sometimes not, the Gospel of John, the Letter of James, Galatians, and Matthew).

Augustine's ideal readers (and in this case also his actual ones upon first display of this work) do not have a written version of the work commented upon before them. This would have been effectively impossible in Hippo in the second decade of the fifth century; it would have been vastly too expensive to provide manuscripts of the Bible to everyone, and most of those congregated to hear Augustine would not have been able to read them if they'd had them. But it is quite likely that his hearers would have had the relevant passage from John's letter in their minds, either in its substance or verbatim, so that whenever Augustine quoted it or paraphrased it (even without saying that he was doing so) the appropriate echoes would have been raised. For one thing, they would probably have heard the passage read aloud immediately before Augustine's homily began; it's likely, too, that this would have been far from the first exposure to the letter for most of them. Augustine certainly gives much less information to his audience about the context of a particular verse and its relation to immediately preceding and following matter in the letter than most modern preachers would, and this can only be because he thinks it unnecessary. He gives enough to show that he thinks it important for his audience to have a sense of the letter's thread of meaning, and of where in that thread they are; but he also gives sufficiently little to make it evident that he had higher expectations of what his audience had in mind than is possible now.

Augustine's ideal readers are also expected to resonate to quotations, allusions, and references to other parts of the Bible, either without their being signaled at all, or being signaled only by phrases like "the Apostle Paul says," or "in the Gospel it is said," or "one of the prophets says." It is not that Augustine expects his ideal readers to have enough of the Bible at command for it to be possible for him simply to quote the first word or two of a verse and have his hearers complete it in their heads (as Buddhist commentators typically do with the verse root-texts upon which they comment). His quotations from other parts of the Bible almost always make sense as given, without appeal to their context; but it is also clear that he means to conjure their context by his quotations and allusions, and that he feels confident he can do so.

Finally, and obviously, Augustine's ideal readers are not expected to be literate, and are not expected to enjoy or to want the elevated rhetorical tone and the complex constructions beloved by Tertullian. Augustine was, of course, perfectly capable of such flights: there are plenty of them in the *De Trinitate* and in the *Confessions*. But in this work, as in many of his biblical commentaries, the style is plainer. The tone is still strongly hortatory (see, e.g., the exhortation on avarice in x.4), but the constructions are simpler and the parallelisms, multilayered metaphors, and serpentine synecdoches are few.

Ideal Readers in Roman Africa

These studies of four works composed in Roman Africa, coupled with what is known about the period's material culture of books and bookmaking, and about its pedagogical practice, strongly suggest (as with the Buddhist works discussed in chapter 5) that writing was not then of great importance for the composition and display of literary works, and that while many works were stored in writing, this was done for reasons that had not much to do with their redisplay. For Christians in Roman Africa, as also for Buddhists in classical India, learning a work was mostly a matter of ears, memory, and mouth.

Cyprian's and Augustine's anthologizing, and Augustine's treatment of I John, are clearly the work of religious readers—as also was, without doubt, their use in the pedagogy of the catechumenate. Tertullian is a harder case; his work is written for readers in the narrow sense, it seems, and though its relationship to a religious account of things is evident enough if you know much about the broader context of his work, it can't be denied that the formal properties of the *Adversus Marcionem* make it a work that could have been used by consumerists in a consumerist fashion. But he provides the possible exception that shows the general acceptability of the rule that Christian literary works in Roman Africa were composed by religious readers for religious readers.

Conclusion

THIS BOOK HAS BEEN ABOUT reading in the service of the creation, maintenance, and development of a religious account. This kind of reading is almost lost among those educated in universities, no matter where in the world the universities are found. Even the memory that it once existed is almost gone. There are several ironies in this. One, most pressing for scholars of religion, is that the very intellectual activity that makes possible and largely constitutes the study of religion in universities also makes it effectively impossible to understand what is studied. The gaze of those who practice *religionswissenschaft* is systematically wrenched away from what they study and toward its epiphenomena by the very practices that promised to reveal the thing-in-itself. The balance-beam gymnast, elegantly poised and pivoting, does not look at the floor as she does her somersaults; if she does, she falls. And this is the situation of scholars of religion: they cannot look squarely at what they study because to do so would mean losing both the ability and the desire to study it as they've been trained to do. They are trained to consume with delicacy, wit, and sophistication, and to show their delicacy by writing with exquisite creativity. But Agag, king of the Amalekites, came before Samuel with delicacy, and was hacked in pieces for his pains (I Samuel 15:32–33). And this is what looking at the fact of religious reading does to consumerist readers of an intellectual bent. They can look away, typically by constructing (preferably with a punning epigram and a slew of sparkling paradoxes) a frame of reference that both forces and justifies the aversion of the gaze; or they can look at the fact of religious reading, of its subsumption of everything it encounters into itself, and have the wraithlike insubstantiality of their own identity blown away, dissipated into ineffectual tendrils of smoke.

Face a starving man on the street. If you see him for what he is, you have three choices, one praiseworthy, one damnable, and a third that only pretends to be a choice and is really a refusal to see. You can serve the starving man, feed him back to health, and love him; you can kick him in the face and walk on; or you can inculcate airy and abstract theories of benevolence, explaining how this poor fellow got to be as he is, and how the system ought to be righted so that he and his like are fewer. But the third option requires that you no longer see the starving man; your gaze has been wrenched away from him toward a phantom. If you still see him for what he is, you can only feed him or kick him in the face. Your choice is between the meet, right, and proper thing, and the sinful and wicked thing. Clear sight of a starving man creates a forced option, just as clear sight of religious reading creates a forced option. But university-trained scholars of religion have abandoned clear sight, and have done so, paradoxically, in the name of gaining it. This is their peculiar form of damnation: not to be able to see what they claim to want to see, and (worse) to prevent others from seeing it by claiming that what they see is what's really there. And the abandonment of clear sight has all the negative effects of kicking the starving man in the face without its sole virtue: honesty.

University-trained scholars of religion are not alone in this particular circle of hell. There are philosophers there, too, looking for the foundations of knowledge, for a place to stand upon the desirability of which all reasonable people can agree. Such searches suffice to prevent the prosecution of the intellectual enterprises they were designed to serve. They issue in the realization on the part of the clear-sighted (Ludwig Wittgenstein, for example) that the very most philosophy can do for and by itself is to demonstrate the impropriety and unrealizability of some intellectual ambitions. The deep and strictly idolatrous philosophical desire that informs the search for foundations is to find justifications for reading this and not that (Richard Rorty instead of Augustine), doing this and not that (maximizing the free flow of trade goods across national boundaries rather than writing commentaries on the Torah), being this and not that (Christian rather than Buddhist), justifications that will carry conviction to all reasonable human beings. Such a desire cannot be realized, and is a direct outflow of the pride that turns from God and toward itself; in so doing, it empties its possessor's thought of all efficacy and, in the end, all existence. Its flames, such as they are, consume themselves and leave only a cold, fine-grained, smothering gray ash. The results are entirely predictable. First, the end of careful and precise constructive reasoning such as can be seen in the works of such as Augustine, Aquinas, Suarez, Asaṅga, Dharmakīrti, Udayana, Ratnakīrti, Gaṅgeśa, Vedāntadeśika, and Newman. This is bad enough. But then, what's left of philosophy becomes a tool in the hands of something else; and this something is global capitalism, impelled by the desire for profit whose principal institutional form is that quasi person, the transnational limited liability corporation, now more massive even than Hobbes's Leviathan. When the intellectual identity given by religious reading is gone, all that's left is appetite, unhampered, undirected, uneducated, unfettered. The act of consumption is the only remaining deliberate act.

Too many of the philosophers, scholars of religion, historians, literary critics (and others) created by the university remain trapped in the iron cage of the intellectual's vocation. In this captivity they share a fundamental characteristic. It is the desire to mention (but never to use) the vocabulary, the conceptual tools, and the practices of what they study. Mention preserves distance; its typographic sign is the quotation mark, and its prevailing tone lies somewhere between the irony of the satirist and the affectless *obiter dictum* of the newspaper obituary writer. Use requires no framing device; mention tries always to provide one. Users are agents upon the stage, and their comments are also and always contributions and interventions. Moreover, they know it: users of a particular vocabulary (lovers whispering endearments to their beloveds, Cyprian compiling the words of God for the people of God to memorize and place in their hearts, Śāntideva compiling *buddhavacana* for those who have taken refuge in the triple jewel and want to use it as a template for practice) contribute constructively to the purposes of that vocabulary, are subject to it as they do so, and know all these things to be the case. Those who mention (analysts of the rhetoric of love who do their work only in order to manufacture Valentine cards that will sell; historians for whom Cyprian, Śāntideva, and all their works are instruments only for scholarly publication and the increase of their own reputation) attempt never to contribute constructively to the purposes of that which they mention, and if pressed for the goals in the service of which their own acts of consumption and production occur can in the end only point incoherently to the mouth and the belly, to the instruments of appetite.

If your vocabulary and your purposes are the consistent and repeated object of mention by those whose purposes are not yours; if those mentioning acts are expressions of a veiled but voracious appetite, the insatiable desire of the consumerist reader; and if the economic order of the world is such that appetite is its moving force, its principal power and potency—if all this is the case, you will be at first marginalized, then forced into a museum, and in the end, having been completely consumed, excreted as a sterile turd. For religious readers, all these hypotheticals are actual: this is how things are. Religious reading is almost, but not quite, at the point of extinction; the principal agent of its destruction has been, and continues to be, the institutional forms produced by the expansive forces of global capitalism, among which are the university. The university treats what comes within its grasp with the same unnuanced deadness that McDonald's and Exxon give to what comes within theirs: the former consumes in the service of witty display, and requires the same of its acolytes; the latter consumes in the service of profit, and requires the same of its servants. Every university scholar who sits at the feet of a pundit, a *paṇḍita*, a sanskritic religious reader, not in order to further the goals of the tradition of religious reading the pundit represents but to consume his skills for other purposes (the purposes of the university) hastens the end of what the pundit represents. The fact that university scholars of religion cannot, by virtue of their training, see what they study means that when they look at religious reading and see something else, and when they do so with the power of the consumer in their hands and on their tongues, they inevitably contribute to its destruction.

Indologists and anthropologists have done more to destroy traditional Sanskrit learning than ever Christian missionaries could. Each one sent to "the field," as it is graphically called by anthropologists (a virgin field ripe for ploughing, a field of dreams upon which fantasies can be written, a new field—that last, best hope of university scholars—to be creatively written up, a field, above all, to sow with your own seed, to make your own, to consume, to eat, and so to destroy), is one more nail in the coffin. The same is true, mutatis mutandis, for Africanists and Africa, Hawaiianists and Hawaii, and so on down the line. The damage done by university scholars to religious readers is not only great and inexcusable, but also dishonest—this last because it pretends benevolence and respect while bringing only manipulation and destruction. That unreflective and naive university scholars may believe in their own benevolence, and that their religious counterparts may believe in it too, and as a result not realize their own danger and not resist it with the vigor it deserves—these things do not alter the facts. Those who welcome their own destruction should be alerted to the nature of what they welcome (an especially large and fertile cuckoo's egg), not helped to embrace it.

University scholars, therefore, in their role as creatures of global consumerism, have made major contributions to the eradication of religious reading as an intellectual or cultural force of significance. It exists still in small pockets in the Christian world: I have seen it among some Benedictines in the United States and Europe, among some Jesuits in India, among some Baptists in the American South, and among some Mennonites in the American Midwest. But it has no significant place in the practice of any church. It has some cultural weight, still, among Orthodox Jews in the United States and Israel, where I have also seen it; but, at least in the United States, it is becoming increasingly marginalized. It exists still, to my observation, among Tibetan Buddhist intellectuals, but they are few, and mostly in exile. There are small pockets of it yet to be found among Hindus in India (I have seen one or two from afar), but they will probably not long survive the combination of Indologists and the Ford Motor Company (which began production in India in 1997). And it seems (though I have not been there to see) that in at least some parts of the Islamic world, religious reading has roots. But even there it defines itself more and more as the needed response to the West's intellectual and material consumerism, and not in terms of its own resources. And such a move is, in the long run, a guarantee of death.

Such is the situation of religious readers: almost everywhere on the verge of extinction, and even where not quite that far gone, uneasily aware that the juggernaut of McDonald's and Kentucky Fried Chicken is about to knock them flat, even while the vampires from the university are growing fat on their blood. What is to be done?

Before making some recommendations, tentative and probably hopeless though they must be, a preliminary objection must be addressed. Isn't it the case, it might be said, that communities of religious readers are dangerous? Aren't they insular, xenophobic, misogynist, and violent? Haven't they repudiated, along with rationality and the open market, basic human rights? And isn't it they who pronounce sentences of death upon writers who've offended them, shoot, bomb, and otherwise maim those who do things they don't like, and advocate (often violently) unpleasant forms of racist and nationalist violence (Christians in Ireland, Buddhists in Sri Lanka, Hindus in India, Muslims in Iran, Jews in Israel, and so on)? Shouldn't right-thinking people then be glad of their impending end?

Acts of violence are almost always sinful: they involve conscious decisions to maim, kill, or otherwise mistreat images of God, and there are almost no situations in which such actions are justifiable. The same is true of misogyny, racial and ethnic hatred, and so on. But the question is not whether some religious accounts provide those who offer them the resources to oppose these things, for it is obviously the case that they do. Christian voices in Ireland, Buddhist voices in Sri Lanka, and Muslim voices in Iran have been raised, in the name of those religions, against violence, ethnocentrism, and racial hatred. The question is rather whether there is a tight connection, one that permits reliable prediction, between offering a religious account and engaging in the kinds of unpleasantness mentioned in the preceding paragraph. Is there the kind of connection that obtains between, say, having a household income of more than $200,000 per year in the United States and voting for the Republican Party? Or the one that obtains between living in Manchester or Newcastle in England and voting for the Labour Party? Asking the question in this way should make it obvious that there is no such connection. No generalizations with predictive power can be offered about the likelihood that those who offer religious accounts will use organized systematic violence (or the threat of such) in pursuit of their goals. There are some who do; there are many who do not; and there is no tight connection between the two variables. Everything depends upon the particulars of the religious account offered.

There's more substance in the claim that religious readers are insular. They must be, at least in the sense that they use a hierarchy of values that elevates some works over others as intrinsically worth reading. It follows from this that they value the identity given them by their religious reading over all else. And this is certainly a species of insularity, one that sits well with the judgment (and its concomitant practices) that there are insiders and outsiders, that the boundaries between them are fairly clear, and that they ought to be maintained. Many temples in India these days post signs forbidding entry to non-Hindus; Christians do not welcome non-Christians to participate in the celebration of the Eucharist; Tibetan Buddhists often will not let you study a particular work unless you've had the proper initiations. These are all forms of insularity. But they are entirely proper, best likened to the exclusion from the marriage bed of anyone but the spouses, and certainly not a moral reason for rejoicing at or conniving in the continuing extirpation of religious readers.

There are, then, no defensible grounds for objecting in principle to religious reading and religious readers. Since there are no such reasons, and since one part of the burden of this book has been to suggest by example that there are real benefits to religious reading, benefits of a cognitive, moral, and practical kind that are not otherwise obtainable, it's reasonable to ask what might be done to preserve and nurture religious reading, and to advocate it.

There are two possibilities. I can mention them only schematically here; their full exposition would require another book or two. First, there is the possibility that local and translocal religious institutions (churches, synagogues, monasteries, temples) might recover the traditions and practices of religious reading that all of them harbor and have at their root. Second, there is the possibility that universities might make room for religious readers within their walls. A very few words about each of these.

For churches, synagogues, and temples actively to encourage religious reading is, as things now are, an act of resistance. It is *pratiśrotra*, against the grain. All the arrows point in the other direction, toward consumerism. But nonetheless, it could be done. The first and primary tool would have to be a recovery of catechesis in the very broadest sense of that word: I mean the idea that, in order to be a member of a religious community, you need to have some information and some skills written on your heart and engraved on your memory, and that it is a central part of the task of your community to teach you that information and that skill. Good intentions and warm feelings, a passion for justice and a love of humanity—these things are desirable and virtuous, but they have nothing directly to do with being Christian or Jewish or Buddhist. Being these things requires (though is not exhaustively constituted by), as does marriage, knowing your spouse: knowing a good deal about her, remembering her name, her likes, her dislikes, and her history; and having the skill to behave toward her in a way that both expresses and deepens your love. To be Christian or Jewish or Buddhist is to have an institutional form as your spouse, an institutional form with a history. Catechesis is the tool whereby these institutional forms make spouses of their members. Refusing to offer and receive catechesis means, in the end, a refusal of marriage, of intimacy, and of the nourishment that only these things can bring. Recovering catechesis is perhaps the greatest challenge that religious institutions face. If they can begin to do it there will be some hope for the recovery and deepening of religious reading, and some hope also for human existence in institutional forms that are not subject to the profit motive and to cost-benefit analysis.

The second possibility is that universities might provide a home or a haven for religious readers. I made some comments on this in chapter 3. It is a bare possibility, but scarcely more. A university in North America or Western Europe could, coherently, provide institutional support for readers who want to spend their lives teaching and learning the Torah and its exegesis, and to do so self-consciously in the service of the account of things that such an activity presupposes and implies. So also, mutatis mutandis, for readers who want to do the same with the Gospel, or with the *buddhaśāsana*, the doctrine and discipline of Buddhism. There are no longer theoretical reasons that make such support questionable. But there are many practical and attitudinal ones, and these change, usually, much more slowly than does theory. It's up to those in universities, most especially those who make the study of religion their avocation, to see, if they can, what their current practices are doing, where they are leading, and how they might be amended.

This book has been (always implicitly and sometimes explicitly) a jeremiad against the pedagogical and reading practices of the academy, and more especially against the attitudes and techniques of professional scholars of religion. It's therefore at least mildly paradoxical that I, its writer, am someone trained by, in, and for the modern academy; that I've held academic positions for the past fifteen years; and that I submitted this book for publication to a major academic press, and am grateful and happy that it was accepted and has been published. Aren't I, then, a member of the professional class whose practices I despise? Aren't I also sheltered and paid by an institutional form whose existence I'd be happy to see come to an end? And aren't I therefore guilty at the very least of biting the hand that feeds me? The answer to all these questions is yes, which means that there is indeed a paradox of sorts at the heart of a work like this, one that cannot be completely removed. The paradox is not, however, disabling in either an ethical or a practical sense. This is principally because the academy, as I suggested in chapter 3 as well as in this conclusion, has among its virtues the professed desire to support and encourage intellectual work whose central convictions and aims are at odds with its own self-understanding. This is why it may be possible for the academy to provide a haven for religious readers. It is also why it may be possible for the community of professional scholars of religion to pay heed to the recommendations contained in this book.

For both religious institutions and universities the imperative is the same: *tolle, lege*—take and read.

Notes

1. RELIGION

1. Michel Despland's *La religion en occident* (Montreal, 1979) has provided me with much of what I know about the history of the use of the term 'religion'. Karl Barth's observations, mostly in §17 of *Die kirchliche Dogmatik* (Munich, 1932–1967), on the difficulties for Christians of thinking about Christianity as a religion have influenced me, as also has George Lindbeck's *The Nature of Doctrine* (Philadelphia, 1984). A different strand of Christian thinking about religion is evident in Schubert Ogden's *On Theology* (Dallas, 1992), and *Is There Only One True Religion or Are There Many?* (Dallas, 1992), where formal and a priori definitions of religion are given. These have been influential mostly in the negative sense, as an important and challenging instance of how Christians should not think about religion. I've benefited, too, from Clifford Geertz's important and much-reprinted essay "Religion as a Cultural System," first published in M. Banton, ed., *Anthropological Approaches to the Study of Religion* (London, 1966), 1–46.

2. See Thomas Nagel, "What Is It Like to Be a Bat?" in his *Mortal Questions* (Cambridge, 1979), 165–180.

3. On unsurpassability see Lindbeck, *Nature of Doctrine*, 47–52.

4. J. H. Newman's *Essay on the Development of Christian Doctrine*, first published in 1845, is the classic example of an argument for the view that unsurpassability requires the essential doctrinal features of an unsurpassable account to change only in form or degree of explicitness, not in substance. Its thought underlies what I say in this section.

5. Dan Sperber, *Rethinking Symbolism* (Cambridge, 1975), 87–88.

6. On knowing how and knowing that see Gilbert Ryle, *The Concept of Mind* (Harmondsworth, 1990; first pub. 1949); J. L. Austin, *Philosophical Papers* (Oxford, 1961), especially chapters 3 and 4.

7. Ryle, *Concept of Mind*, 46.
8. Ryle, *Concept of Mind*, 58.
9. The principal influences upon the version of the Christian account offered here are Augustine, J. H. Newman, John Donne, George Herbert, and Karl Barth.
10. C. A. Patrides, ed., *The English Poems of George Herbert* (London, 1974), 76–77.

2. RELIGION AND LITERARY WORK

1. On the relations between the written and the spoken see M. A. K. Halliday, *Spoken and Written Language* (Oxford, 1985).
2. *[S]ed quia verberato aere statim transeunt, nec diutius manent quam sonant, instituta sunt per litteras signa verborum.* Augustine, *De doctrina christiana* (ii.4), ed. R. P. H. Green, *Augustine's De Doctrina Christiana* (Oxford, 1995), 60.
3. Rolf Köhn, "Latein und Volkssprache, Schriftlichkeit und Mündlichkeit in der Korrespondenz des lateinischen Mittelalters," in J. O. Fichte et al., eds., *Zusammenhänge, Einflüsse, Wirkungen* (Berlin, 1986), 340–356.
4. The general theoretical literature on orality and literacy that I've consulted includes Jack Goody and Ian Watt, "The Consequences of Literacy," *Contemporary Studies in Society and History* 5 (1963), 304–345; Jack Goody, *The Interface Between the Written and the Oral* (Cambridge, 1987); Eric Havelock, *Preface to Plato* (Cambridge, 1963); idem, *The Muse Learns to Write* (New Haven, 1986); Marshall McLuhan, *The Gutenberg Galaxy* (Toronto, 1962); Walter J. Ong, *The Presence of the Word* (New Haven, 1967); idem, *Orality and Literacy* (London, 1982); David Olson, *The World on Paper* (Cambridge, 1994).
5. Edward Gibbon, *The Decline and Fall of the Roman Empire*, ed. Hugh Trevor-Roper (New York, 1993; first pub. 1776–1788), 1:242–243.
6. Gibbon, *Decline and Fall*, 1:245.
7. Goody and Watt, "Consequences of Literacy."
8. See especially Ong, *Orality and Literacy.*
9. Olson, *World on Paper*, 68.
10. Olson, *World on Paper*, 101.
11. See Elizabeth Eisenstein, *The Printing Press as an Agent of Change* (New York, 1979); Robert Darnton, *The Business of Enlightenment* (Cambridge, Massachusetts, 1979); C. A. Read et al., "The Ability to Manipulate Speech Sounds Depends on Knowing Alphabetic Writing," *Cognition* 24 (1986), 31–44.
12. The most substantial body of work that raises problems with monolithic views about the significance of writing and reading treats the uses of both in Europe from late antiquity to the high middle ages. In gaining a toehold on this topic I've found the following works useful: Mary Carruthers, *The Book of Memory: A Study of Memory in Medieval Culture* (Cambridge, 1990); M. T. Clanchy, *From Memory to Written Record: England 1066–1307* (2d. ed., Oxford, 1993); Joyce Coleman, *Public Reading and the Reading Public in Late Medieval England and France* (New York, 1996); John Dagenais, *The Ethics of Reading in Manuscript Culture* (Princeton, 1994); Dennis Green, "Orality and Reading: The State of Research in Medieval Studies," *Speculum* 65 (1990), 267–280; idem, *Medieval Listening and Reading* (Cambridge, 1994); Martin Irvine, *The Making of Textual Culture* (Cambridge, 1994); Rosamond McKitterick, *The Carolingians and the Written Word* (Cambridge, 1989); idem, ed., *The Uses of Literacy in Early Mediaeval Europe* (Cambridge, 1990); Brian Stock, *The Implications of Literacy* (Princeton, 1983); Paul Zumthor, *La lettre et la voix de la 'littérature' médiévale* (Paris, 1987). In addition, Rosalind Thomas's *Literacy and Orality in Ancient Greece* (Cambridge, 1992) raises questions about the applicability of monolithic views to ancient Greece; and Ruth Finnegan's *Literacy*

and Orality (Oxford, 1988) and *Oral Poetry* (Bloomington, Indiana, 1992) contain some useful observations on method.

13. Milman Parry's papers are collected in *The Making of Homeric Verse*, ed. Adam Parry (Oxford, 1971). Albert Lord's chief works are *The Singer of Tales* (Cambridge, Massachusetts, 1960); *Epic Singers and Oral Tradition* (Ithaca, 1991); *The Singer Resumes the Tale*, ed. Mary Louise Lord (Ithaca, 1995). Further bibliographic guidance may be had from Edward R. Haymes, *A Bibliography of Studies Relating to Parry's and Lord's Oral Theory* (Cambridge, Massachusetts, 1973), and John Miles Foley, "The Oral Theory in Context," in idem, ed., *Oral Traditional Literature* (Columbus, Ohio, 1981), 27–122. A significant early criticism of the theory is John Smith's "The Singer or the Song? A Reassessment of Lord's Oral Theory," *Man* 12 (1977), 141–153. On Parry's and Lord's uses of the Greek material consult John B. Hainsworth, *The Flexibility of the Homeric Formulae* (Oxford, 1968), and David M. Shive, *Naming Achilles* (New York, 1987). Lord's last (posthumous) work, *The Singer Resumes the Tale*, 187–202, contains an interesting though fairly desperate response to criticisms made by Dennis Green in "Orality and Reading."

14. See Larry D. Benson, "The Literary Character of Anglo-Saxon Formulaic Poetry," *Publications of the Modern Language Association* 81 (1966), 334–341; Donald Fry, "Caedmon as a Formulaic Poet," in J. J. Duggan, ed., *Oral Literature* (New York, 1975), 41–61; idem, "The Memory of Caedmon," in Foley, *Oral Traditional Literature*, 282–293; Werner Hoffman, *Mittelhochdeutsche Heldendichtung* (Berlin, 1974).

15. Arthur F. Grimble, *Return to the Islands* (London, 1957); John Smith, *The Epic of Pābūji* (Cambridge, 1991).

16. The Parry/Lord theory has not been without its influence upon studies of the uses of writing in ancient India. See Lance S. Cousins, "Pāli Oral Literature," in Alexander Piatigorsky and P. T. Denwood, eds., *Buddhist Studies Ancient and Modern* (London, 1983), 1–19; Rupert Gethin, *The Buddhist Path to Awakening* (Leiden, 1992); idem, "The Mātikās: Memorization, Mindfulness, and the List," in Janet Gyatso, ed., *In the Mirror of Memory* (Albany, 1992), 149–172. Oskar von Hinüber's *Der Beginn der Schrift und frühe Schriftlichkeit in Indien* (Wiesbaden, 1989) and his *Untersuchungen zur Mündlichkeit früher mittelindischer Texte der Buddhisten* (Wiesbaden, 1994) also show the effects of the theory. But there are also other bases for making deterministic and monolithic judgments about the effects of the introduction of writing in India. See, for example, Goody, *Interface*, 110–122.

17. The best recent work on the uses of writing in ancient India is Harry Falk's *Schrift im alten Indien: Ein Forschungsbericht mit Anmerkungen* (Tübingen, 1993). I rely heavily upon it in what follows. I've also benefited from von Hinüber's works mentioned in n.16, as well as from Gérard Fussmann's "Les premiers systèmes d'écriture en Inde," *Annuaire du Collège de France: Résumé des cours et travaux* (1988–1989), 507–514.

18. On the evidence of the pottery shards from Sri Lanka see K. R. Norman, "The Development of Writing in India and Its Effect Upon the Pāli Canon," *Wiener Zeitschrift für die Kunde Südasiens* supplementary vol. (1993), 239–249. Norman draws on work by S. U. Deriyanagala that has not been available to me.

19. On the evidence of the Vinaya about writing see von Hinüber, *Untersuchungen*, 22–54; Falk, *Schrift*, 270–283.

20. I've used the edition of the fragments by E. A. Schwanbeck, *Megasthenis Indica* (Amsterdam, 1966; first pub. 1846). There is a translation by J. W. McCrindle, *Ancient India as Described by Megasthenes and Arrian* (London, 1877).

21. Opposed interpretations of fragment #34 are in von Hinüber, *Mündlichkeit*, 19–21, and in J. D. M. Derrett, "Two Notes on Megasthenes' INDIKA," *Journal of the American Oriental Society* 88 (1968), 776–781. I follow von Hinüber.

22. Takakusu Junjiro, transl., *A Record of the Buddhist Religion as Practised in India and the Malay Archipelago (A.D. 671–695)* (Oxford, 1896), xi–xii (Müller wrote the introduction to this volume).

23. Richard Salomon, "On the Origin of the Early Indian Scripts," *Journal of the American Oriental Society* 115 (1995), 271–279, at 278.

24. Translated from the Pali given by Falk, *Schrift*, 285.

25. There's a good bit of work on the question of how and why Christian monks read between late antiquity and the transformation of European intellectual life with the recovery of Aristotle and the development of high scholasticism in the twelfth and thirteenth centuries, and some of this has influenced the discussion given in this section. I've especially benefited from Paul F. Gehl, "Competens Silentium: Varieties of Monastic Silence in the Medieval West," *Viator* 18 (1987), 125–160; Jean Leclercq, "Meditation as Biblical Reading," *Worship* 33 (1958–1959), 562–569; Monica Sandor, "Lectio Divina and the Monastic Spirituality of Reading," *American Benedictine Review* 40 (1989), 82–114; Ambrose Wathen, "Monastic *Lectio*: Some Clues from Terminology," *Monastic Studies* 12 (1976), 207–215. Less directly on this question, but essential for deeper background, are the works on medieval European uses of writing and reading mentioned in n.12.

26. [Bhikkhu] Pāsādika and Lal Mani Joshi, eds., *Vimalakīrtinirdeśasūtra* (Sarnath, 1981), 505.

27. George Steiner, *Real Presences* (Chicago, 1989), 193.

28. Jean Leclercq et al., eds., *S. Bernardi Opera*, vol. 1 (Rome, 1957), 89–90.

29. Translated from F. S. Schmitt, ed., *Anselm: Opera Omnia*, vol. 3 (Edinburgh, 1946), 84.

30. Sitansusekhar Bagchi, ed., *Mahāyānasūtrālaṅkāra of Asaṅga* (Darbhanga, 1970), 2.

31. P. L. Vaidya, ed., *Mahāyānasūtrasaṃgraha*, part 1 (Darbhanga, 1961), 89. This is a standard trope in Indian Buddhist literature.

32. René Gothóni, "Religio and Superstitio Reconsidered," *Archiv für Religionspsychologie* 21 (1994), 37–46, at 44.

33. Anne C. Klein, *Path to the Middle: Oral Mādhyamika Philosophy in Tibet* (Albany, 1994), 26.

34. Richard Rorty, *Consequences of Pragmatism* (Minneapolis, 1982), 90–109.

35. Fredric Jameson, *Postmodernism* (Durham, North Carolina, 1991), 275–276.

36. Geoffrey H. Hartman, "Midrash as Law and Literature," *Journal of Religion* 74 (1994), 338–355, at 343.

37. See Alvin Plantinga, "Augustinian Christian Philosophy," *Monist* 15 (1992), 291–320.

38. There's been a recent explosion of interest in the arts of memory as these were developed in the West. Francis A. Yates's *The Art of Memory* (London, 1966) and Herwig Blum's *Die antike Mnemotechnik* (Hildesheim, 1969) were the seed for more recent studies, and among these I've profited from Carruthers's *Book of Memory* (see n.12), which is now the standard work on mnemotechnique in medieval Europe; Jonathan Spence's *The Memory Palace of Matteo Ricci* (London, 1985); Frits Staal's *The Fidelity of Oral Tradition and the Origins of Science* (Amsterdam, 1986), on mnemonic practice in India; and Patrick Hutton's "The Art of Memory Reconceived: From Rhetoric to Psychoanalysis," *Journal of the History of Ideas* 48 (1987), 371–392, on Vico on memory, which, though still tied too closely to Ong's views on orality and literacy, is theoretically provocative.

39. Translated from Charles H. Buttimer, ed., *Hugonis de Sancto Victore: Didascalicon* (Washington, 1939), §iii.11.

40. George Steiner, *No Passion Spent* (New Haven, 1996), 14.

41. I rely here upon my own unsystematic reading in Augustine's sermons, and on Roy Deferrari, "St. Augustine's Method of Composing and Delivering Sermons," *American Journal of Philology* 43 (1922), 97–123, 193–219; Christine Mohrmann, "Saint Augustin prédicateur," *La Maison Dieu* 39 (1954), 83–96; and William Harmless, *Augustine and the Catechumenate* (Collegeville, Minnesota, 1995).

42. On memory capacity see George A. Miller, "The Magical Number Seven, Plus or Minus Two: Some Limits on Our Capacity for Processing Information," *Psychological Review* 63 (1956), 81–97; idem, "Information and Memory," *Scientific American* (August 1963), 42–46; Donald A. Norman, *Memory and Attention* (New York, 1969); idem, *Learning and Memory* (San Francisco, 1982).

43. Hugh's *De tribus* is translated by Carruthers, *Book of Memory*, 261–266. I've relied on this translation.

44. See J. W. de Jong, ed., *Nāgārjuna: Mūlamadhyamakakārikāḥ* (Madras, 1977).

45. Harry Gamble, *Books and Readers in the Early Church* (New Haven, 1995), 1–41.

46. On literary works and stupas in India see Gregory Schopen, "The Phrase 'sa pṛthivīpradeśaś caityabhūto bhavet' in the Vajracchedikā," *Indo-Iranian Journal* 17 (1975), 147–181.

47. On literary works and stupas in China see Katherine R. Tsiang Mino, "Bodies of Buddhas and the Princes at the Xiangtangshan Caves: Image, Text, and Stupa in Buddhist Art of the Northern Qi Dynasty (550–577)," Ph.D. dissertation, Department of Art, University of Chicago, 1996.

48. Gamble, *Books and Readers*, 237.

49. On the changes in manuscript production that began to take place in the high middle ages see Richard and Mary Rouse, *Authentic Witnesses* (Notre Dame, Indiana, 1991), 221–255.

50. On the uses of vocalization in reading and composition see Josef Balogh, "Voces Paginarum: Beiträge zur Geschichte des lauten Lesens und Schreibens," *Philologus* 82 (1927), 84–109, 202–240; Paul Saenger, "Silent Reading: Its Impact on Late Medieval Script and Society," *Viator* 13 (1982), 367–414.

51. For the German text see Elias Canetti, *Die Blendung: Roman* (Munich, 1992; first pub. 1935), 18. I follow, with some minor modifications, the translation by C. V. Wedgwood in Canetti, *Auto-da-fé* (New York, 1982), 22.

52. See Dagenais, *Ethics of Reading* (see n.12), passim.

53. On dictation as a tool of book production see T. C. Skeat, "The Use of Dictation in Ancient Book Production," *Proceedings of the British Academy* 42 (1956), 179–208. There are also some scattered but useful comments in Giles Constable, ed., *The Letters of Peter the Venerable* (Cambridge, Massachusetts, 1967).

54. See Antoine Dondaine, *Les secrétaires de Saint Thomas* (Rome, 1956).

55. Dondaine, *Secrétaires*, 1:15–25; Carruthers, *Book of Memory*, 3–6; Kenelm Foster, transl., *The Life of St. Thomas Aquinas* (London, 1959), 36–38, 44–45, 51; Jean-Pierre Torrell, *Initiation à Saint Thomas d'Aquin* (Paris, 1993), 351–355.

56. Dondaine, *Secrétaires*, 1:126–145.

57. Dondaine, *Secrétaires*, 1:205.

58. For Origen's habits of composition see G. A. Williamson, transl., *History of the Church from Christ to Constantine* (Harmondsworth, 1965), 262–263. For Augustine's see Gamble, *Books and Readers*, 133–139; Brian Stock, *Augustine the Reader* (Cambridge, Massachusetts, 1996).

59. For Jerome and scribes see Saenger, "Silent Reading," 371–372; Evaristo Arns, *La technique du livre d'après Saint Jérôme* (Paris, 1953). For Guibert see M. C. Garand,

Guibert de Nogent et ses secrétaires, Corpus Christianorum, autographa medii aevii, vol. 2 (Turnholt, 1995).

60. On ancient shorthand see Herbert Boge, *Griechische Tachygraphie und Tironische Noten* (Berlin, 1973); Harald Hagendahl, "Die Bedeutung der Stenographie für die spätlateinische christliche Literatur," *Jahrbuch für Antike und Christentum* 14 (1971), 24–38.

61. Peter Ackroyd, *Dickens* (New York, 1990), 423.

62. Daniel E. Perdue, *Debate in Tibetan Buddhism* (Ithaca, 1992), 28.

3. THE CONTEXT OF RELIGIOUS READING

1. Much of what I say about institutions for religious reading is indebted to George Steiner's utopian sketch of houses of reading in his *Real Presences* (Chicago, 1989). Steiner's thoughts about these seem even less developed than mine, and some of what he says is marred by hyperallusive preciosity. But nonetheless, he sees more deeply into the question of the importance of institutional form than anyone else I've read; and he understands what religion is because he knows how to read (the same can be said of Stanley Fish), which is often a better route into understanding religion than being (conventionally) religious.

2. On the rejection of authority (institutional and other) in modernity see Jeffrey Stout, *The Flight From Authority* (Notre Dame, Indiana, 1981); Alasdair MacIntyre, *Whose Justice? Which Rationality?* (Notre Dame, Indiana, 1988); idem, *Three Rival Versions of Moral Enquiry* (Notre Dame, Indiana, 1990); Nicholas Wolterstorff, *John Locke and the Ethics of Belief* (Cambridge, 1996).

3. John Locke, *Essay Concerning Human Understanding*, ed. Peter H. Nidditch (Oxford, 1975, based on the 4th ed. of 1700), iv.20.17.

4. Flannery O'Connor, *Collected Works* (New York, 1988), 1058.

5. Translated from P. L. Vaidya, ed., *Śikṣāsamuccaya* (Darbhanga, 1961), 26.

6. On the rise and development of the western university Heinrich Denifle's *Die Universitäten des mittelalters bis 1400* (Berlin, 1885) and Hastings Rashdall's *The Universities of Europe in the Middle Ages* (Oxford, 1895) are the standard nineteenth-century histories, and I've used both with pleasure and profit. Both emphasize the importance of the connection between institutional innovation and changes in techniques for the composition, storage, and display of verbal works. More recently see G. R. Evans, *Old Arts and New Theology* (Oxford, 1980), on the beginnings of theology as an academic discipline. George Makdisi, in *The Rise of Colleges* (Edinburgh, 1981) and in "Baghdad, Bologna, and Scholasticism," in J. W. Drijvers and Alasdair A. Macdonald, eds., *Centres of Learning* (Leiden, 1995), 141–157, shows the influence of Islamic institutional forms upon early European universities; he takes much further what was only suggested by Denifle and Rashdall. On the modern western university I've found Derek Bok's *Beyond the Ivory Tower* (Cambridge, Massachusetts, 1982), and *Universities and the Future of America* (Durham, North Carolina, 1990) helpful. J. H. Newman's *The Idea of a University* (first delivered as lectures in 1852) is still fundamental and essential background.

7. On judicial attempts to rule religious reading out of the public sphere and out of the institutional setting of the university Mark De Wolfe Howe's classic study, *The Garden and the Wilderness* (Chicago, 1965), provides essential background for the understanding of the establishment clause and its interpretation. On strictly historical and jurisprudential matters I've benefited from Leonard Levy's *The Establishment Clause* (New York, 1986) and Harold J. Berman's "The Religion Clauses of the First Amend-

ment in Historical Perspective," in W. Lawson Taitte, ed., *Religion and Politics* (Austin, Texas, 1989), 96–110. See also Stephen L. Carter, *The Culture of Disbelief* (New York, 1994), together with several of the essays in William W. van Alstyne, ed., *Freedom and Tenure in the Academy* (Durham, North Carolina, 1993), and those collected in Noel B. Reynolds and W. Cole Durham, Jr., ed., *Religious Liberty in Western Thought* (Atlanta, Georgia, 1996). Franklin I. Gamwell's *The Meaning of Religious Freedom* (Albany, 1995) is an eloquent, though in my judgment finally unconvincing, philosophical defense of a construal of the clause's intent that sees it as friendly to religion.

8. The Religious Freedom Restoration Act was effectively ruled unconstitutional by the U.S. Supreme Court in the summer of 1997, largely on fourteenth-amendment grounds: the Court took the legislature to be *ultra vires* in specifying the meaning of the Constitution rather than redressing wrongs to it. Many states are now writing their own legislation on the matter.

9. Richard Rorty, "Religion as a Conversation-Stopper," *Common Knowledge* 3/1 (1994), 1–6.

10. The epistemological discussion here relies heavily upon William P. Alston, *Epistemic Justification* (Ithaca, 1989); idem, *Perceiving God* (Ithaca, 1991); and Alvin Plantinga, *Warrant* (New York, 1993). Plantinga's trilogy (only two volumes published to date) is especially comprehensive and valuable in this respect: the first volume contains extensive bibliographic guidance to work in the field. An associated question of considerable importance is that of the epistemic importance of testimony: C. A. J. Coady, *Testimony* (Oxford, 1992), is important here, as is Richard T. De George, *The Nature and Limits of Authority* (Lawrence, Kansas, 1985).

11. Plantinga, *Warrant*, 2:29.

12. Locke, *Essay*, iv.17.24.

13. Fredric Jameson, *Postmodernism* (Durham, North Carolina, 1991), 393.

14. For Augustine on the value of submission to authoritative direction in religious reading see especially *De magistro* [On the Teacher] and *De utilitate credendi* [On the Usefulness of Believing].

4. THE FUNDAMENTAL GENRES OF RELIGIOUS READING

1. There's little literature of historical or theoretical interest on the idea of commentary or commentary as such. Edward Hobbs, *The Commentary Hermeneutically Considered* (Berkeley, 1977), is disappointing. There's better material on specific commentarial traditions. On commentary in Judaism I've used Michael Fishbane, *Biblical Interpretation in Ancient Israel* (Oxford, 1985); idem, ed., *The Midrashic Imagination* (Albany, 1994); Steven D. Fraade, *From Tradition to Commentary* (Albany, 1991); Daniel Boyarin, *Intertextuality and the Reading of Midrash* (Bloomington, Indiana, 1990). There's a huge body of work on Latin Christian literature, and on works in Greek from late antiquity, but only a tiny proportion of it pays attention to theoretical questions connected with the composition and use of commentaries. Most useful is the collection edited by Alastair J. Minnis and A. B. Scott, *Medieval Literary Theory and Criticism c.100–1375* (rev. ed., Oxford, 1991). On Chinese commentarial materials the best place to begin is with John B. Henderson, *Scripture, Canon, and Commentary* (Princeton, 1991). See also Daniel K. Gardner, "Modes of Thinking and Modes of Discourse in the Sung," *Journal of Asian Studies* 50 (1991), 574–603; Stephen Jay van Zoeren, *Poetry and Personality: Reading, Exegesis, and Hermeneutics in Traditional China* (Stanford, 1991); Richard Lynn, *The Classic of Changes* (New York, 1994). There is now much work on Indian commentaries: see chap. 5 n.4.

2. Among discussions of commentary by biblical scholars I've profited from: Bernhard W. Anderson, "The Problem and Promise of Commentary," *Interpretation* 36 (1982), 341–355; Karlfried Froehlich, "Biblical Hermeneutics on the Move," *Word and World* 3 (1981), 140–152; idem, "Bibelkommentare—Zur Krise einer Gattung," *Zeitschrift für Theologie und Kirche* 84 (1987), 465–492; René Kieffer, "Was heisst das, einen Text zu kommentieren?" *Biblische Zeitschrift* 20 (1976), 212–216; Norbert Lohfink, "Kommentar als Gattung," *Bibel und Leben* 15 (1974), 1–16. In order to place the debate among biblical scholars in a broader context it's worth consulting some of Peter Stuhlmacher's work, notably "Neues Testament und Hermeneutik: Versuch einer Bestandsaufnahme," *Zeitschrift für Theologie und Kirche* 68 (1971), 121–161; "Thesen zur Methodologie gegenwärtiger Exegese," *Zeitschrift für die neutestamentliche Wissenschaft* 63 (1972), 18–26; *Biblische Theologie des Neuen Testaments*, vol. 1 (Göttingen, 1992), 1–39.

3. Jonathan Z. Smith, *Map Is Not Territory* (Leiden, 1978), 299–300.

4. Anderson, "Problem and Promise," 343.

5. Fishbane, *Biblical Interpretation*, 285.

6. Fraade, *From Tradition to Commentary*, 1–2.

7. All three works are edited together in Dwarikadas Shastri, ed., *Abhidharmakośa and Bhāṣya of Ācārya Vasubandhu and Sphuṭārthā Commentary of Ācārya Yaśomitra* (Varanasi, 1981).

8. Hobbs, *Commentary*, 31.

9. For an extract from Dayānanda's work see my *Christianity Through Non-Christian Eyes* (Maryknoll, New York, 1990), 197–203.

10. See John Searle, "Reiterating the Differences: A Reply to Derrida," *Glyph* 1 (1977), 198–207; Jacques Derrida, *Limited Inc a b c . . .* (Baltimore, 1977).

11. Jonathan Z. Smith, *Imagining Religion* (Chicago, 1982), 45.

12. Translated from Michel Foucault, *L'ordre du discours* (Paris, 1971), 26–27. See also idem, *Naissance de la clinique* (Paris, 1963), xii.

13. The text is edited by Bagchi, *Mahāyānasūtrālaṅkāra*.

14. The best survey of the development and uses of the florilegium in the West is Henry Chadwick, "Florilegium," in *Reallexikon für Antike und Christentum*, vol. 7 (Stuttgart, 1969), cols. 1131–1159: this treats the genre from its pre-Christian origins in the Near East to its development in Greece and its appropriation by Christians; it also offers a definition of the genre (1156). It should be supplemented by the surveys given by Ekkehard Mühlenberg, "Griechische Florilegien," *Theologische Realenzyklopäedie*, vol. 11 (Berlin, 1983), 215–219, and Franz Brunhölzl, "Lateinische Florilegien," ibid., 219–221. See also Henri-Marie Rochais, "Florilèges Latins," *Dictionnaire de Spiritualité*, vol. 5 (Paris, 1964), cols. 435–460; idem, "Florilegia," *New Catholic Encyclopedia*, vol. 5 (New York, 1967), 979–980. Among more specialized works on particular anthological traditions, I've profited from Birger Munk Olsen, "Les classiques latins dans les florilèges médiévaux antérieurs au XIIe siècle," *Revue d'Histoire des Textes* 9 (1979–1980), 47–121; 10 (1980–1981), 115–164; Jacqueline Hamesse, *Les auctoritates Aristotelis: Un florilège médiéval* (Louvain, 1974); Henri-Marie Rochais, "Contribution à l'histoire des florilèges ascétiques du haut moyen age Latin: le Liber Scintillarum," *Revue Bénédictine* 63 (1953), 246–291; Richard and Mary Rouse, "The Florilegium Angelicum: Its Origin, Content, and Influence," in J. J. G. Alexander and M. T. Gibson, eds., *Medieval Learning and Literature* (Oxford, 1976), 66–114; idem, *Authentic Witnesses* (Notre Dame, Indiana, 1991). Finally, there are a number of useful essays on florilegia in a volume published by the Louvain Institute for Medieval Studies: *Les genres littéraires dans les sources théologiques et philosophiques médiévales* (Louvain-la-Neuve, 1982).

15. Minnis and Scott, *Medieval Literary Theory*, 229.

16. W. D. Ross, *Aristotle* (4th ed., London, 1945), 59.

17. On the idea of quotation see the discussion in Boyarin, *Intertextuality*, and Stefan Morawski, "The Basic Functions of Quotation," in C. H. Van Schooneveld, ed., *Sign, Language, Culture* (The Hague, 1970), 690–705.

18. Ludwig Wittgenstein, *Philosophische Untersuchungen//Philosophical Investigations* (New York, 1953), §309.

19. Rouse and Rouse, "Florilegium Angelicum," 89.

20. George Steiner, *No Passion Spent* (New Haven, 1996), 7–8.

21. On the commonplace book in general (an understudied genre) see John McNair, "Stephen Batman's Commonplace Book," Ph.D. dissertation, University of Colorado, 1977; Peter Beal, *'Notions in Garrison': The Seventeenth-Century Commonplace Book* (Chicago, 1987); Max W. Thomas, "Reading and Writing the Renaissance Commonplace Book: A Question of Authorship," in Martha Woodmansee and Peter Jaszi, eds., *The Construction of Authorship* (Durham, North Carolina, 1994), 401–415. Most recently (and this book reached me too late for me to make proper use of it), see Ann Moss, *Printed Commonplace-Books and the Structuring of Renaissance Thought* (Oxford, 1996).

22. Beal, *'Notions in Garrison'*, 1.

23. John Locke, "A New Method of a Common-Place-Book," in *The Works of John Locke* (12th ed., London, 1824), 2:441–459. There exist versions in French (published in the *Bibliotheque Universelle* in 1686) and Latin; it's not quite clear in which language Locke first composed the essay.

24. Locke, "New Method," 450.

5. COMMENTARY AND ANTHOLOGY IN BUDDHIST INDIA

1. For the study of Indian Buddhist literature there are as yet no standard works of reference like the patrologies mentioned in chapter 6. The most useful reference works are the *Catalogue-Index of the Tibetan Buddhist Canons* (Sendai, 1934), more briefly known as the Tōhoku Catalogue, and the *Répertoire du canon bouddhique sino-japonaise*, compiled by Paul Demiéville, Hubert Durt, and Anna Seidel (Paris and Tokyo, 1978). Nakamura Hajime's *Indian Buddhism: A Survey with Bibliographical Notes* (Delhi, 1987) is a handy work of reference, as are Edward Conze's *Buddhist Scriptures* (New York and London, 1982), and Peter Pfandt's *Mahāyāna Texts Translated into Western Languages* (Köln, 1983). Heinz Bechert's *Abkürzungsverzeichnis zur buddhistischen Literatur* (Göttingen, 1990) suggests standard abbreviations for citing Buddhist works and contains much useful bibliographic information about them.

2. On the content and nature of the Tibetan canonical collections see Kenneth Ch'en, "The Tibetan Tripiṭaka," *Harvard Journal of Asiatic Studies* 9 (1945), 53–62; Paul Harrison, "A Brief History of the Tibetan bKa' 'gyyur," in José Cabezón and Roger Jackson, eds., *Tibetan Literature* (Ithaca, 1996), 70–84; Dudjom [Rinpoche], *The Nyingma School of Tibetan Buddhism*, transl. Gyurme Dorje and Matthew Kapstein (London, 1992), 1:88–109.

3. The only relatively clear case of a commentary in the *Kanjur* is a work called *Vimalaprabhā* ('Pure Radiance'), a commentary (*'grel bshad/ṭīkā*) on a tantra called *Kālacakra* (Tōhoku #845). But even this isn't found in all the xylographic editions of the *Kanjur*. See Imaeda Yoshiro, *Catalogue du Kanjur tibétain de l'edition de 'Jang sa-tham* (Tokyo, 1982), 185.

4. Work of various sorts on commentary in India is slowly increasing in quantity and quality. I have profited especially from the following: Paul Dundas, "Somnolent Sūtras: Scriptural Commentary in Śvetambara Jainism," *Journal of Indian Philosophy* 24

(1996), 73–101; Jan Gonda, *Vedic Literature* (Wiesbaden, 1975), 26–43; Laurie L. Patton, *Myth as Argument: The Bṛhaddevatā as Canonical Commentary* (Berlin, 1996); Jeffrey Timm, ed., *Text in Context: Traditional Hermeneutics in South Asia* (Albany, 1991); Katherine K. Young, *Hermeneutical Paths to the Sacred Worlds of India* (Atlanta, 1994); Kamil Zvelebil, *The Smile of Murugan* (Leiden, 1973), 247–263 (on Tamil commentary); Norman Cutler, "Interpreting the Tirukkūraḷ: The Role of Commentary in the Creation of a Text," *Journal of the Royal Asiatic Society* 112 (1992), 549–566; Francis X. Clooney, *Seeing Through Texts* (Albany, 1996). Louis Renou's *Histoire de la langue Sanskrite* (Lyon, 1956), chapter 4, makes some useful general comments on the method of Sanskrit commentary, as does Frits Staal's "The Sanskrit of Science," *Journal of Indian Philosophy* 23 (1995), 73–127.

5. Narayana Sastri Khiste, ed., *The Kāvyamīmāṃsā of Rājaśekhara* (Benares, 1931), 31. All quotations from this work in the next several paragraphs are found on this same page.

6. Dundas, "Somnolent Sūtras."

7. The phrase comes from Vātsyāyana's comment upon *Nyāyasūtra* iv.2.47.

8. On methods of education in India in the period generally, Radha Mookerji, *Ancient Indian Education* (Delhi, 1987; first pub. 1947), provides a good basic reference. This work may usefully be supplemented by C. Kunhan Raja's *Some Aspects of Education in Ancient India* (Madras, 1950). Both are moved to some extent by a hopeless attempt to demonstrate the unrivalled excellence of premodern Indian pedagogy, but nonetheless contain useful information.

9. On the Vinaya rules in general (with passing comments on those having to do with education) see Mohan Wijayaratna, *Buddhist Monastic Life*, transl. Claude Grangier and Steven Collins (Cambridge, 1990); Richard Gombrich, *Theravāda Buddhism* (London and New York, 1988), chapter 4.

10. On the *bhāṇaka* system for reciting works see my study "Indian Buddhist Meditation-Theory," (Ph.D. dissertation, University of Wisconsin-Madison, 1983), 33–38.

11. On the so-called Buddhist councils the standard studies are Eric Frauwallner, *The Earliest Vinaya and the Beginnings of Buddhist Literature* (Rome, 1956); André Bareau, *Les premiers conciles bouddhiques* (Paris, 1958). Charles Prebish's "A Review of Scholarship on the Buddhist Councils," *Journal of Asian Studies* 33 (1974), 239–254, and "Buddhist Councils," in Mircea Eliade, ed., *The Encyclopedia of Religion* (New York, 1987), 4:119–124, may also usefully be consulted.

12. Ramchandra Pandeya, ed., *Madhyānta-Vibhāga-Śāstra* (Delhi, 1971), 3–6.

13. I. B. Horner, transl., *Milinda's Questions* (London, 1969), 1:22–24.

14. Guiseppe Tucci, *The Religions of Tibet*, transl. Geoffrey Samuel (Berkeley and Los Angeles, 1980), 10.

15. James Legge, transl., *A Record of Buddhistic Kingdoms* (Oxford, 1886), 43.

16. On the endowment and support of the Buddhist monastic institution at Bsam-yas see Gary W. Houston, *Sources for a History of the bSam yas Debate* (Sankt-Augustin, 1980); Tucci, *Religions of Tibet*, 9; idem, *Minor Buddhist Texts*, part 2, Serie Orientale Roma 9/2 (Rome, 1958), 56.

17. On Gopala I's activity in endowing monasteries see Lalmani Joshi, *Studies in the Buddhistic Culture of India* (2d. ed., Delhi, 1977), chapter 4.

18. On the development of translocal institutions in Buddhist India (and especially on Nālandā) I've benefited from Joshi, *Buddhistic Culture* (which treats the material and intellectual culture of Buddhist India); Sukumar Dutt, *Buddhist Monks and Monasteries* (London, 1962); Debala Mitra, *Buddhist Monuments* (Calcutta, 1971); Upendra Thakur, *Buddhist Cities in Early India* (Delhi, 1995). These works vary greatly in quality. They

all use a combination of information derived from archaeology with that derived from accounts composed by Chinese pilgrims to India, but they do so with very different notions about what counts as good historiography. On the whole, the works by Dutt and Joshi are the most useful. On Nālandā specifically there is still some use in Hasmukh D. Sankalia, *The University of Nālandā* (Madras, 1934).

19. Li Rongxi, transl., *A Biography of the Tripiṭaka Master of the Great Ci'en Monastery of the Great Tang Dynasty* (Los Angeles, 1995), 95.

20. Details of Yijing's travels in the vicinity of Nālandā are in Takakusu Junjiro, transl., *A Record of the Buddhist Religion as Practised in India and the Malay Archipelago,* (A.D. 671–695) (Oxford, 1896), 8–9, 63–65, 117, 154–157, 165–166, 173–185, 192.

21. Details of Dharmasvāmin's visit to Nālandā are in George Roerich, ed. and transl., *Biography of Dharmasvāmin* (Patna, 1959), 29–35, 64–65, 90–97.

22. The epigraphical and archaeological evidence relevant to Nālandā is treated in Hirananda Shastri, *Nālandā and Its Epigraphical Material* (Calcutta, 1922); idem, "The Nālandā Copper-Plate of Devapāladeva," *Epigraphica Indica* 17 (1923–1924), 310–327; idem, "Nālandā Stone Inscription of the Reign of Yaśovarmmadeva," *Epigraphica Indica* 20 (1929–1930), 37–46.

23. Samuel Beal, "Two Chinese-Buddhist Inscriptions Found at Buddha Gaya," *Journal of the Royal Asiatic Society*, New Series 13 (1886), 552–572.

24. Rongxi, *Biography*, 94–95.

25. Rongxi, *Biography*, 90–95.

26. Takakusu, *Record*, 103–104.

27. Takakusu, *Record*, 175–176.

28. Takakusu, *Record*, 182–183.

29. Roerich, *Biography*, 95–96.

30. Dwarikadas Shastri, ed., *Bodhicaryāvatāra of Ārya Śāntideva* (Varanasi, 1968).

31. On the material culture of the book Henry Falk, *Schrift im alten Indien: Ein Forschungsbericht mit Anmerkungen* (Tübingen, 1993), contains the most thorough and up-to-date bibliography. Louis Renou and Jean Filliozat, eds., *L'Inde classique: manuel des études indiennes* (Hanoi, 1947, 1953), 2:709–712, is a good introductory survey. I've also used Jeremiah Losty, *The Art of the Book in India* (London, 1982), and D. B. Diskalkar, *Materials Used for Indian Epigraphical Records* (Poona, 1979). Bapurao S. Naik, *Typography of Devanāgarī* (Bombay, 1971), although mostly about typography, has surprisingly thorough and useful comments (in vol. 1) on the history of writing in India, and (in vols. 2–3) on the influence of typography upon the display of material in Sanskrit. A. F. R. Hoernle, "An Epigraphical Note on Palm-Leaf, Paper and Birch-Bark," *Journal of the Royal Asiatic Society of Bengal* 69/1 (1901), 93–134, though now almost a century old, is still unrivalled as an account of the different materials used to write upon in classical India.

32. Losty, *Art of the Book*, 6.

33. Rongxi, *Biography*, 121.

34. Hoernle, "Epigraphical Note," 124.

35. E. C. Sachau, transl., *Alberuni's India* (London, 1888), 2:71.

36. C. D. Dalal and R. A. Sastry, eds., *Kāvyamīmāṃsā of Rājaśekhara* (3d ed., Baroda, 1934), 50–53.

37. On the scribal caste see Romila Thapar, *Interpreting Early India* (Delhi, 1992), 14–15; Stephen Hillyer Levitt, "The Indian Attitude Towards Writing," *Indologica Taurinensia* 13 (1985–1986), 229–250.

38. On the lack of change in conventions of displaying textual material on palm leaves, see the mss. of widely differing dates reproduced in Mimaki Katsumi et al., eds.,

Three Works of Vasubandhu in Sanskrit Manuscript (Tokyo, 1989), and in Chr. Lindtner, *Nāgārjuniana* (Copenhagen, 1982), 292–327.

39. Subas Pani, *Illustrated Palmleaf Manuscripts of Orissa* (Bhubaneswar, 1984), provides some beautiful examples of decorated manuscripts; but even here the decorations aren't principally intended to aid the reader in reading.

40. Ernst Steinkellner, "Zur Zitierweise Kamalaśīlas," *Wiener Zeitschrift für die Kunde Südasiens* 7 (1963), 116–150.

41. I quote and translate from the edition by Bhikkhu Pāsādika, *Nāgārjuna's Sūtrasamuccaya* (Copenhagen, 1989). Parenthetical numbers in my text are references to the pages of this edition. Pāsādika has also published a translation of the SS in eighteen parts in *Linh Son: Publication d'Études Bouddhologiques* 2–20 (1978–1982). I've consulted this with profit.

42. On the authorship of the SS see Lindtner, *Nāgārjuniana*, 172–173; Amalia Pezzali, *Śāntideva* (Florence, 1968), 80–97; Ishida Chiko, "Some New Remarks on the Bodhicaryāvatāra Chap. V," *Indogaku bukkyōgaku kenkyū* 37/1 (1988), 34–37.

43. See Lindtner, *Nāgārjuniana*, 175–178; Anukul C. Banerjee, "The Sūtrasamuccaya," *Indian Historical Quarterly* 17 (1941), 121–126.

44. This passage merges and summarizes P. L. Vaidya, ed., *Mahāyānasūtrasaṃgraha*, part 1 (Darbhanga, 1961), 77, 78–79.

45. Étienne Lamotte, ed. and transl., *L'Enseignement de Vimalakīrti* (Louvain-la-Neuve, 1962), 131–138.

46. The original is at Vaidya, *Mahāyānasūtrasaṃgraha*, 345.

47. I quote and translate from P. L. Vaidya, ed., *Śikṣāsamuccaya* (Darbhanga, 1961)—parenthetical numbers in my text refer to the pages of this edition. I've also profited from the English version by Cecil Bendall and W. H. D. Rouse, *Śikṣā-Samuccaya* (Delhi, 1981; first pub. 1922).

48. For an example of traditional Buddhist hagiography on Śāntideva see Losang Norbu Tsonawa, transl., *Indian Buddhist Pandits* (New Delhi, 1985), 60–64.

49. Examples of contemporary historical treatment of Śāntideva are Pezzali, *Śāntideva*, 3–45; J. W. de Jong "La légende de Śāntideva," *Indo-Iranian Journal* 16 (1974), 161–182.

50. Not all of these are also present in the Tibetan version, which sometimes gives an unabbreviated excerpt where the Sanskrit uses *peyyālam*. It is no longer possible to decide whether some or all of these instances are due to Śāntideva, to later copyists, or to the Tibetan translators.

51. I quote and translate from Sylvain Lévi's edition, *Vijñaptimātratāsiddhi: deux traités de Vasubandhu* (Paris, 1925)—parenthetical numbers in my text refer to the pages of that edition. I've profited also from the French translation by Lévi, *Une système de philosophie bouddhique* (Paris, 1932), the German one by Hermann Georg Jacobi, *Triṃśikāvijñaptibhāṣya des Vasubandhu mit bhāṣya des ācārya Sthiramati* (Stuttgart, 1932), and the (unreliable) English one by K. N. Chatterjee, *Vasubandhu's Vijñapti-Mātratā-Siddhi* (Varanasi, 1980).

52. For traditional biography of Sthiramati see Tsonawa, *Indian Buddhist Pandits*, 37–38; Rongxi, *Biography*, 126; [Lama] Chimpa and Debiprasad Chattopadhyaya, transl., *Tāranātha's History of Buddhism in India* (Atlantic Highlands, New Jersey, 1980), 179–181, 399–400; Ernst Obermiller, transl., *The History of Buddhism in India and Tibet by Bu-Ston* (Leipzig and Heidelberg, 1932), 2:147ff.

53. For modern historical work on Sthiramati see Leslie Kawamura, "Vinītadeva's Contribution to the Buddhist Mentalistic Trend," Ph.D. dissertation, University of Saskatchewan, 1975, 46–48; Sylvain Lévi, "Les donations des rois de Vallabhi," *Bibliothèque de l'École des Hautes Études, sciences religieuses, études de critique et d'histoire,*

second series 7 (1896), 75–100; Erich Frauwallner, "Landmarks in the History of Indian Logic," *Wiener Zeitschrift für die Kunde Südasiens* 5 (1961), 125–148, at 136–137.

54. I quote and translate from the edition by Padmanabh S. Jaini, *Sāratamā: A Pañjikā on the Aṣṭasāhasrikā Prajñāpāramitā Sūtra* (Patna, 1979)—parenthetical references in my text are to the pages of this edition. There is, so far as I can tell, no translation into any European language.

55. On Ratnākaraśānti's life see Chimpa and Chattopadhyaya, *Tāranātha's History*, 295, 313–314, 428; Obermiller, *History of Buddhism*, 1:31.

56. John Makransky, "Controversy Over Dharmakāya in Indo-Tibetan Buddhism," Ph.D. dissertation, University of Wisconsin-Madison, 1990, 1:189.

57. For the AA I've used Th. Stcherbatsky and Ernst Obermiller, ed. and transl., *Abhisamayālaṅkāra-Prajñāpāramitā-Upadeśa-Śāstra* (Leningrad, 1929); for the 8,000 P. L. Vaidya, ed., *Aṣṭāsāhasrikā Prajñāpāramitā with Haribhadra's Commentary Called Āloka* (Darbhanga, 1960).

58. Vaidya, *Aṣṭāsāhasrikā*, 153–160.

59. Vaidya, *Aṣṭāsāhasrikā*, 153.

60. Stcherbatsky and Obermiller, *Abhisamayālaṅkāra-Prajñāpāramitā*, iv.32–34.

6. COMMENTARY AND ANTHOLOGY IN ROMAN AFRICA

1. On the history, geography, and administrative structure of Roman Africa I've profited from A. H. M. Jones, *The Later Roman Empire* (Oxford, 1964). Auguste Audollent's *Carthage Romaine* (Paris, 1901), though old, is the most detailed study I've found of the material culture of a Roman African city. Indispensable background to the world of late antiquity can be found in Peter Brown's works, especially *Religion and Society in the Age of Augustine* (London, 1972), and *The Making of Late Antiquity* (Cambridge, Massachusetts, 1978). A. T. Olmstead's "The Mid-third Century of the Christian Era," *Classical Philology* 37 (1942), 241–262; 38 (1942), 398–420, raises some still useful questions about the nature of social life in the empire at that time.

2. I take this from Susan Raven, *Rome in Africa* (3d ed., London, 1993), 122.

3. On the extent and nature of the Christian presence in Roman Africa see Michael Sage, *Cyprian* (Cambridge, 1975), 1–46, together with the literature cited there. On the judicial status of the African Church in the period Charles Saumagne's *Saint Cyprien: Évêque de Carthage* (Paris, 1975) is very useful. On daily life and material culture in the Church, I've made use of Daniel Sullivan, *The Life of the North Africans as Revealed in the Works of Saint Cyprian* (Washington, 1933); R. Fluck, "La vie de la communauté chrétienne au IIIe siècle à travers la correspondance de Saint Cyprien," *Jeunesse de l'Eglise* 4 (1945), 89–124; Victor Saxer, *Vie liturgique et quotidienne à Carthage vers le milieu de IIIe siècle* (Rome, 1984).

4. On the language and genres of Latin Christian literature in the period from 194–430, Paul Monceaux's massive *Histoire littéraire de l'Afrique chrétienne* (Brussels, 1966; first pub. 1901–1923) is still worth consulting. I've also used the standard patrologies and histories of Latin literature: Johannes Quasten, *Patrology* (3d. ed., Westminster, Maryland, 1986–1988); Berthold Altaner and Alfred Stuiber, *Patrologie* (7th ed., Freiburg, 1966); Eligius Dekkers, *Clavis Patrum Latinorum* (3d ed., Rome, 1995); Gian Biagio Conte, *Latin Literature: A History*, transl. Joseph B. Solodow (Baltimore, 1994). I've also found Timothy David Barnes, *Tertullian: A Historical and Literary Study* (2d. ed., Oxford, 1985), useful on third-century literature generally, as also is R. A. Markus, "Paganism, Christianity and the Latin Classics in the Fourth Century," in J. W. Binns, ed., *Latin Literature of the Fourth Century* (London, 1974), 1–21.

5. Conte, *Latin Literature*, 596.

6. See Pierre Hadot, *Marius Victorinus: recherches sur sa vie et ses oeuvres* (Paris, 1971).

7. See William Harris, *Ancient Literacy* (Cambridge, Massachusetts, 1989).

8. My basic work of reference on the question of education in the empire has been Henri-Irénée Marrou, *Histoire de l'éducation dans l'antiquité* (6th ed., Paris, 1965). I've also consulted Stanley F. Bonner, *Education in Ancient Rome: From the Elder Cato to the Younger Pliny* (Berkeley and Los Angeles, 1977); Alan D. Booth, "Elementary and Secondary Education in the Roman Empire," *Florilegium* 1 (1979), 1–14; M. L. Clarke, *Higher Education in the Ancient World* (London, 1971); Martin Irvine, *The Making of Textual Culture* (Cambridge, 1994).

9. [*I*]*am vero unum et unum duo, duo et duo quattuor odiosa cantio mihi erat*, Augustine, *Confessiones*, I.13, ed. C. P. Goold (London, 1912), 42.

10. Quintilian, *Institutio oratoria*, i.3, ed. H. E. Butler, *The Instituto Oratoria of Quintilian* (London, 1958), 54.

11. Booth, "Elementary and Secondary Education," 8–9.

12. Bonner, *Education in Ancient Rome*, 331.

13. Harris, *Ancient Literacy*, 235–236.

14. Suetonius, *De vita caesarum*, viii.18, ed. Henri Ailloud, *Suétone: vies des douze césars*, vol. 3 (Paris, 1932), 62.

15. Bonner, *Education in Ancient Rome*, 132–133.

16. On the material culture of the book, I've relied primarily upon the following: Harris, *Ancient Literacy*; Harry Gamble, *Books and Readers in the Early Church* (New Haven, 1995); David Diringer, *The Book Before Printing* (New York, 1982); Colin H. Roberts and T. C. Skeat, *The Birth of the Codex* (London, 1983).

17. On Pliny's account see Roberts and Skeat, *Birth of the Codex*, 12.

18. Roberts and Skeat, *Birth of the Codex*, appendix.

19. On scripts and punctuation I've consulted some of the standard works on paleography: Franz Steffens, *Lateinische Paläographie* (Freiburg, 1903–1906); E. M. Thompson, *Introduction to Greek and Latin Palaeography* (Oxford, 1910); E. A. Lowe, *Palaeographical Papers* (Oxford, 1972).

20. Roberts and Skeat, *Birth of the Codex*, 45–46.

21. Roberts and Skeat, *Birth of the Codex*, 54–61; Gamble, *Books and Readers*, 59–66; Harris, *Ancient Literacy*, 294.

22. Gamble, *Books and Readers*, 49.

23. Tertullian, *De idololatria*, x.1, ed. A. Reifferscheid and G. Wissowa (Brepols, 1954), 1109.

24. Tertullian, *De idololatria*, x.6, ed. A. Reifferscheid and G. Wissowa (Brepols, 1954), 1110.

25. Augustine, *De catechizandis rudibus*, §13, ed. I. B. Bauer (Brepols, 1969), 135.

26. There's much useful material on Augustine's attitude to reading in the first book of the *Confessions*. A recent and thorough study of the matter is Stock's *Augustine the Reader*. Compare Irvine, *Making of Textual Culture*, 169–189.

27. On Jerome and reading see Harald Hagendahl, *Latin Fathers and the Classics* (Göteborg, 1958), 312–328; Gamble, *Books and Readers*, 175.

28. Markus, "Paganism," 2.

29. On the Christian catechumenate in the period, I've worked principally from Saxer, *Vie liturgique*; William Harmless, *Augustine and the Catechumenate* (Collegeville, Minnesota, 1995); Michel Dujarier, *A History of the Catechumenate* (New York, 1979).

30. Augustine, *De catechizandis rudibus*, §9.

31. Harris, *Ancient Literacy*, 304–305.

32. Harris, *Ancient Literacy*, 320–321; Gamble, *Books and Readers*, 220–221.

33. Dujarier, *History*, 43ff.

34. Dujarier, *History*, 101.

35. Harmless, *Augustine*, 274–292.

36. R. Vander Plaetse, ed., "[Augustine's] Sermo de symbolo ad catechumenos," in Corpus Christianorum, series latina, vol. 46 (Turnholt, 1969), 179–199, at 185.

37. Saxer, *Vie liturgique*, 109.

38. I quote and translate from the edition by R. Weber and M. Bévenot, *Sancti Cypriani Episcopi Opera*, Corpus Christianorum, series latina, vol. 3/1 (Turnholt, 1972), 3–179. Parenthetical page numbers in the text are of this edition. I've benefited also from consultation of the translation by Ernest Wallis, "[Cyprian's] Three Books of Testimonies Against the Jews," in *Ante-Nicene Fathers*, vol. 5 (Peabody, Massachusetts, 1994), 507–557.

39. Michael A. Fahey, *Cyprian and the Bible* (Tübingen, 1971), 15–16.

40. Saumagne, *Saint Cyprien*, 188–190.

41. Michael M. Sage, *Cyprian* (Philadelphia, 1975), 382–383.

42. I quote and translate from Franciscus Weihrich's edition, *S. Aureli Augustini Hipponensis Episcopi Liber Qui Appelatur Speculum*, Corpus Scriptorum Ecclesiasticorum Latinorum, vol. 12 (Vienna, 1887), 3–285. I cite the work parenthetically by chapter number. So far as I can tell there is no translation into any European language.

43. I quote and translate from Claudio Moreschini's edition, *Tertulliani: Adversus Marcionem* (Milan, 1971), citing by book, chapter, and paragraph (i.1.1, e.g.). I've also benefited from Peter Holmes's translation, "The Five Books Against Marcion," in *Ante-Nicene Fathers*, vol. 3 (Grand Rapids, Michigan, 1980), 269–474. The partial edition and translation by René Braun, *Tertullian: Contre Marcion* (Paris, 1990–1994) has also been useful for its prefatory material, though it had not at the time of writing progressed as far as book 4.

44. I quote and translate from Paul Agaësse, ed., [Augustine's] *Commentaire de la première epître de S. Jean*, Sources Chrétiennes vol. 75 (Paris, 1961), which also contains a French translation, citing by tractate and section (ii.8, e.g.). I've also consulted the translation by H. Browne, "[Augustine's] Homilies on the First Epistle of John," in *Nicene and Post-Nicene Fathers*, vol. 7 (Peabody, Massachusetts, 1994), 459–529.

45. Agaësse, *Commentaire*, 15.

46. Agaësse, *Commentaire*, 15–16.

47. On the meaning of 'tractate' see Gustave Bardy, "Tractare, tractatus," *Recherches de Science Religieuse* 23 (1946), 211–235.

48. Agaësse, *Commentaire*, 20.

Index